PLEIADES

CONNECTION

RETURN OF THE PHOENIX

VOLUME I

BY

GYEORGOS CERES HATONN

"dharma"

A PHOENIX JOURNAL

Library of Congress Cataloging-in-Publication Data

Hatonn, Gyeorgos Ceres
PLEIADES CONNECTION--RETURN OF THE PHOENIX
ISBN 0-922356-31-9

First Edition Printed by America West Publishers, 1991

Published by

AMERICA WEST PUBLISHERS
P.O. Box 986
Tehachapi, CA. 93581
1-805 822-9655

Printed in the United States of America
10 9 8 7 6 5 4 3 2 1

TABLE OF CONTENTS

iv

DEDICATION

REC #2   HATONN

TUESDAY, DECEMBER 18, 1990   7:55 A.M.   YEAR 4 DAY 124

To Albert Monette is this dedicated, in behalf of all of you readers who would question and ask. All are seeking Truth and Light and we humbly honor those who speak out and allow interchange beyond the personal debate. These documentations are set forth to give you thought material to measure growth and understanding, for confusion reigns at the time of unveiling of the mysteries of this wondrous experience journey through life. We are all moving through various veils of learning and growth-- each from the higher plane given to assist the ones in less understanding and those higher than we, give unto us--IT IS THE PATH BACK UNTO ONENESS WITH GOD, WITHIN THE WONDROUS CREATION.

I salute you!

1

INTRODUCTION

This will be a bit tedious as an "Introduction" because I wish to share insight of a much higher understanding rather than simply dump you into your relationship with your brothers from Pleiades. To understand your connections with more advanced brothers you must understand that you are simply struggling within the learning processes of growth into the wholeness of God/Creation Love and Balance.

I herein DEDICATE this volume--this "Introduction" to one, Albert Monette of Joshua Tree, California. I ask that his most recent correspondence be reprinted here in full. We must all learn to separate that which is the whole into pieces of "chewable" size. Whatever is written in the Journals in no way discounts the truths which have been brought forth prior to our accounting. I have utilized Al's correspondence dealing with the subject of "Loving thine enemies into change" and I am humbly grateful to this man for his in-depth thoughts on the subject material and his sincere and time-consuming expression of his thoughts.

It may appear that we enjoy scattering the tatters of pain upon you as a sleeping society--nay, but you must awaken unto that which IS. Then, and only then, can you move into the effection of change and within the truth of actions and intent. Unfortunately, thus far, the Journals of necessity have had to contain the shocking uncloaking of the evil and pain upon your place. Now, we may also move more quickly into the spiritual aspects of balance through the individual attachment unto that which is truth in spiritual development.

To be released in the very near future is a three volume projection from Sananda through a beloved servant, "JOY", who outlays in brilliance and glory that which is both individual and massively encompassing for humanity. I have requested that America West publish the material and make it available unto you. You see, we of the higher energies most certainly work in concert. For those of you who need confirmation and "proof" however, all does not come from a single source. Neither may it come as ONLY through THE JOURNALS. This set of writings, you will find, totally balance the JOURNALS in truth but bear the truth of spiritual necessity and "how to" of a distant receiver--not working in conjunction with Dharma. This does two things--it spreads the responsibility and allows all of you readers to understand the diversification of the bringing forth of truth and the fact that if truth is truth--it varies not from pen to pen. This series, as indicated, I believe will be entitled: SOLUTIONS FOR OUR TOTAL GLOBAL SPIRITUAL STARVATION. I apologize in that you will have to contact America West for further information for I have naught to do with the material. I believe it shall be available around the first of the year--at least the first volume.

In direct response to Al Monette I would ask that he, and YOU, recognize that most of the JOURNALS come forth from my own projections as a COMMANDER in only slightly advanced form than are you of Earth plane. Things of physical manifestation must be tended in the manner of presentation--physically. Spirit is ultimately ALL, but man must come again into recognition of that which is placed asunder and then he can grapple with regaining balance from the chaos. This means, dear ones, that the chaos MUST BE CONFRONTED, ISOLATED AND BROUGHT AGAIN INTO ORDER!

I ask that we write portions from the letter in italics, Dharma, and I shall respond in ( ) in formal type style for I do wish to respond as I move along. I further request that this be placed at the forefront of the next Express. I am pained that Al presents the publishing of this document in the form of a formal challenge but none-the-less it bears the thought of the multitudes and therefore shall be handled as such. I do suggest that you ones would not, however, write such challenges unto say, "Bo" Gritz and/or Alvin Toffler. Perhaps the very fact that you do handle the information differently indicates great impact on the consciousness--I sincerely hope so. Salu.

December 14, 1990:

The Phoenix Journals/Express offers us truthful but negative information which enlightens us as to what the "Dark Forces" are doing to control us, however this form of information also has a tendency to instill in our minds, condition us or incline us to:

a) Hate, anger, resentment, revenge and hostilities.

(Do you cast blame upon the Journals, dear friend? Are these emotions absent in your lives as is? Do these feelings only stem from learning truth of circumstance or is, perhaps, the problem already present in over-abundance?)

b) Lose faith, hope and trust in our brothers.

(Do you have faith, hope and trust in your brothers? If so, why has your world become so ill that the truth hurts so much? Have your "brothers" not gained the deserving of loss of these higher qualities to great extent? Is it the JOURNALS AND EXPRESSES that have single-handedly presented this new phenomenon of mistrust unto you the people? I think perhaps you give unto us a bit more than our share of credit for there have been some very daring authors and speakers bringing like truths unto you regarding your plight. Or, is it that this information is somehow unacceptable from the Hosts of Heaven and precursors of God's return to your placement? You ones of Earth cannot have it both ways--you must come into the light or remain ever in the darkness for that is simply the way of it.)

c) To become fearful, combative, offensive or defensive.

(Do you speak for self or for all of your brethren? We have not received other material of such content other than to thank us for the new feelings of "we must do something about this situation". It is not the feelings which are erroneous and should be subjugated--it is the action taken in thoughtful RESPONSE instead of REACTION. Our mission is to awaken mankind--he has had the lessons of LOVE (totally misunderstood by all save a tiny few) and he has only gotten deeper into the mire--therefore, it must be assumed that mankind has lost his way and he must see where he is in order to regain a path, be it positive or negative in portent.)

d) Reject, blame, judge and condemn our brothers.

(I would hope this is not true, but I am confident the statement is all too true! I would hope, rather, that you look within and see what rejection, blame, judgment and condemnation is appropriate for SELF and then, only then, can correction be brought about. It is never the brother at "blame"; it is YOUR PERCEPTION AND RESPONSE AND AL-LOWANCE OF THAT BROTHER WHICH PRECIPITATES THE PROBLEMS IN WHICH YOU NOW FIND SELVES.)

e) See the gloomy side of life and have a negative frame of mind!

(I most surely do hope so! Do you indicate that there is no gloomy side of life nor negative perspective except now that the JOURNALS have brought the causative factors into focus? Could it be that you of the lie want to continue to hide the gloom and negative aspects under the carpets to be out of sight? Will this legacy of refusal to focus on the CAUSE be sufficient to the generations to come--for that which you in your genera-tion fail to correct?)

f) Feel disappointed, frustrated, disgusted and depressed without destiny.

(Oh, beloved brothers, NO, NO, NO! Be totally disappointed, frustrated, disgusted and depressed with that which has come to be about you. BE IN GLORIOUS PRAISE OF THAT WHICH IS YOUR DESTINY! GOD AND TRUTH ARE YOUR DESTINY AS YOU CORRECT THAT WHICH HAS PRECIPITATED THE CIRCUMSTANCE AS YOU DE-SCRIBE OF IT. IF YOU BELIEVE IT CANNOT BE DONE, YOU HAVE LIMITED GOD AND CREATION. RELEASE THE NEGA-TIVE SHACKLES AND REJOICE IN THE TRUTH AND KNOWL-EDGE THAT WITH GOD ALL IS POSSIBLE AND SHALL BE SET TO RIGHT AS SOON AS MAN UNDERSTANDS.)

g) Feel divided, rather than united and integrated for Peace, Love with harmony and balance.

(You are already totally divided, disunited and unintegrated. You have no Peace, true Love or Harmony--certainly you have no Balance.! You must understand that which IS, lest you continue your path of the downward spiral while those--who understand how to manipulate these tatters--de-stroy the remainder of the course chosen by you ones as experience. IF YOU ALLOW IT, IT SHALL COME UPON YOU. ONLY TRUTH

SHALL GIVE YOU FREEDOM FOR ONLY THROUGH THE KNOWLEDGE OF THAT WHICH IS IN TRUTH GIVES YOU IN-STRUCTIONS FOR THAT ACTION WHICH MUST BE TAKEN.)

h) Lose sight that we are all part of the ONENESS as well as an extension of the INFINITE, DIVINE source of Cosmic Conscious-ness, LIGHT and LOVE.

(If we have failed in this projection, then I bend in humble apology for ultimately this is ALL there IS! For not one moment nor word of projec-tion is it intended to indicate a separation of the above outlaid connection. THIS IS <u>WHY</u> YOU MUST TAKE CONTROL AND COME INTO UNDERSTANDING OF TRUTH SO THAT YOU REGAIN THE POWER OF THIS WONDROUS CONNECTION AGAINST WHICH NO DARKNESS CAN PENETRATE, MUCH LESS, PREVAIL!)

i) Be narrow-minded and biased, rather than open-minded, to see other points of view, different than ours, in order to find a solution to our problems, disputes, disagreements or differences.

(I know not to what you refer. It is time to be narrow-minded and biased toward Truth and God. It is a LIE OF LIES projected upon you ones that you must accept that which is heinously done unto you and your species by those who project "total open-mindedness" and "accept ALL things good or bad" in majority rule and/or allowing! You have all but de-stroyed your entire species and planet through this type of action and/or inaction. Is it not equally "right" to take a stand for God as it is to AL-LOW all manner of EVIL to surround and destroy you? Have we ever suggested you not debate, bring public the points in question, disagree or have differences of opinions? Nay, please brothers, do not effort to dump blindness upon your higher brothers! Stand responsible--RESPONSIBLE--for your blunders and errors; do not denounce us for pointing out the truth which has so completely deluded and eluded your attention. Can you not be gracious unto these ones who bring forth this truth in actual line of gun-fire and targeted destruction and death? Can you sit in your sanctimonious and pious blinders and cast stones at these ones who stand forth and give ALL THEY HAVE OF WORLDLY GOODS AND PLACE THEIR VERY LIVES ON THE EXECUTION BLOCKS IN ORDER TO SERVE GOD AND <u>YOUR DESTINY!</u> Please, I ask for more from each of you than that attitude. I am accused of repetition and boring repeating of, "YOU ARE GIVEN FREE-WILL <u>CHOICE</u> AND IT IS UP TO YOU THAT WHICH YOU WILL DO WITH THIS TRUTH!" Does this actually portend intent as you have laid it forth?)

j) Instead of the above negative emotions, let us learn to pray for, forgive and love our brothers and sisters.

Have we forgotten what Matthew 5:44 states?

"But I say unto you, Love your enemies, bless them that curse you, do good to them that hate you, and pray for them which despitefully

5

use you, and persecute you". <u>*AREN'T THE DARK FORCES OUR*</u>
<u>*BIGGEST ENEMY?*</u>

(Do you also believe in eye for eye and tooth for tooth--death for death regardless of cause, etc.? Why do you ones so selectively present your Biblical passages unto us? Is not each grouping upon your place claiming truth of their own "Holy Books"? Could it be that ones deny GOD in favor of man's interpretation of that which is correct and usually mistranslated? I care not which, but let me also do a little quoting from that same good book! Let us look at JAMES 4:" .... You are like an unfaithful wife who loves her husband's enemies--the evil pleasures of this world--makes you <u>an enemy</u> of God? I say it again, that if your aim is to enjoy the evil pleasure of the unsaved world, <u>you CANNOT</u> also be a friend of God."

And, how about 1 JOHN 2: "... Stop loving this evil world and all that it offers you, for when you love these things you show that you do not really love God...." As we have gone along with these JOURNALS we have efforted to remind you over and over and over again--you must love your brother and love your enemy--but you must abhor, disdain and despise evil actions. Did the Master Teacher not cast the money-mongers and changers from out the temple? Well, is not the planet, herself, the temple? Is not your own self, within, the temple of God? Would you misunderstand LOVE AND ALLOWANCE for the keeping of that which is evil, deceitful and corrupt within???? Do you perhaps confuse the precious creation for the actions thereof? "If thine wife gives you a dish of food with salt rather than sugar in the pie, do you hate your wife for the error--or do you cast aside the pie as that which it is, unpalatable?" Would you be expected to eat it? Suppose the error is of poison--wouldst you go ahead and eat it? If you would, oh brother, then you do not understand the lessons of God.)

The Dark Forces represent the following:

1. The Bolshevik/Zionists and supporters.
2. One-World Government Cartel/Elite and supporters.
3. Trilateral Commission and supporters.
4. The Council on Foreign Relations & supporters.
5. The Communist Party and supporters.

(So be it, as far as it goes. You have said, it appears, that which we have brought to your attention. Wherein lies the problem?)

To refresh our memories, let us define "<u>*UNCONDITIONAL*</u>
<u>*LOVE*</u>*", shall we? Unconditional Love is a total acceptance of all entities, whether they be positive or negative without blame, without judgment, without condemnation and without expectations.*

(Dear ones, it is one thing to "accept" the presence of these entities--it is quite another to continue to allow the actions of the entities to destroy others of God's Creations, enslave and prostitute the nations as well as the peoples and planet herself. To ALLOW THESE ACTIONS INDICATES

6

SANCTION OF THE ACTIONS AND IT IS UPON THIS MISCON-
CEPTION OF THE MASSES THAT THE WOULD-BE CON-
TROLLERS THROUGH EVIL ARE ABLE TO ACCOMPLISH THEIR
HEINOUS DEEDS!)

*All this negative information, <u>even if truthful</u>, which the readers
receive in <u>The Phoenix Journals</u> or <u>Express</u> is compounding the situation and our problems on this planet. As we all know, negative
emotions and thinking encourage the negative or dark forces of energy to continue whatever they're doing! Instead... educate the
readers, with more emphasis on how we may all improve or generate more LOVE and raise our Spiritual Consciousness. By the
way, we need this desperately at this time.*

*We should all know that the negative or dark forces of energy can
not operate and flourish in an environment filled with love! The
more love we can generate on this placement, the quicker we can
eliminate or rid ourselves of these negative and dark forces of energy, which try to manipulate, control and enslave mankind. You
may want to call these forces the "False Jews", The 13th Tribe,
The Khazars or the Zionists or even the Satanic Forces! But whatever name you use, they are all "Dark Forces of Negative Energy",
are they not?*

(We call them by their proper labels SO THAT YOU THE PEOPLE DO
NOT MISINTERPRET AND LABEL THE PRECIOUS AMONG THE
RABBLE. As for the projections that LOVE will cure all--ah yes, it
would do so, no doubt about it. I suggest, however, that there are thou-
sands of books suggesting that we simply love one another and the bad
monsters will "just go away". No, they will not for you must know who
and what are the bad monsters to impact them in any manner what-so-
ever, Love or Hate included. AS MAN COMES AGAIN INTO UN-
DERSTANDING OF GOD AND CREATION HE WILL AUTOMATI-
CALLY BEGIN TO TURN AGAIN INTO TRUTH AND LOVE; HE
WILL DO THIS BY RECOGNIZING THE ERRORS AND LIES
THRUST UPON HIM SO THAT HE CAN UNDERSTAND THAT
PORTION OF HIS ACTIONS AND BELIEFS THAT HAVE LED HIM
ASTRAY IN THE FIRST PLACE!

(We do not suggest that you do not "Love the evil MAN--but despise his
evil"! Most ones involved in, say, the Zionist "movement", are totally
unaware of truth of the situation. If we do not give unto you the explanation and point out the difference, how are you to come into truth in time
to allow for a Godly destiny? This is why we are presented unto you, so
that, at what you will classify as "judgment", you beloved ones of the
planet shall have some idea as to the truth of your circumstance--'tis what
is "within" which shall be coming into inspection by self and God. God
now decrees that "the time of ignorance" is to be put behind you as a
species--it is graduation time.)

If you dear folks in Tehachapi mean well, and I am sure you are out to do the Will of The Infinite, Divine and Creative Source, if you are dedicated to serve mankind and are out to promote Peace, Love, Truth and The Light, then kindly print this letter with your response, whatever it may be, in The Phoenix Journals, for all to read and discern for themselves with our "FREE WILL".

If you are truly Light Emissaries filled with Truth and Love and you're not afraid of losing a few dollars from the sale of these books, then you will not reject or ignore this request.

Should you decide to refute this letter, then sadly you will be showing your true colors. This letter has been written with sincerity and Love for all concerned.

(So be it! There is gross misunderstanding, however, as to who is who and what is what. The ones who write and publish only do so as WE ask them to do so. They do not make the decisions for they work in true service unto the God who brings this message of truth unto you. They remain hundreds of thousands of dollars in debt for the presenting of this information so it is not of kind service unto them to suggest they would withhold truth or sharing in order to glean "a few dollars" by not printing your thoughtful information. We KNOW that your message is sent with great LOVE FOR ALL CONCERNED, ESPECIALLY YOUR FELLOW-MAN, so please KNOW that we KNOW! Further, please understand that even though you did not fully understand WHY YOU FELT COMPELLED TO SEND THIS DOCUMENT--GOD KNOWS AND APPRECIATES YOUR RESPONDING TO HIS CALL THAT OTHERS MIGHT SHARE THE EXPRESSION YOU WOULD TAKE THE TIME TO PRONOUNCE.

Please accept our humble dedication unto you, brother, for service which might appear to be responded with egg on the face. Nay, it is giving a forum for expression which is not of such value simply stated unto the ethers.)

May the abundant Blessings from God-Light be with you always, and may you all have a beautiful, holy and happy holiday season.

In Divine Love and Affection,
Albert Monette
60353 Latham Trail
Joshua Tree, Ca. 92252

(I give his address for he has given us permission to print same, along with his documents (permission on file). Be in appreciation to ones like this brother who will sort and attempt understanding that all of you might find your way in truth without fear of countering or questioning. God expects use of that wondrous gift given unto you of the human species--only through thought and sharing can you perfect that wondrous gift and again come into oneness with thine own Source. I would hope that ones of you readers who have appreciation in a special manner, might write unto this one in the same Love as given forth from him unto you. He simply fears that you as a creation will be somehow misled as to the ultimate purpose of soul journey. I honor this man greatly and give humble appreciation unto his service.)

P.S. I'm not saying that no one should read the Phoenix Journals or Expresses nor that we shouldn't be keeping an open-mind to Political Truth's presented in these writings! I'm only trying to emphasize the idea that we shouldn't forget what Jesus, Esu, Emmanuel or Sananda stated in Matthew 5:44. We should have a firm and solid foundation and be Spiritually prepared to comprehend the meaning of "Unconditional Love" and not lose sight of this!

Unfortunately, the average person or reader and Church goer is not Spiritually prepared, so they quickly forget the Scriptural passage from above and they do not fully comprehend the full or true meaning of Love. SO BE IT!

(Ah, and so be it! Let us not be misunderstanding the intelligence and ability of human intent--we must not place limits on that which man can grasp and will grasp as truth is unfolded. He has simply lost his bearings, his way, and will rekindle Spiritual Oneness as he remembers. We are ALL BUT ONE and to lessen the ability or intent of ONE only lessens ourselves within the ALL. WE MUST CONFRONT THE ERRORS IN THE LIGHT OF TRUTH, CORRECT THE ERRORS THROUGH THE LIGHT OF TRUTH IN LOVE, FORGIVENESS AND UNDERSTAND-ING--THEN THE REVERSAL SHALL COME AND AGAIN WE CAN JOIN IN THE ONENESS IN RETURN INTO THE WHOLENESS OF OUR SOURCE. AHO!)

This requires an understanding of placement in the Universe, the Cosmos and Source of journey through heritage, ancestry and awakening to the unfolding of the MYSTERIES! NOT THE MYSTICISM! GOD AND CREATION ARE NOT MYSTICAL--THEY ARE WONDROUS MYS-TERIES IN THE PROCESS OF UNVEILMENT! MAY WE SHARE THIS WONDROUS REVELATION AND UNVEILING TOGETHER!

I am Hatonn

CHAPTER 1

REC #1   HATONN

WEDNESDAY, NOVEMBER 21, 1990   6:52 A.M.   YEAR 4 DAY 97

LET US REMEMBER TOGETHER

I am Hatonn, come in the Radiance of the Lighted Source! I am come forth as truth-bringer and to awaken you, my brethren, from your lodges and beds. I come, that you might be given to understand that which has been brought to you prior to this and mostly denied--while persecuting those who brought the truth unto you. I come as one--no longer to simply "test the waters" but to actually participate in preparation for the returning of God to your placement. I tend to want this job done well and, therefore, may appear a bit abrupt in the alarm-clock ringing! Remember that God is quite capable of doing that which He deems appropriate for, as Creator, His truth is manifestation.

I speak as a representative of those from your home galactic system who have now again come to help you through a time of transition and change for your planet has gone about as far as She can go without horrendous consequences. I only ask audience for reason is a gift unto man--FROM GOD--and I see and understand not why you find it difficult to believe God has others in such a magnificently ordered universe! So be it, for it shall be outlaid and again, as with prior truth-bringers, you may accept or deny--but I suggest to you, THE STORY IS YET UNFINISHED AND YOU AS A SPECIES ARE IN GRAVE TROUBLES! GOD WOULD NOT LEAVE HIS CREATIONS IN IGNORANCE AND WITHOUT ASSISTANCE--GOD WILL NOT ABANDON HIS CREATIONS-- EVEN IN ILLUSION--SO PERHAPS YOU CAN READ TRUTH WITH AN OPEN MIND AND THEN YOU SHALL BE ABLE TO FIND YOUR OWN LEVEL OF UNDERSTANDING AND CONFIRMA- TION. THANK YOU.

Some of you will have instant understanding of things I will briefly cover- -others will have a complete blockage of perception. I make no effort herein to do other than outlay a few "space-brother" aspects for it is time to make known our presence and purpose as come from God and there is no intention to mislead nor frighten your species. Our wings are of the "silver clouds" of ancient reference and we are come to help you find your way HOME!

The last Great Teacher to come upon your place as Wayshower, went to prepare a place for you--we are now come to prepare a place for His re- turn upon Earth--it is the time of sorting and separation; may you be given understanding in your individual aspects to comprehend this which I give unto you. We come in the open revelation and service unto the ONE

GOD OF CREATION--MOTHER/FATHER/ALL-CREATOR AND WITHIN THE GLORY OF THE CREATION. OUR INTENT BEARS NO FORCE, FEAR NOR EVEN PERCEIVED HARM. THE HARM AND FEAR IS BORN OF MAN IN THE DENSITY OF EARTH PLANE. YOUR CONSPIRATORS, AGAINST HOLY GOD, SHALL PROJECT OTHERWISE TO MISLEAD AND CONTROL YOU--GOD COMES ONLY IN LIGHT WITH ALL SECRETS REMOVED. SE-LAH. "IN THE BEGINNING WAS THE WORD--AND THE WORD IS GOD!" SO BE IT! AMEN.

Some of the things I shall outlay for you will seem quite primitive for I speak to all, and some of your fellow creations may possibly not be able to think and treat with spirituality and understanding that which we bring. At this time of awakening unto truth, most still lay captured too much in the issues of purely human inclinations of feelings, physical participation and indoctrined "instructions" as given forth by other humans who would mostly set forth to control of him in some manner or another.

We do not force our way into the thoughts of another--it is not even of importance to penetrate the thoughts of others than those who would find this truth for truth IS and will stand on its own merits for infinity.

I make no objection to your perceptions that there are false speakers who claim contact from our brotherhood--they have their intent to play games and cause you to disbelieve truth when it is brought unto you. There must always be caution and concern, when "UFO" contactees pretend their friends from the stars, among other things, communicate with telepathy! If they pronounce any instruction that deviates from the LAWS OF GOD AND THE CREATION--they do not bring forth total truth and, there-fore, must be considered deceivers. God will give only truth for your consumption. These "speakers" do exist. Their communication was ei-ther originally telepathic, or they simply allowed the flapping of their tongues in self-projection and/or entertainment. Some of the so-called "speakers", "channels"--whatever you label them, are simply deceivers and the facts can always be witnessed. All of those could-be contactees who USE others are but dupes and it is not for any of us to judge.

We come not as regards the "Christian RELIGION". We come in truth and knowledge of that which IS--it bears on Christ-ness and perfection of the Sacred Infinite Circle but we come not as "religious" anything.

Although many deceivers exist as "receivers", there are many who have had and still have contact. There are thousands who have witnessed and been given the privilege to actually photograph the presence of the broth-ers from the cosmos. Only a very, very few have actually had personal, physical contact with the higher brotherhood--and they have been discred-ited and persecuted--so, personal appearances which all of you demand, did not work either. It has reached the point that ones having personal contact have simply ceased to speak out and tell what they witness. The misinformation troops have had a field day in the deception business! Ones who have come from our domain are badly used and misprojected.

11

"Little Gray Aliens" indeed! Come to dismember and terrorize you? "Hold your government hostage?" Dear ones, come, come!

Some of the cosmic brotherhood come from different worlds and systems than do we for there is now a window of perception which allows participation and observation of your planet--but it is still cosmic law--KEEP HANDS OFF! Some come from other races unto your place on expeditions and have collected different things which could serve their investigations. Some have participated in conjunction with various earth people to research necessary information regarding evacuation of your place if need be and to be ground crew at the arrival of the cosmic brotherhood. Some "aliens" look exactly like you for they are your ancestors and some are quite different in appearance having evolved into the "selection" of natural evolution to be best suited for their own experience and environment. They have come to many recently, in your current generations, to bring truth of spirituality and work with you in silence of understanding until comprehension is full enough to be acceptable. If one comes from and in service to God--He/She/It comes in total love.

Some of these members of the brotherhood are quite new at space travel, and so perform their expeditions to expand their knowledge and understanding. Hereby, it also can happen that they come into contact with Earth humans quite unexpectedly, and then never return.

These are not hungry and thirsty for might and power and such, and are happy to finally have some calm and order in their own worlds of experienced existence. It can also happen that they, here and there, take communication with Earth humans, bring them within their craft and sometimes examine them very carefully. But any being capable of coming a great space distance from out of your solar system is technically oriented indeed and would inflict no pain nor trauma. The humans thus participating are, in every instance, released for there is not intent to harm you ones in any manner what-so-ever. If ones coming from space at this time of planetary evolution and transition, are able to reach your orb--they are allowed entry only through the absolute guidelines of the Cosmic Code of behavior. In every instance--any visitor from "out here" is more humane than any upon your place in the form of human as you recognize the label.

There have been some quite barbarous creatures who have also traveled through the cosmos, and have come to Earth, too, many being power hungry and quite wicked indeed--how do you think evil was introduced upon your place--from a snake in an apple tree? They have sometimes kidnapped earth humans, as well as other planetary human beings from other systems, and abduct them away to their home planet. There these poor creatures might then have been caused to be placed on exhibition, etc.--as you do with aliens who are captured voluntarily or involuntarily--by your governments.

It is now come to be that in these times of closing cycles upon your planet that the evil is already perfected upon your sphere--working now in your own density of perception--you are already infected and infested and you must awaken to your plight for YOU have let the demons within. These ones carry great power in some instances and they are malignant in nature for they use the power of "feelings" and other physical human characteristics and movements which are often quite strange for them and thus, a life means very little to them for they do not abide by Cosmic Law--although now, they cannot get off your planet in these closing days of sorting and separation. This is why I tell you again and again that, "It is what is already on your planet which you must attend--not we who come in these days of perception, to assist you!"

Many deceivers have come forth with their fantastic UFO tales and gained great publicity but there are MANY who do not deceive. There are ones who have encountered our ships and even have made contact and physical radio contact with our craft or other ships from strange visitors. These ones have been discredited and often simply "murdered" to stop the stories of truth and ones sent from the CIA, etc., to start cover-up stories to denounce and spread panic and fear. The worst scenarios are yet to come as your Conspirators and One World Global Cartel sets up actions which will be blamed on the space brotherhood--I ask you to mark my words NOW for it shall be in the coming.

Earth human is very difficult to convince of anything and you are so focused and centered on the false projections that you no longer know which is false and which is truth--so you cling to the physical elements--but I remind you that life-span is only averaging about 75 years of counting seasons and I suggest that there is something of which you are not aware, afoot. If it is not of the physical plane as you know it, does it not stand to reason that it might perhaps come from the Heavens, as you refer to the Cosmos? If you are EXPECTING A RETURN OF GOD, AND YOU HAVE, BY MAJORITY PROJECTION, STATED, YOURSELVES, THAT IT IS "SOON" OR "NOW"--WHAT IS IT THAT YOU DO NOT UNDERSTAND? WHY WOULD YOU DENOUNCE THE VERY TRUTH-BRINGERS WHO WOULD BRING YOU INTO TRUTH AND BRING ABOUT THE RETURN OF GOD WHICH YOU EXPECT? HOW LONG WILL HU-MAN OF EARTH DENY GOD? HOW LONG WILL YOU CHOOSE RIDICULOUS FABRICATIONS WHEN THE TRUTH OF THAT WHICH IS COMING IS SO MUCH MORE PERFECTED AND WONDROUS? ALL OF YOU WISH TO TAKE YOUR HUMAN FORMS; WOULD IT NOT BE MORE CREDIBLE TO SUGGEST TAKING THEM TO PLACES PREPARED FOR HUMAN FORM THAN TO RESIDE ON FLOATING CLOUDS WHERE HU-MAN FORMS WOULD SIMPLY FALL BACK TO EARTH? I SUGGEST IT IS NOT "OUR" TRUTH WHICH IS IN QUESTION, BROTHERS!

BROTHERS ARE NOT SUPER-BEINGS

Most of the assistants from the cosmos are NOT super-beings, as Earth men like to call them in their imagination. Most are not even teachers, missionaries, or way-preparers for that matter--only a few for, with God, it requires very few! There is an obligation in duty to preserve the existing life already developing in this universe. This means that we endeavor to keep order and maintain peaceful presence.

Now and then, especially we, your Pleiadian brothers, make contact and open communication with inhabitants of different worlds, search out single ones and give explanations unto them that you might become informed of that which you perceive to be beyond you. Most of your cosmic brothers are only "advanced" from your status and the contacts are for the purpose of allowing growth and the ability to realize that you are not the only thinking creatures in the universe.

I, Hatonn, come as an etheric being "leader", experiencing in a format which can be better understood as the times of transition come and the higher beings make presentation upon your place. Our roots, yours and mine, are in the Pleiades and therefore the fleet most involved with your evolution is from Pleiades--YOU ARE *HUMAN* AND THAT REQUIRES *PHYSICAL* CARE.

CLARIFY MATERIAL INFORMATION

In the bringing of historical knowledge to fill in some of your missing links, I must point out that I have the information per scanner--I am a Commander--not an historian and do not even wish to spend this time in contemplation of such, but the barrage of inquiries are great and I will share that which is most frequently under question.

What about longevity in the other experiences? Man can become a thousand, or even hundreds of thousands, of years old, in your mode of counting, *when he reaches a certain level of spiritual development and evolution. BUT BEYOND THIS STATE, THE SPIRIT NO LONGER NEEDS A MATERIAL BODY. HE THEN DOES LIVE IN PURE SPIRIT AND WITHIN SUCH HIGH SPHERES THAT ONE CAN NO LONGER COMMUNICATE WITH HIM IN TYPICAL HUMAN MANNER.*

I would give you some comparison at this point for your own historical research projects. The 1,000 or so years of average experience of ones of Pleiades coincides with that reported for the average longevity of Earth humans PRIOR to that which is known as the "Great Flood", when the dense vapor envelope surrounding the Earth came down in torrents everywhere for scores of days. Loss of the vapor envelope reduced the atmospheric protection of Earth's creature species from the harsh radiations of your sun, and the lifespans of all creatures decreased dramatically and rapidly to well under a century for humans. Vegetable and plant yields were reduced accordingly.

Oh you ask, "Well, how did the sun get through the vapor envelope?"

14

Very simply--your sun was young and easily pierced the veil.

Perhaps you could better understand the possibilities herein in considering the historical documentation and myths that your ancestors, when they were upon your place long ago, your 1,000 year Biblical longevities might now take on more meaning and acceptance in perspective. Loss of atmospheric protection has shortened your lifespans in great measure and you accepted this restriction, in concept, by limiting your own creative ability to have it otherwise. You chose shorter lifespans rather than bring about natural evolutionary alterations which would give protection--then, in the perception of limitations of time and space--you forgot and accepted that which was thrust upon you.

You ARE having trouble with your ionosphere--but it is not that which the scientists of the Conspirators outlay for you. What you are being told by the controllers upon your place is to intimidate and frighten you--what is happening in the ionosphere is of a magnitude and "cause" beyond your Earth projections and worse, your more learned scientists know what it is and what could be done to shore it up and yet, are not allowed to do so.

You will note through the ages that even drawings of space creatures appear and have protective coverings about their beings--these are not in the form of bubble suits as you would recognize them relative to your astronaut uniforms. From Pleiades, for eons there is ability to encapsulate both the craft and the person when out of the vehicles within energy fields which give protection from your atmospheric environment which causes the same level of aging and damage as is done to Earth humans. In Pleiades, for instance, to be some 500 "years" of age is but barely bordering on approaching mid-life and would more likely be still considered very youthful. Furthermore, it might be advantageous for you of Earth to understand something about your brothers and sisters, who come from Pleiades most predominantly--they are beautiful in human form which surpasses your own physical stature and beauty--it would be most advantageous to have them for ancestors for they are wondrous indeed, as relative to yourselves. They are not unlike you--nor or they monstrous beings of mutant origins--they are a more perfected reflection of your races.

Fear of monsters and mutants are thrust into your minds by those who would control you in fear and terror. There is no basis in fact.

JMMANUEL

A perplexing aspect of your unfolding truth unto you, is your refusal to even look at that which contradicts in any manner that which you have been told--BY MAN, IN MAN'S NAME AND WITH AND THROUGH MAN'S TRANSLATIONS. *HOW CAN YOU LEARN IF YOU REFUSE TO LOOK?*

Why does it disturb man so much to come into truth regarding extrarestrial (which means--not of terrestrial; nothing more and no lesser). Ones stand in the pulpits of your "Churches" and pronounce that his or her knowledge is directly from God or Christ--do you now denounce your own truth of the projection by discounting extraterrestrials and/or communication with them? By all definitions, God and/or Jesus Immanuel are extraterrestrials as you define the term--both are etheric and "speak" to "receivers" in this same manner! Why do you pronounce our words to be of evil, Satanic content and methods?--Satan is a very physical, earthy worker, brothers--who is he more apt to tamper with--YOU OF EARTH-BOUND WHO CAN STILL BE DECEIVED OR WE, WHO ALREADY KNOW HIM FOR THAT WHICH HE IS?? EARTH IS IN THE AGE OF CHAOS AND SATANIC RULE--WHO DO YOU BELIEVE MIGHT BE GIVING YOU A SONG AND DANCE?

Extraterrestrials have had many experiences in events as outlaid in that which you call your Bibles. I again make reference to the scriptum about Jmmanuel (Immanuel, Emmanuel, Iisa, Essa, Esu, "Jesus").

The scriptum is a document written by one, Judas Ischarioth, one of the few disciples with an education, my friends. He could read and write. The facts are such that his written words bear the truth and the projectors of the false history as projected upon you, would be in great panic to have truth presented and blow away the lies. Because Earth man doesn't like the truth does not in the least change the truth of it for TRUTH *IS!* EARTH MAN CONFUSES THE HISTORICAL TRUTH OF ONE, JU-DAS ISCHARIOTH AND ONE, JUDA IHARIOTH. Is this such a hard disclosure to accept that perhaps in 2,000 years someone might make translation and typographical errors? Come now, allow him who is without error to cast of the first stone! I can only suggest that you obtain and read carefully indeed, <u>AND THEY CALLED HIS NAME IMMANUEL</u>. The Master "Jesus", as you label him, oversaw the translation of the Arabaic scrolls--there are some misunderstandings of projections in some instances due only to lack of common definition of translated words. If you become enslaved to a point of record some 2,000 years past, you miss the point of the Christ's manifestation at that time. He came to teach, lead and show you the fact of immortality. He experienced as a human and suffered as a human--YOU OF THE HUMAN MISSED THE POINT OF THE JOURNEY!

I am speaking of Pleiadian perspectives at this time--I speak of more spiritual matters in depth elsewhere--for we serve differing purposes and missions, your Pleiadian brothers and myself! We are from two different levels of dimension and I believe we will clarify that matter by the ending of the writings.

Another sarcastic projection thrust at this scribe and other receivers is, "How is it that these extraterrestrials always speak the exact and proper language?" Simple indeed--THEY DO IT THE OLD FASHIONED WAY--THEY LEARN THEM! Most can speak or understand "universal language" but many cannot decipher clearly in Earth dialects and when contact is made it is with ones whose language is studied and communications can be clearly translated. I, on the other hand, being etheric in experience, need no language and as I communicate, as with Dharma, I utilize frequency beams and "pulse" information which her mind is programmed to receive and place into English and sometimes into Native American--specifically Lakota Sioux extraction because the ancient truths shall come forth onto paper from a Lakota Sioux receiver of the oral teachings and the documents must be compatible. Dharma does not speak native language in any manner what-so-ever--nor any other language save English.

Pleiadian extraterrestrials must learn languages. They possess all Earth languages, present and past, that were ever spoken and/or utilized. They have detailed knowledge of them in most different ways. From them, language training courses are given. This work is performed by language-"scientists" and machines, similar to what you call computers. Machines of similar sort serve then to transmit the desired language and instill it into the student--directly. This is performed in a machine-induced hypnotic-like state, and by this method the language terms and senses become implanted and registered. The processing of a new language requires about 20-30 days. Then there is allowed another week or so to practice correct usage--in all, a new language can be quite well perfected in about a month of your counting.

Is this so difficult to comprehend? For several years now, on your own place, language institutes are using recorders and sleep-learning techniques. These techniques are in great use in the training of your so-called surveillance (spy) groups and is called programmed learning. Further, you have developed Robotoids who are totally programmed with imitation memory banks and are constantly manipulated by pulsed beam mechanisms for ongoing control of input and manipulated actions. Why would it be difficult to believe that higher societies than your own, would have perfected the technology?

Dharma, allow us to close this segment at this point. There are physical things to be accomplished and we must allow you to "live" in your Earth format also. Tomorrow is labeled "Thanksgiving" and I recognize great thanks and appreciation for allowance of participation and we acknowledge the need for comradry with brothers and families. Go do that which needs doing in the physical and we will meet with this document this evening. I cannot give you the day off, chela, for we must write at least once per day as our time grows shorter and we must come into understanding regarding the information--therefore, I ask you to allow time for our work. I, too, have no words to express my thanks and appreciation to you with such willing hands to serve--may we all bow in wondrous gratitude unto God for his Grace and may He accept our joy and gratitude in the wondrous participation of our service. May we be given understanding into that which is unfolding before us. Salu.

Hatonn to clear, please. I remain on circuit--go in security. Saalome'

CHAPTER 2

REC #1   HATONN

THURSDAY, NOVEMBER 22, 1990   9:11 A.M.   YEAR 4 DAY 98

<u>GIVING THANKS</u>

FROM DHARMA: On this day of focusing appreciation I need within, to express without my gratitude and humble thanks for being allowed to participate in this unfolding, incredible experience called LIFE! At this time of historical transition, to be allowed to even be present is beyond my expression capabilities--to participate is a gift above all gifts. I express, on behalf of we, the Earth ground-team, our collective recognition of the honor and love bestowed upon us. We come, as do you, in service unto God, fellow-man, nation and truth--may your will be done, Grandfather, for you have walked with us while we have grappled our way through the veil and into flickering memories of our purpose.

There is nothing we would not do for you in the light of truth if you but ask us, for too long have we only asked of you and the brotherhood. May we assume the responsibility of this mission in the glory and truth handed into our care for the sowing of the seeds of truth upon the fertile ground-- if you can give unto us such a gift--may we never be found intentionally negligent of the commission.

We ask, and give, our own truth and blessings unto all our relations that we do not, for even one moment, forget their passage is filled with confusion and, as we grow, Grandfather, may we find the path and move some of the pebbles out of the path of our brothers.

Thank you for walking with us, and may we come into understanding for it is difficult to be hu-man in this day of chaos of which there seems to be no understanding and may we come home soon in fulfillment of that which you have sent us to do. May we ask only for our brother and then hear that which you give us to do that his way might be easier and truth come into his being. May your will always be that which we acknowledge and bear action, for in the knowledge of that truth we, too, shall come into the lighted halls of your lodge and rejoin our family. We are homesick and lonely for our home but may we serve well that our arrival back to our place among the stars shall the bear glory, love and peace which moves always beyond our understanding. May your will be done and may your power reveal itself in each of us that we act, always, in your truth and light. May our lodges be always in perfection, within, that you find a place of perfection in which to dwell.

In appreciation unto the councils and the Sacred Circle of Infinity to be allowed to serve, I ask your continued guidance and presence as we journey forth upon this planet in the mission granted unto us. Thank you, Grandfather, for your sheltering wings, for sometimes we are so lonely and the way seems impassable and impossible--may we always be given to persevere and see the way as you would have us walk, within the wondrous Creation. May we represent our brothers of the tribes from the Heavens and we ask that you of the unseen tribe be in knowledge of our love and service unto you.

I am humbled to be allowed to be your hands for I have so little else to give and you have given all. Hear us, Grandfather, that we not be a blind voice in the dark, but rather, a knowing example and presence within the Light.

In behalf of my brothers and sisters, I petition you to accept our gratitude for you have gifted us with ALL there is. May we keep this ever present in our consciousness- - -.

AHO

* * * * * * * * * * *

TODAY'S WATCH

Hatonn present, to walk with you ones within the light of which you give appreciation. We can only bind as into ONE, the prayer of petition that we might serve together as we walk through this journey home. Salu.

I would not take time this day to speak of many world events for you are capable of seeing the facade on this day of projected banterings and harangues. I do, however, ask that you follow the trail of the Russian representative on his journey to high level meetings with China! This is indeed important. There is much going on behind the sham of turkey dinners and crass facade but allow us to give appreciation for the brotherhood which does come forth on the special days set aside for unity. May the peace and love of your holiday season override the clang of battle and war cries. Every turn into the direction of God is blessed indeed.

PLEIADES CONNECTION

We have often spoken of your connection with Pleiades and for a while we shall write about these attachments for your brothers from the stars have great insight which they willingly share with you ones who are still grappling with the dark corners of memory.

Your brothers from Pleiades have witnessed those of you who were and are unable to determine the truth or were frightened when confronted with it; this serves no purpose for terrestrial man nor themselves. The fear

19

should never be present in any manner as all men hold the truth within themselves and must only know this to find it. A human may deliver himself from all manner of ignorance if he generates the will to seek truth and then does so.

Wisdom is the light and wherever the light flashes upward, there darkness and ignorance disappear. Ignorance is the essential darkness and can only be overcome by the light of wisdom. Further, little brothers, wisdom is the mark of a human who has recognized the existence of spirit and works with and according to the Creational laws, for wisdom and the spirit are two factors which react as one, much in the same way as the sun and light of the sun. Both give warmth and both give light. Wisdom is the mark of the existence of the spirit and disguises itself in the qualities of truth, knowledge, love, beauty, grace, harmony and peace.

You ones of Earth desire to remain bound to passing "time" but you cannot measure "age" by that which you perceive as passing years. The "human" may be very old as witnessed by the exterior perception, but this is only a passing state. A century ago human was not old and a century for this present moment he will not be old--only the physical body can age in any manner what-so-ever for the spirit only renews and grows in knowledge and experience. The spirit remains forever young and is never subjected to the appearance of age, for age is like youth and every other experience, it is only a passing state of being.

YOU WANT TO HOLD IT ALL

You ones of Earth-bound attachments dream and ponder and wonder about your brothers of space. You ponder about whether or not they are "out there" and if so, how can they reach you and how can you reach them--you want ideas you can understand and yet, there is no mysticism regarding these states of actions and being but only mystery--until the puzzle is accomplished.

You want to know about propulsion systems and physical elements of construction of ships and be reminded of how it is where you came from so that you might be reminded of that which makes you lonely and home-sick--you want to remember the "whys" and "hows" and you are impatient to move on and yet you lock yourselves into the cement of that which you have created to shackle you to the physical experience.

I can speak of the general of that which you consider "physical" for your brothers move about in a most physical manner, for the most part, having learned to overcome the compression of the dimensions as they differ. We, of the etheric presence move by the projection of intent through thought so I shall not go into that deeply at this writing for we need to speak of your connections with your kindred.

Let us consider propulsion for the largest number of questions come forth

20

as "How can you travel such distances--how do your craft function?" For travelling through cosmic space, a drive is necessary which surpasses the speed of light by millions of times. But this propulsion can only come into action when the speed of light has already been achieved. From that it follows that a further drive is necessary regulating normal speed up to that of light. This means that a starcraft, or beamship as referred to by the Pleiadians, requires two drive mechanisms, first the normal which accelerates up to the speed of light, and then a second for the hyperdrive, as you might refer to it. A drive then, which generates a million-fold, and even billion-fold, the speed of light, thus producing the hyper-speed by which hyper-space is pierced and penetrated. This is a space in which the mass seems to increase in relationship to the speed attained. So time and space simply collapse, and they become zero time and zero space. This actually means that time and space cease to exist. Thusly, distances of numerous light-years are traversed in a mere fraction of a second--with no lag of time.

The actual "time" required to make a journey, say, from Pleiades to Earth is in the speeding up to light speed and the slowing down again at destination. In thought transference there is no time involved what-so-ever except the split seconds required for disassembly and reassembly. The actual time of physical transference by craft is less than ten minutes of your calculations for such a distance.

You will not be given statistics of detail as to function because you ones have enough toys beyond your ability to control without bringing them into outer-limits of the cosmos. It is not in the best interest of the cosmic brotherhood that Earth human be given the ability to penetrate the cosmic spaces--you have all you, and we, can handle right on your orb and solar space. To great extent, however, many of the problems have been overcome by some of your Earth scientists and the Soviets, as you call them, have developed great technology in space flight and solar exploration. The U.S. has done very well, also, but you all utilize the wondrous technology to produce wars and not grow in grace, peace, exploration for knowledge and brotherhood in love. In time, you will be given to solve the problems yourself--when the sequence of growth becomes safe for the universal existence.

Your thrust systems, of course, will work on the basis of light pulses from light emitting drives. Light-emitting drives work for normal propulsion and move the beamships to nearby planets and a safe distance away from an orb and then another drive is activated when the distances are great. We could refer to this second drive mechanism as a hyper-propulsion system, which surpasses time and space. It is a bit hard to describe these systems in Earth terms for your language is different and so are the labels given to such minerals as mercury, which is utilized as well as the various programming crystals necessary for craft apparatus. We refer to things such as "tacheons" which are generated and harnessed in both drive systems with only differing magnitude and attitude.

Pleiadians predominantly utilize disc-shaped craft, especially for long distance travel, because of the aerodynamic qualities. Once in motion, we ride a "boundary layer" much similar to the principle applied to Tesla's bladeless turbine/pump. The boundary layer, for brief explanation, is the tiny distance, let us say, between the wing of an aircraft and the atmosphere passing across the surface--there is a totally static area untouched by the atmosphere itself to the surface. Once in motion there is nothing that touches the skin surface of the vehicle. The disc-like form, therefore, vouches the least resistance, and also offers the largest surface which rides the energy currents, to enable the drives to be most efficient.

GRAVITY OF GRAVITY

This is a bit easier to discuss, and further, is no longer a secret to Earth scientists. The beamship is completely surrounded by a protection-beam-girdle (excuse me, ladies). This allows every interference to simply glide away, without pushing. The same also occurs in the cosmos, which swarms with particles. Therefore, the beam-protection screen functions to protect the ship against all influences and resistances, with anything contacting the screen becoming pushed aside or disintegrated -- as the boundary layer spoken of above. All things which would otherwise penetrate or are resistance-offering are simply diverted without evoking pressures in any manner. Resistance must be eliminated to reach sufficient speeds for distance travel.

Removal of this protecting screen brings into play another very important effect which is of great importance--especially to passengers and crew; the glide-away effect of the beam-protection-screen diverts the gravity and attractive forces, and the beamship in effect becomes a micro-planet which can travel at near lightspeed through any atmosphere without any risk at all.

The gravity of a planet does not influence the beamship; the passengers feel nothing abnormal and there is no force levied against their beings-- just as if they were on a home planet where the balance is adjusted by natural selection and where the planetary gravity is in accordance with their anatomical capabilities.

In the beamship itself the gravity, of course, is balanced to the passengers and is completely controlled. When passengers on spacecraft from other worlds move in atmospheres alien to them, or on hostile planets with unbearable gravity and atmosphere, they must utilize controlled environment coverings, light "aura" shields and transportable instruments and apparatus to measure, maintain and produce protection for the beings.

These things will be, and some already are, developed on your planet but Earth human must develop behavior balance before all technical knowledge is allowed perfection for as I stated prior--Earth man always utilizes the wondrous inventions and higher scientific knowledges in detrimental ways. As you develop, the menace is ever present of the Earth human exercising his technical knowledge, abilities and inventions for evil intent and power-control motives. This continues to happen over and over again, not only with Earth humans, but with other humanoid beings on other worlds as well. As man develops these techniques which will allow him into the outer cosmos, he will not longer be allowed to continue this behavior without recourse--he will not be allowed to fly from planet to planet intending to capture and control and become victor over another race.

In cosmic space many dangers of many proportions lurk where other cosmic inhabitants are not helplessly exposed to attack by other races. There could follow deadly defeats for the Earth humankind, and complete slavery, which could equal the falling back into the primary existence.

Is could also be possible that the planet Earth could be completely destroyed, because there are inhumane and hostile as well as humane races inhabiting planets, etc., in the cosmos as well as humane and advanced races.

When Earthman desires to take his barbarous thirst for power, material possessions and control into the cosmos, then he must count on his complete destruction, and no other creatures from other planets will come to his assistance for he will be the aggressor and such behavior will not be allowed according to cosmic order.

Earth human must understand that his world is in transition and herein comes the separation and sorting. Some will transcend the accepted dimension but many will be sorted into other placements while the Earth orb heals and renews. As Earth man moves into cosmic space, let it be known that there are other races who will not allow themselves to be under attack, exploited, or forced into servitude, as is usual behavior among the nations of your Earth. They will defend themselves with power, which will remain for a long time, infinitely superior to all technical means of the Earth human being. Where this is not the case, they may well be under the protection of other and more developed intelligences whose techniques approach perfection.

Peace will be preserved and death and destruction will not come to universal order and this must be given as information to Earth human, for his spiritual wisdom is still poorly developed indeed.

Earth man must face himself that he and his forefathers have brought all of mankind and the Earth herself to the brink of ruin and, prior to this current time, has had to evacuate the planet in panic and flight on numerous occasions--to return in a primitive state indeed.

There have been occasions in the cosmos when power-hungry and barbaric characters experienced in your solar system and roamed the spaces with limitless hate and unquenchable thirst for power. In one such instance they destroyed themselves to the last man, and no creature survived the conflict. They destroyed their own planet with a vast explosion which ignited the very atmosphere and nothing remained of that planet save the many thousands of asteroids, which still today circle around your sun--as memorials to the deadly unreasonability of human creatures to following the laws of God and The Creation as laid down for guidelines. This planet was known by several names, one of which was Maldec, and another, "Malonia". This is not intended, by the higher brotherhood, to ever again be allowed--the system is still in upheaval after eons of interim sequence. You will end your cycle of experience in different manner for the chaos is not acceptable.

Your planet must unify--but it must unify in light under God and in balance and harmony with others of the universe. This New World Order-- Global One World Plan is the most destructive of all unifications upon your planet for it is birthed in evil intent, control, greed and intent to depopulate the planet by any means necessary. Brothers, you have come a long, long way--unfortunately the journey has been, for the most part, in the wrong direction--away from God and not toward His Presence. The actions have caught up with you and you endure a time of chaos and unbalance which threatens your destruction--may truth and knowledge flow in time to make the necessary changes to return to sanity.

Man must return to spiritual balance and come into love within the highest definition. One cannot clothe love into words, for love is the same as bliss and joy, a state without a place or limit. It perishes nor can it be shaped or manipulated into that which it is not.

A spiritually developing person is a noble artist of precious spirit, filled with love, endowed with knowledge, logic and above all, wisdom. His wisdom is an always present light, shining even into the depths of darkness. It is not as the light of day which can be overcome by the darkness of night--it is ever present and surrounds all.

As man comes into spiritual awareness that wonders which abound are but the spiritual force exercising perfection, as all too often occurs, the human conceals a wonder behind a mysterious veil because he lacks logical explanation. Something unexplained is always a mystery in consideration- -it does not mean that it is *"mystical"*--ONLY UNEXPLAINED AND NOT YET UNDERSTOOD!

The only thing limiting the progress of the Earth human is the Earth human himself! You are limited by time and space perception and therein you differ greatly--for with the brothers of the cosmos--there is only the immediate--the "now". So be it.

Let us begin to act in each moment as if it were unlimited and as if space were infinite--for so it is. Whatever the perceptions of the moment, know that it can be changed in the flickering of an eye if man but chooses to so do. As we journey together into the cosmos, the bindings of the past experience must be left aside and only the positive lessons learned be brought forth in habit and character. To change thine world there only needs be one changed--YOU! PONDER IT.

May we walk in Grace, together, this day. Come with me, chelas, for I know the way. Salu.

I move to standby, Dharma, that you might join with your family. May there be renewal of intent and direction as we focus on our mission within the Glory of WHAT *IS*!

God has come forth in perfection and because He IS; so shall we become! Saalome'.

Hatonn, to stand-by. Clearing frequency, please. Thank you for your service this day. Salu.

CHAPTER 3

REC #1   HATONN

FRIDAY, NOVEMBER 23, 1990   8:28 A.M.   YEAR 4 DAY 99

Hatonn present to speak; I come in total service unto God, The Creation and unto you, my brothers. May understanding be sharpened that comprehension come quickly and our work accomplished. In the light shall we stand strong that the darkness may be removed from this wondrous, but weary, land.

DESTINY IN YOUR HANDS

Earth brother, for the present, the destiny of lifestream and the placement of your experience rests with full weight upon your own shoulders. However, should a time arise where an aberration or probable cataclysm comes in imminent, irreversible track that would affect the depths of cosmic space beyond the conscious thoughts of the Earth-human, it shall be that involvement from the advanced brotherhood will be activated.

Those humans present upon your planet who are willing and/or have turned unto God and The Creation Laws, shall be evacuated at such occurrence for most of you are our "ground crew" and will come rapidly into the remembering thereof. God would never--NEVER--leave his focused children without assistance and instruction.

COMMUNICATION

Over and over you ones ask "WHY?" this or that. Most especially "Why do you speak only through a translator--why not speak directly to us in first person?" Because you are not attuned to "hear". Ones anger at us for not giving forth the frequency for radio contact of this scribe, for instance. We have no objection to giving forth the frequency and you can tune it in on your wave bands--but what do you expect to hear? Do you expect to hear David Brinkley giving forth with dissertations regarding Cosmic and Earth current events?

We send to specific receivers who are placed at most particularly chosen locations--at critically located crystal formations. There is nothing mystical about the procedure of actual communication for the patterns are put forth in frequency pulses on specific wave frequencies which are not necessarily closed circuits. But herein the problem arises in such circumstances as is present with scribes--their purpose is to put to print the information as given. We give it in projected format of universal codes

26

(pulsed signals). The receiver receives the signals which are then translated by the individual into language native to the receiver. I would not, for instance, have Dharma, who only converses in English--receive Germanic dialects. Why would we do that when we can utilize a German speaking native to receive in German language? We broadcast in what you could refer to as vision sequence and code pulses which are instantly translated by the receiver. IF YOU TUNED IN TO THE EXACT FREQUENCY UTILIZED FOR, SAY, DHARMA--YOU WOULD PICK UP HIGH PITCHED (SHRILL), MOST DISAGREEABLE ELECTRONIC TONES WHICH WOULD BE ANNOYING INSTEAD OF INFORMATIVE. THERE WILL ALSO BE WHAT YOU CALL "STATIC" FROM INTERFERENCE WHICH A RECEIVER IS CAPABLE OF DISREGARDING. We do not work in great secrecy or mystical hoopla--it is simply that the receivers are trained to handle the apparatus, so to speak.

The higher energies are, of course, capable of communicating with any and all, but space brothers do not and the receiver must be acceptable to communication. It has nothing to do with capability but everything to do with free-will action and privacy. Pleiadians (since this is the race in topic) do not penetrate thoughts unless invited to do so. More of you of Earth request that communication than you might be aware of at your level of consciousness, and even though the use of invisible modes of contact are available for usage, the presumption of interference is forbidden. To do so would be to violate two highly regarded principles: privacy and free will, put as simplictly as possible. Both are considered most important to the development of an individual or society and terrestrial man must be allowed to make conscious decisions and then *learn* to be responsible for that which he creates.

Thought transmission is the purest form of communication, as the conversation may not be manipulated into something it is not! Changes in intent and content are manifest through the translation into languages. This is why, as we move into the realm of need of absolute understanding while reducing error projection through language, this local group of Earth humans sit together and physically read the documents and hear the portions read aloud whereby we can clarify, repunctuate and attend misrepresentations to the best of group contemplation. I personally attend every word and witness whether or not the understanding is penetrating the understanding faculties of the individuals. It makes for very long hours of intense attention--please accept that we are projecting as clearly as allowed and as is possible. Our full intent is to allow total truth, but remember dear ones, we come in service within fallible species and are restricted to alien language and alien identification of more technical and scientific materials.

For instance, there will be less than one in a million who would even begin to understand projections of mathematical configurations and grid harmonics and therefore we do not outlay such material which would simply bore the masses into deeper sleep. How many of you even care to look at the surface and cross-sectional areas of the earth in terms of nautical miles, or minutes of arc, and consider the values in regard to distance on the surface to see the interesting facts which emerge? Well, let us see! The cross-sectional area is equal to 37127665.09 square nautical miles. The harmonic reciprocal of this number is 26934093.

The surface area is equal to 148510660.36 square nautical miles. Each quarter of the earth's surface is therefore equal to 37127665.09 square nautical miles. The harmonic reciprocal again being 26934093. Now, how many of you simply fell in love with the foregoing? I thought not! We will enclose some of such information for we will be bringing keys to unlocking information cells for certain ones--but it will mean nothing to the receiver nor to most readers in the general populace. Believe me, chelas, to expect "proof" from cosmic brothers on the basis of technical knowledge or holographic projection simply is unrealistic in suggestion-- for it means naught to man unless he is in understanding of that which he is receiving. We are bringing truth unto the masses in these Journals--that means more than 6 billion individuals! Technical information shall come forth in other formats unto ones with understanding--and I assure you the book sales of such volumes is quite limited indeed.

HARMONY IN THE STARS

I have written some of the information which will be given herein in past Journals but it so pertinent to the subject of Pleiades that I must give it forth again. I shall endeavor to not be boring or repetitious to the point of losing you completely. You must begin to know your historical roots, however.

> **HERMES:** "Listen to your inner selves and look into the infinity of space and time. There reverberate the song of the stars and the harmony of the spheres.
>
> "Each sun is a thought of Creation, each planet a mode of that thought. In order that you may know divine thought, O souls, you painfully descend along the paths of the seven planets and their seven heavens and ascend once again.
>
> "What do the stars do? What do the numbers say? What do the spheres revolve? O souls that are lost and saved, they relate, they sing, they revolve your destinies."

PLEIADES

Most commonly the Pleiades are today referred to by their ancient Greek name, Pleiades, (Plea' ya dez). These suns carry names from all areas of your history. The Romans called them the "Virgins of Spring", the Australians labeled them the "Young Girls", and many civilizations denoted them as the "Falme", typical of the god Agni, who represented the source of fire, and the Bible refers to them as the "Seven Stars", or simply as the "Pleiades". At this time of your cycle (ending November) in the hours near the changing of your day, the Pleiades will be almost directly overhead in perception. The golden radiance "star" perceived just beneath the constellation as seen from Earth sphere--is the Starship "Phoenix"! Salu!

The Greeks refer to the cluster of stars that have guided people, far removed from each other, in agriculture and commercial affairs simply by rising and setting, as the Seven Sisters. These are honored in the Court of the Cariatids (as pronounced in English) in the stone remains of the Acropolis in Athens. Their brilliance and twinkling communication has been the source of wishful admiration and critical observation on every continent, in every age of man. They have been worshipped by some, celebrated by others, and recognized for their wondrous beauty and sweet influence by almost all. Why? Because they call to you as a whisper from home and homeland!

> *JOB* 38:31: "Canst thou bind the sweet influences of the Pleiades or loose the bands of Orion?"

> *AMOS* 5:8: "Seek him that maketh the seven stars and Orion, and turneth the shadow of death into morning, and maketh day dark with night: that calleth for the waters of the sea, and poureth them out upon the face of the earth: The Lord is his name."

Pleiades (The Seven Sisters) are located in the constellation of Taurus, the bull. Clearly visible in the northern hemisphere on winter nights, they resemble a tiny reproduction of the Little Dipper and are often called such--actually, in Greek, they are often referred to as the "micro-dipper" These are one of the most carefully studied regions of the firmament. Man of Earth is drawn to them as if to a magnet by iron shavings.

These wondrous orbs have enraptured minds for centuries of your counting and we give honor to your 18th century comet hunter, Charles Messier, who was first to chart and identify them. The primitive equipment of the day often allowed amateur astronomers to mistakenly label stationary objects as comets so, to assist his fellow celestial watchers, Messier worked diligently from his observation atop the Hotel de Cluny in Paris, France. In 1771 he published his first catalogue of some forty-five non-cometary objects and it was in this register that the Pleiades were designated the label of M-45. Now for you ones who keep up with such happenings, the alien recently "taken" by your CIA in Virginia, comes from the system designated as M-31. These are simply designations by Earth man to more easily place the heavens into a grid system.

Many astronomers have charted many suns in the area of M-45. There are several thousand in this tiny sector of which some two hundred and fifty are recognized as members of this galactic cluster, the rest lie in the depths of space beyond the system. Once all of the more faintly visible stars have been examined, the total shall be far greater--closer to some half million.

This celestial group is easily tracked by first locating the giant red star--which is visible beyond Starship, known as Betelguese, which appears in the Orion constellation as the "shoulder" of the Great Hunter. Next finding Aldebaran, a first magnitude star in Taurus, draw a line between the two. Extend the line in a northwest direction almost an equal distance past Aldebaran. Here it will terminate just south of the beautiful Seven Sisters. This is an attempt to visualize from Earth perspective but will be accurate enough in description in your language to allow identification. Herein, to the publishers, place a copy of the diagram as described, please.

This tightly grouped cluster of suns is in your own galaxy, six of the seven are discernible by the unaided eye. Alcyone is the brightest. It has a magnitude of 2.9 and is classified as a B-5, blue-white star whose primary element is helium with an approximate temperature of some 13,000 degrees Centigrade. The magnitude of these luminous orbs range from the meek twinkling of Sterope (Asterope) which is also blue-white, but is what is labelled B-8 with an apparent magnitude of 5.9, to the brilliance of Alcyone, which is thought by some to exceed your sun's refulgence a thousand times or more. As difficult as it may be for your minds to fathom, this light, which you categorize and classify and gaze into the heavens to search out, has been traveling toward you for one and a half centuries before you of Earth perceive it. I am herein efforting to speak in Earth perception for it is sufficient for our purposes of becoming acquainted.

HISTORICAL DOCUMENTATIONS

It is not accidental that the predominantly recorded system is Pleiades. Cave paintings, hieroglyphics, legends, mythology, and written languages have depicted these shimmering beams as a positive force through civilization's history. Their position in the expanse of darkened heavens throughout key times in the calendar year does not fully account for the remarkable influence attributed to them.

> *POPE: "For see: the gath'ring flocks to shelter tend, And from the Pleiades fruitful showers descend."*

> *MANUDER:* "When the constellations were first designed the Pleiades rose helically at the beginning of April and were the sign of the return of spring."

The beauty and peaceful connotations of these mysterious wonders are referred to in text, both past and present, as the Seven Stars, yet one of them is not visually seen. Almost a universal tradition, therefore, suggests that one of them has been misplaced or is hidden, and was so deemed the "Lost Pleiad" by the Greeks. Now, for some proof of purchase--how would a missing star be classified and spoken of--and far later in historical documentation be proven--if there was not ancient attachment? How can you relate to something unknown? Therefore, it follows that it had to have been "proven" and "known" at some time historically. It seems quite amazing that ALL cultures of antiquity were aware of the seventh star, which is masked from the view of the inhabitants of Earth!

Could it be that the future is only the past again, entered through a different gate of perception?

The repeated acknowledgement will be fully understood and explained as the jigsaw puzzle is assembled--for now, most of the pieces are still a bit scattered and some are still missing completely. There is little room for doubting, however, that since the dawn of your recorded time, these stars have been a most powerful influence and are believed, upon your place, to be a powerful influence and to hold at least a portion of the responsibility for molding the destiny of humanity.

Throughout time thousands of cultures, religions, and beliefs have been introduced to this delicate planet you call home in this present experience. Many of these ideals and ideas conflict or contradict one another and existing in every single one is a positive/negative flow of information. However, in all of the societies and civilizations that have been researched for this connection, one topic remains alluded to as a consistent enlightening force, found in the earliest texts and legends, it is the mystifying cluster of suns...called Pleiades.

You will find that tracking the source of verbal legend is most difficult, of not impossible--until the oral tradition and teachings are brought forth and unfolded as we will now be doing--here and through the Lakota Brother, Little Crow , of the Lakota Sioux in permission and commission from Wakan Tanka/Tunkonshila (Grandfather), here at the closing of the Sacred Cycle. In proper sequence of information projection with the Journals, THE SACRED HILL WITHIN will come forth as confirmation of this truth within the Journals as a gift unto man from Creator/Creation that you might know your Source and your Roots.

SHOCKER

You can find truth in the hereditary conversations, from most unrelated areas of your world, which correctly reflect upon the Pleiades as the "Center of the Universe", the "Seat of Immortality", and the "Home of God". Intangible as these sources might be, it is only circumstantial that these legacies left a definite mark in diverse civilizations. Well, let us move beyond circumstantial and into correlations exhibiting evidence of a massive contact with Pleiadian cosmonauts somewhere in your past, little brethren.

LET US PEER INTO HISTORY:

The Hopi named them "Choo ho kan", meaning those who cling together, and they, too, consider themselves direct descendants of the inhabitants of the cluster. The Hopi, as well as the Navajo and other cultures dispersed around the world, used a calendar that allowed them to chart the seasons, special events, and ceremonial rites with uncanny accuracy. They used a system based on a 260 day "Sacred Round", or minor cycle, and a 365 day year, a major cycle which equaled a period between the midnight culminations of the Pleiades. Any day calculated on these cycles would not repeat itself for 18,980 days (or, 52 years).

In the Kiva of the Mesas, Sacred Temple of the Mesas, the Hopi ceremoniously "light the new fire". This occurs every 52 years when the temple's sacred points align with the stars, Choo ho kan. All fires are extinguished throughout the nation and rekindled from a sacred fire produced by the holy men. The young men of the tribe learn the importance of the Pleiades early in life, for initiation into the spiritual ways takes place only when the cherished cluster is directly overhead at night--so you see, this is a most powerful time of the annual cycle!

The Dakota Ehanni stories, which are tales of the world previous to the Dakota emergence, speak of the Tayamni, the home of their ancestors, and the reason for the seven tribes...the Pleiades. The Seven Sisters play a major role in their history as well as their present day culture. In May, the month of Hanblaceya (I believe I translate correctly as `vision quest'), the Dakota communicate with the spirits. Astronomy tells you that the Pleiades rise with the sun in May and the Dakota oral history tells you that the home of the spirits is the Pleiades. The older Dakotas say that when you die, your spirit goes to the Milky Way and turns south---south to the Seven Stars.

The Navajo named the sparkling suns the "Dilyehe", home of the black god and the Osage believe their society was once pure of spirit and journeyed from the stars to Earth.

The Iroquois believe the twinkling orbs represent seven young people who guard the holy seed throughout the night. Prayers for happiness were addressed unto them, and during ceremonial rites, the calumet was symbolically presented to them. After all, these stars were the home of their ancestors.

There is a lovely legend among the Native Americans as exemplified in a tale from the Onondaga:

"A long time ago a party of hunters journeyed through the woods in search of a good hunting ground. Having found one, they proceeded to build their lodges for the winter, while the children gathered together to dance and sing.

32

"While the children were thus engaged, an old man dressed in white feathers, whose flowing hair shone like silver, appeared among them and bid them cease dancing lest a mysterious force befall them, but the children danced on unmindful of the warning, and presently they observed that the were rising little by little into the air.

"One of them exclaimed. `Do not look back for something strange is taking place'. One of the children disobeyed this warning and, looking back, became a falling star. The six other children reached the high heavens safely and can now be seen dancing in the Pleiades...the stars they became."

The Hohokam, a Pima word meaning "that which has vanished", disappeared from the arid Arizona desert they had so successfully irrigated and tamed. Although no one knows why they vanished or where they went, legend claims they returned to their home in the stars--to Pleiades.

The Creeks claim to have come to Earth from the stars in spirit form to become flesh and blood. Each year a medicine man who has served the apprenticeship of seven years performs the "green corn dance" where he takes seven ears of corn from seven fields of the seven clans to insure a healthy harvest.

The intent is to bring forth **THE SACRED HILL WITHIN***, in seven volumes--in length for reading in one sitting appropriate per each revealing.*

These wondrous connections could go on for volumes of material--each attached and coming from all directions of your planet; Australian Aborigines, Mayans, Aztecs, Incas and on and on, but the document would become unwieldy and I would like to focus on that which is better recognized and known today.

I would, however, like to give you one more illustration of the connections and point out the diversity of geographic location for original belief traditions: Huang-Ti, the "Yellow Emperor" of China (2697-2587 BC), is considered by many Taoists to be a miraculous being who succeeded in attaining immortality. During his reign utensils of wood, clay pottery and metal were manufactured; boats and carts were constructed and utilized and the medium of currency was originated. Provinces of the vast country were mapped, accupressure and accupuncture became sciences, and the Emperor is generally acknowledged as the father of holistic medicine. Huang-Ti claimed that much of this rapid development began because of conversations held in court with his **consultants....**_**beings from the Pleiades**_.

I would like to herein point out that in 1975 AD, on your planet, contacts from Pleiadian persons began in regular sequence. The original thrust was in Switzerland which was a non-warring country, neutral in political arenas and open of mind. There have been photographs, materials for scientific study, etc., left for you to examine. These have caused great pain and suffering for the contacts. Work has been discounted and disinformation thrust upon a deceived public. We herein intend to repeat the information and again, man can do that which he will with it. I would however, stress the suggestion that you consider this information most carefully indeed. You as a species locked to the planet Earth had better come to grips with your circumstance and look beyond the lies thrust upon you by your controllers--you are in the time of Kali (chaos) and if you look into your prophecies, you will find this is very nearly the closing time of the cycles. When that loop closes it will be a "hot time in the old town tonight"!

SEPARATION IMPOSSIBLE

As you come into understanding of beginnings, you will desire to argue and denounce connections with star beings and etheric angelic beings--so be it. You can "desire" all ye wish--it will not change truth.

You are descendents of that which was referred to as the ones from the skies who could "fly"--in many and varied manners. You are what has been referred to as the clan of the winged ones, or more generally put: The Bird Tribes. Is it not time to preen your flight feathers? Salu. Hat onn to stand-by as we close this segment. Thank you for your service. Saalome'

CHAPTER 4

REC #1   HATONN

SATURDAY, NOVEMBER 24, 1990   5:25 A.M.   YEAR 4 DAY 100

Hatonn present in the Light and in service unto God and unto man. May our truth be ever present and may we find understanding in our projections.

I am sorry to call you forth at such an early hour again, Dharma, for the fatigue is taking toll, but other ones shall simply have to tend of the Earthly matters for I cannot sacrifice the day of writing in order to have guests--please lean upon me and I will give you strength and energy to do that which we need do. Aho.

TODAY'S WATCH

Allow us to bypass "Today's Watch" for we must do a segment for the Journal. I do, however, ask that you be cautious as the surveillance has been increased as have the bombardments of elf's to your place. There was a deliberate focus of sonic blast against this place yesterday and apparently more are in the staging; keep the protection and security tight as so many come and go through the dwelling.

Naught has changed as ones come and go in curiosity and non-decision. Remember, ours is not a mission of entertainment nor social picnics--it is the time of decisions within the group, most especially, and ones functioning for their own selfish reasons, within, are erring greatly for this is NOT the place to find fulfillment of self indulgence in Earth physical fun and games. Those who use another in controlling power for self will find the welcome mat turned upside downward for ours is a place of production and one cannot put him/her-self above another nor take the precious time remaining in drifting in directionless wandering. It is a time of definite choices and maturity--if ones just wish to play games of "Catch the Gold Ring", it must be done elsewhere. So be it.

DOMES AND TERRAIN

I will take this opportunity to discuss structures intended for the most efficient utilization of space and functionability since we will have guests which are working in perfection of the domed structures. The subject is expecially applicable to the point of Pleiades so the segment will not be lost to the Journal.

First I shall be reminding you of expected events of "Natural" nature which shall be making themselves increasingly difficult with which to deal over the time of transition. Man-triggered or nature-triggered makes no difference if the winds are blowing at a steady 150 miles an hour, dear ones. Dwellings cannot stand long against such assault. As man continues to tamper with the atmosphere and devastation of the lands all manners of changes shall come upon the orb--but allow us to speak of the the "why" of domed architecture and underground structures.

Adequate layers of earth or cement are barriers against many of the elements which may come upon you--i.e., radiation, extreme temperatures, winds and, if made properly--water. If introduced fragments of metalic powder or particles the shield shall guard against microwaves and several types of particle beams. Further, the shape of the building itself will deflect, instead of allowing piercing by, projectiles.

Your goal must be to build downward within the earth where feasible but remember, if you utilize care, an above ground shelter can serve many varied needs.

In time you must be prepared for the "possible" for you will not be given the extent of such possible hazards to life of physical beings. Therefore, you will wish to utilize the optimum advantages of architecture as pertains to asthetic desirability as well as durable and protective styles.

Architectural shape, lighting and heating forms are most critical. Also the mode of living must be considered most carefully for no matter if a man survives if he is rendered mad or infirm by his environment.

MATERIALS

Please, you who are self-styled builders and engineers; do not come forth saying a thing can or cannot be done--REMEMBER, IF IT CAN BE CONCEIVED, IT CAN BE ACHIEVED. Do not, for instance, tell me that compressed earth is not possible for use as shelter roof. It not only is possible for such use but fitted properly will stand against ALL elements-- be they ones that shake, rattle or roll. I suggest you look at the architecture of the great cathedrals for the principle of arches and domes never fails if structured properly with balance and proper infrastructure.

If the world as you know it never changes you have nothing to concern about--but, if it does, you face having no metals with which to fabricate domes and no way to refine or roll the finished product if you do. You must move to that which you can produce for self--and anything short of that need is but frosting for your cakes.

Let me paint a vision for you as regards that which is practiced in the more progressive planets of your homeland. We are speaking of a solar system wherein, as with your system, each planet varies--with one exception. There is availability of inter-planetary interchange for the most part and the backward planets do not inter-mingle much with the more advanced brotherhood of the solar system of Pleiades, for instance. I would interject herein that on some of the habitable planets of Pleiades, the societies are in growing above that which is bringing Earth to her knees. But in many societies the humans were evacuated to safety off their own planets and placed in security in other compatible facilities in which to continue physical experience. These planets remain as isolated and landlocked as does Earth. TO PLAY AMONG THE STARS IN THE UNIVERSAL COSMOS REQUIRES INTEGRITY, GODLINESS AND AN ADHERENCE UNTO THE LAWS OF GOD AND CREATION.

I prefer that you ones turn from the attitude of "simple survival" and move in the direction of change because it is a "better way" in which to live. If you move into the "better way" it matters not that which comes to pass.

Let us consider "typical" Pleiades living for the "ordinary" inhabitants in a suburban setting or "rural" environment for, within the cities, the principals of architecture are the same but of course the needs are different and therefore the setting differs.

A typical family will have a considerably large dwelling of any size desired--mostly underground. The typical tunneling is in the shape of a spoked wheel which can be enlarged, closed off or done in any desirable manner pleasing to the family and according to means available. Homeless brothers are not acceptable! Facilities are provided wherein the homeless are housed for participation in upkeep.

We do not speak of an unchanging planet which is ongoing in pastoral sublimity--we speak of a changing planet whereupon humans dwell and the lands and people are in constant change as the planet changes. Earthquakes, etc. are as prevalent, or more so, than on Earth orb.

The "main" living quarters of food preparation center, family gathering quarters, entertainment room (living rooms), pools and atriums are in the central "hub". Sleeping rooms and baths are located off the hub in the tunneled "spokes". The areas between the spokes are partially excavated and "finished" into underground gardens. Enough natural formation is always left untouched for a support system of the caving roof.

Near the windows of the housing are located asthetic gardens and beds of plants and shrubs. Growing dens for foodstuff are then in mid=segments between spokes. The garden for the most used kitchen "vegetables" is grown adjacent to the kitchen area. The energy of our suns is harnessed and underground lighting is plentiful anywhere we wish it. The lighting is on automatic cyclic "timers" for balanced optimal growth and rest.

Since clutter is not conducive to mental order, there is abundant storage facility in all dwellings whereby the living areas are kept totally uncluttered.

37

From the main "hub" are exits to the surface as are there exits from every living area to the surface--however, most exit/entrance opening is asthetically and protectively constructed. There is a "garden" room above the hub which can be opened or closed as desired but is more in appearance of a garden setting arranged with natural or formally arranged plant life and/or pools, etc. The pools are available for asthetic reasons, bathing, exercising and in addition, water supply if needed. The sun-room is enclosed in a tranparent glass with high metal content for protection and shielding--however the area can be completely closed off by a sliding shield should radiation protection be necessary. Remember this is not Camelot, Milk and Honey Land or the City with the golden streets and pearly gates--this is a planet much as your own!

Off of each "spoke" room is much storage, a hearth center and a large "bathroom". We recycle water and therefore have abundance which is carefully monitored and unwasted in any manner what-so-ever. All waste materials are treated and returned to natural state and byproducts utilized-- both human and animal.

The alloted amount of land for individual use varies but a typical plot is sufficient to have a luxurious underground dwelling, home park above ground and pasture for animal grazing and domestic stock. There are, however, underground facilities for protection of the stock in inclement weather of any type dangerous to their well-being.

The source of energy is from solar resources; however, "slash" and trimmings of plants and shrubs, orchards and such, are utilized in the "fireplaces" which are the central focus of the dwelling.

Think now, you are living underground -- or, above ground in earthen structures which minimizes changes in temperatures and therefore, a fireplace is more for the needs of soul than for necessary heat.

The materials "re-arranged" from underground excavation are utilized in the structure walling, foundation shoring and above ground retaining walls, fences, planters and such. We compress the material (earth) just as we suggest you do.

Most doors are NOT, but rather screening is utilized by sliding covers or "maze-type" entrances. This gives ability to generalize heating/cooling and reduces need for "hardware" (knobs, hinges, etc.). We have far more energy for use in powering such closures than we have metals which are utilized carelessly for such nonsense.

The cities, of course, are structured greatly underground also but that which protrudes is treated with great care with gardens and natural grounds. A lot of "metal glass" is utilized, I suppose you would call it crystal, but it is as durable and unbreakable as is metal--hence the perception of "crystal cities". The architecture is pyramidal or domed. There is living availability beneath the cities at varying underground levels to house comfortably everyone in the city for safety in natural disasters or accidents. We have a different solar system than do you of Earth and therefore protection must be available against sun flares, etc. The elements can be most extreme for evolution of the planets have, of course, been cyclical such as yours and the inhabitants of these planets have learned just as you must.

As more and more history of your planet is brought to the surface for your attention, you will find that you, too, had such cities in many, many locations. Remember that what you call North America, for instance, is a "new" portion for the most part. As the old continents again rise and old portions of Lemuria and Atlantis are unearthed--you will find designs much as I have described above.

Dharma, find Sipapu Odyssey and write the portion regarding winds and specifically the shifting expected in North America and reprint it herein, please.

FUTURE REVELATIONS

As described:

"......and it is said there shall be winds, and there shall surely be, in the time when it is winter; and the trees shall bow down their boughs, and the winds shall sting with the cold; and there shall be great suffering among the people and they shall fall down and cry for mercy.

"And there shall be a mighty earthquake and it shall split in twain the country of North America, and it shall be as nothing the world has known before, for it shall be that there shall be a great part of the great land of the the north continent go down and a great sea shall form within her center part from the Dominion of Canada into the Gulf of Mexico.

"And there shall be great ocean liners, liners which shall travel within its waters, which will be propelled by solar energy of the next age. But with this, they shall be unable to travel east to west or from west to east, through what is now the Atlantic Ocean, for it shall have a mountain range which has been thrown up from the bottom of the Atlantic; and it shall be extended into the air to the altitude of ten to eighteen thousand feet and it shall be the City of old, for it was the Light of the world. She went down amid a great shock and a great wave; and it shall be that she shall come up the same way as she went down.

"And the west side shall be as the sheer side of granite, and it shall be without foothold; and the way shall be as the eagle flies from the place which is Upper Virginia three hundred miles due east; and at this point it shall be one thousand and eight hundred feet

39

from the waters; and not an entrance through the land shall there be to the east, for it is not for them, which are to be the remnants, to communicate by water; for it shall be with a new science, and a new method shall be given unto them. For there is not a place which is that shall remain the same in its present state.

"And not a person shall be left which is not prepared for that which shall be. And there are many called but few are chosen: for there are none which have been chosen which have not been carefully prepared; and they have been unto themselves true, and they have given credit where credit is due. And now it is given unto them to be the seed of the new Civilization which shall come upon the Earth.

"And within the time which is left before this shall come upon the Earth, it shall be that many will be called: and they shall doubt; and they shall fear; and they shall faint; and they shall fall by the way; and they shall be in no wise, wise, for it is given unto man to fear that which he does not understand--and for that does he wait.

"And it is said that there shall be winds, and there shall be the winds, and they shall be as none the Earth has known; and they shall be as the winds from the sea and from the land all rolled into one great tempest. And they shall be as the winds of the North and the South and East and the West, and they shall tear that which is in their path and they shall be as the reaper who mows down that which is in his path. And they shall sing with the bitterness of the cold. And they shall be as the elements of the earth, for they shall contain both rain and wind; and the hail shall be as big as bird eggs, and it shall split that which it hits.

"And it shall be that the suffering shall be great upon the Earth, for it is given unto man to know suffering. And he has not known such suffering before, and, when it is come upon him, he shall fall down and shall cry for mercy.

"And it shall be that the winds, too, shall be great upon the Earth-- they shall blow East, West, North and South and not a place shall there be upon the Earth which shall escape the winds which bloweth; and when this tribulation has come upon the Earth, it shall be that there shall be many who have kept within the law.

"And with the coming of the winds and belching of fire from within the Earth there shall be - - - MORE!....."

So be it and Selah!

LOOK AT THE POTENTIALS

You must be prepared for the changes for the probabilites remain that man will NOT change of his path and therefore, these things shall come to pass in your time upon the orb. Further, as you change into the transitioned "parallel" and higher dimensioned planet--you will utilize these changes as life-style.

It is not feasible to simply change-out everything--but as you grow and change and it becomes opportune, you change the building modes into the new. As you build shelters, for instance, build them for multi-use if at all possible. As, let us say, current buildings come down for whatever reason--replace them with the new which preserves your natural resources and is inexpensive (not a small concern in time of massive depression). You must learn to rebuild in efficiency and inexpensively for you shall have the economic devastation, food shortages and physical structure destruction coming one upon another and you must learn to utilize "survival methods" and allow beauty and balance as well. For instance, until you have ability to bring forth "free energy", you need the underground facilities to conserve heat and allow cooling according to the extremes as well as sheltering from atmospheric pollution and such. You will need the underground oxygen supply from the underground green-houses. You must structure an ecologically complete system and the planning must be begun whereby all things are in consideration. The spiritual man cannot live by bread alone but the physical man cannot live by spirit alone. Preparations in the planning must be made in the present against the possibilities and probabilities in expectation--at the best, you will not need of the facilities but will have a BETTER mode of life--at the worst--you have protection against that which might come against you, as in the ark atop the waters of the Great Flood.

SHARING OF THOUGHTS

I would like to share some thought provoking ideas which relate to man and his placement which might help define the attitudes and ultimately the plight of human on Earth.

You must stop dishonouring the earth for to dishonour the earth is actually dishonoring the very spirit of man. Man acts out as if he is a creator, which he has ceased to be for the replenishing of creation, and not that of a "user" which he has become. This delusion is robbing him, not only of his natural heritage, but of his future as well.

You abuse land because you regard it as a commodity belonging to you. When you see land as a community to which you simply belong, you may consider using it again with love and respect. The earth you abuse and the living things that you kill will, in the ending, take their revenge, dear ones; for in exploiting their presence you are diminshing that which is

41

conceived as "future". The nation that destroys its very soil, destroys itself.

Everything is perfect coming forth from the Creator; everything seems to degenerate in the hands of man--we must come into awakening of the sleeping destroyers for it is a serious sequence, indeed. The long fight to save wild beauty represents democracy at its very best. It requires citizens to practice the hardest of virtues--self-restraint and self-discipline.

America, for instance, today stands poised on a pinnacle of wealth and power--about to plunge over the edge into the crevass of collapse and depression wherein the power shall be shifted from the people unto the elite. Yet you live in a land of vanishing beauty, of increasing ugliness, of shrinking open spaces, and of an over-all environment that is diminished daily by pollution and noise and blight. The more you get out of the world the less you leave, dear ones, and in the long run you shall have to pay your debts at a time that will be most inconvenient for your own survival. So be it

You must utilize memory and past for that wondrous gift which it provides--LEARNING! Then, you must look forward to that which may come--in anticipation and with forethought--then, dwell in the present moment that you might take action to correct that which is incorrect from the past and become perfection in the anticipated future. In every action, consider that which came before and lessons learned and then consider that which may follow, and then undertake it. A danger foreseen is already half avoided for the time to repair the roof is when the sun is shining and rain not yet upon you---watch it even as regards the proper sequence, (which came first the chicken or the egg?), for in either case you cannot hatch a chicken from a cooked egg. Only those ones who are within a "thing" or "concept" with eyes open to truth can find the safe way out. Look to the end, no matter what it is you are considering. Often enough God gives a man a glimpse of happiness and goal and then allows man to ruin himself--so stay in the path of lighted truth and reap the happiness and security of the goal.

If all of you could but remember, in this passage of confusion and chaos, that the certainty of God giving meaning to life far surpasses in attractiveness the ability to behave badly with impunity.

And I suggest that the following is most true indeed: THOUGH GOD'S ATTRIBUTES ARE EQUAL, YET HIS MERCY IS MORE ATTRACTIVE AND PLEASING THAN IS HIS **JUSTICE!** I further suggest that you who believe you have all the answers and demand that God meet your specifications, I would point out that *no-one has the capacity to judge God. We are all but droplets in that limitless sea of mercy and grace and we had best rember it.* Everyone, whether he is self-denying or self-indulgent; meek or demanding, is seeking after the Beloved Source of Truth and the Word. Every place may be the shrine of love but he temple is within and all searching without shall merit thee only disappointment. God is what man finds that is divine in himself. God is the best way man can behave in any occasion and opportunity of life, and the farthest point to which man can stretch himself. When men vote-in Laws and call them God's and manufacture God--you have just removed God!

There is nothing "good" or "bad"; it is only in the thought perception which makes it so. Salu.

Might we close this segment as you have many ones coming very shortly. May we work in peace and ceaseless endeavor to do the will of God and remain in service according to that will. It is very easy to consider thine own opinions as the direction to be followed and herein I suggest that a good is never productive of evil but when it is carried to culpable excess--IN WHICH CASE IT COMPLETELY CEASES TO BE A GOOD. Everyone keeps placing his own "good" where he can and has as much of it as he can--IN HIS OWN WAY. IN OTHER WORDS--THE MOTTO TOO OFTEN IS, "I PLAN TO DO GOD'S WORK, BUT I PLAN TO DO IT MY OWN WAY ACCORDING TO MY OWN PLAN." Well, I consider it an act of wisdom to consider that your own plan may well not be ideal--look around at what you have created from this attitude!

Hatonn moving to stand-by, Saalome'

CHAPTER 5

REC #1   HATONN

MONDAY, NOVEMBER 26, 1990   8:20 A.M.   YEAR 4 DAY 102

Good morning; in the light of God. Hatonn present to discuss that which happened here on Saturday last. I request that you utilize this writing as an Express, in combination with that which Commander Korton has given through a different receiver. I further request that Thomas sit to receive from Sananda "Jesus" that there be no misunderstanding as regards material issuing forth on the incident. What occurred on Saturday was as nearly a disastrous incident as we have had to date in the political ploys of your world. Because there were some thirty persons (adults) present as witness, perhaps there shall be some level of understanding of truth. Further, there shall be leaked information coming from Edwards Air Force Base and your leaders shall attempt more incitement to war.

THIS WAR, DEAR FRIENDS, IS ATTEMPTED WITH SPACE COMMAND--A MOST FOOLISH MANEUVER INDEED.

INCIDENT IN POINT

Without giving forth tactical security, I shall give a brief description of the incident under discussion.

Please note that this is NOT the first attempt to damage the communications system of the crystal vortex--this IS the first attempt by foreign intervention.

You ones wish to believe that your "cold war" with Russia is over--no, you have heated it up to boiling but it is taking a nasty turn of events in which none of you Earth-based (imprisoned) chelas can win. There seems to be great misunderstanding among your military "professionals" regarding Space Command capabilities and permission to take action.

Commander Korton gave a brief overview of the incident which I ask be combined with this document and with that which Thomas shall briefly receive from Sananda and to be presented as an Express as soon as possible.

At approximately 11:50 A.M., P.D.T, on Saturday, November 24, 1990, in your mode of counting, as some thirty or more persons were gathered at the home of this scribe, a "Cosmosphere" beam-type weapon was discharged with intent to demolish the property and kill all occupants, in addition to intent to destroy the capabilities of the crystal communications/navigation vortex. It is not as simple as simply removing communi-

44

cations linkage with Space Command--the crystal is also utilized by all space-capable craft for navigation, orbit tracking, etc. The instrumentation is remote to insure security.

The entire scenario was an attempt to establish blame on one another. There is an all-out attempt to establish reasonability of attack on Russia-- as we have spoken of at great length--set for early December.

There are at all times a minimum of four Cosmospheres in the area of Edwards Air Force Base in permanent station. There are others also, but we will speak of only these four. There is also a number of Command (ours) craft in the area to protect and monitor this group within which this scribe resides and protect the crystal and the property. Our needs, to now, have been to protect the communications/navigation vortex from ground damage due to quakes, etc. This leaves the surface quite vulnerable to attack--it will no longer be vulnerable for we will enclose it within a full circle shield. This will cause great loss of ability of your own forces to utilize the wondrous facility for we are herein scrambling the signals and will continue to change them at irregular intervals. I suggest you all realize-- for your own elite will not tell you--that your military and that of Russia have basically declared war on Space Command. Therefore, there shall be incidents at frequent intervals in attempt to cause Earth Man to believe that you are under attack from Space Aliens. YOU ARE NOT!

The intent of the incident was to cause us to take aggressive action with shields removed in order to be visible to the public and allow one of your planes (of stealth nature with a dead crew aboard) utilizing young men who have been slain accidentally in Saudi Arabia, to fire upon us without note, and cause us to disable the craft and crash it--thus blaming Space Command for the incident and the death of the crew. It would be obvious for all ones to see from the ground having had attention called to the area by the blast against the scribe's location and crystal. There is great insanity among your Elite groups in effort to gain control of your world at all costs feasible.

The full intent was to get all sides blaming one another. The surveillance Cosmospheres stationed over Nellis Field in Las Vegas, however, informed this sector and plans were outlaid by the "mole" system infiltrated within your military circles.

The Phantom (shielded) craft, which would be "unmanned", would carry a crew of already dead personnel. The attack would be against the crystal and the dwelling thus causing the Space Command to believe it was an attack by Cosmospheres, thereby hoping to bring confrontation between Command and Soviet Command.

The Soviets, being far advanced of you in the U.S.A. in air and space technology, noted the plans and waited. The assault would be thus: there would be simultaneous pulse beam blasts at the dwelling and the communications center from the Phantom which shoud trigger Cosmosphere's pulses at our Command ship, which is only a surveillance craft. The attack was to cause the Spacecraft to become visible and then to stop the intended strike by the crash of the U.S. craft on the property itself, to finish the scenario to perfection. The picture would be a shot down stealth plane with crew lost and done visibly by Space Command--(aliens).

Do you ones actually think that we are so dense? Our Command "reasoned" with these ones for days while this incident was in the planning stage for there were also several diversionary incidents on the planning board had this one been pulled off intact. This location is well known by military and administration leaders. Attempt after attempt has been made against this scribe's life and we of the Command consider it an aggressive act of war. I suggest all of you remember that we come in service of God Creator and you are primitive in comparison to our technology.

We waited until the plane took off from Nellis--I was having a gathering. The Russians had agreed with us to not move forward with the incident, but to simply divert the direction of the U.S. craft and allow it to crash in the Mojave desert away from population. The intent was to bring it down by your forces at any rate either by crashing or explosives. As agreed to, the craft would simply overfly the area, the pulse weapon beam neutralized, and that would be the end of it--"another crash of a training plane".

This is not, however, what happened. Simultaneously, two Cosmospheres opened fire on our shield system, hopefully causing us to withdraw the shield and defend the ground target. So, simultaneously the blast aimed at the dwelling and the crystal vortex and at us by two spheres were enacted. We simply diverted the beam pulse to the ground target but timing was not perfected and the beam had to be diverted to the hillside covering the crystal. We had no need to visualize for either maneuver. The third Cosmosphere was to destroy the U.S. craft--with Space craft visible to appear that we shot down your plane.

We diverted the blast but it damaged the communications system by scrambling much of the communication frequencies. The crystal itself is undamaged and shall be reprogrammed within this day. As the frequencies went wild it has damaged Dharma physically, and we shall need give her healing time over the next few days, please. She is already extremely fatigued and that kind of a tonal assault to her brain is indeed disabling. You of the group will please be patient and bear with her while we decrease gatherings and ask that some of the readings for editing be elsewhere. My frequency is undamaged but she has been terrorized--not for self, but for the possibility of thirty deaths on her property--Oberli has not yet realized the magnitude of the attack.

These attempts at pulling in Space Command into your stupid and heinous warfare will continue to ever-increasing extent. I plead with you ones to pay attention and evaluate carefully that which shall be more regularly coming into your attention. This onslaught is the basis for many of the "world leadership" meetings--"What to do about Space Command!"

What did we do? Ah, funny thing about that--we simply locked onto the U.S. craft with a tracking magnetic tractor beam and returned the confounded thing, dead bodies and all, to Edwards Air Force Base, as well as the Cosmospheres, and we had a dandy understanding right there. I assure you dear ones, whose lives are in jeopardy, that there WAS AN UNDERSTANDING. This does not, however, mean that ones out to "get you" will cease and desist--it DOES mean that we shall now increase surveillance shielding and go on absolute alert over every ground contact on your planet. We shall stick with you of our brothers like super-glue on the duck's back.

SPACE COMMAND IS MOST SURELY ALLOWED AND EXPECTED TO DEFEND SELF, CRAFT, CREW AND GROUND CREW! I SUGGEST ALL MILITARY AND ADMINISTRATION OF COUNTRIES THROUGHOUT YOUR GLOBE--*CLEARLY UNDERSTAND THIS STATEMENT! WE DO HAVE CAPABILITY OF REMOVING ATTACKING CRAFT WITHOUT UTILIZING ONE WEAPON AND THE CRAFT IS GONE FOREVER--FURTHER, WE CAN SET YOUR CREW (IF ALIVE) SAFELY AND VERY CONFUSEDLY ON TERRAFIRMA, INTACT AND WITHOUT MORE THAN CONFUSION OF MENTAL EXPLANATION. I MOST SURELY SUGGEST YOU ACCEPT THIS AS WARNING!*

The merit of being able to blame Space Command was that the Cosmospheres utilize the crystal for tracking also and certainly there is not the desire for being blamed for such a shoot-down. The Cosmosphere crews had no way to know the crew was already dead.

I REMIND YOU WHO WILL READ THIS AND CONTINUALLY ASK FOR "PROOF" AND JUST "DO SOMETHING SO WE CAN BELIEVE"--HOW DO YOU FEEL ABOUT THIRTY PEOPLE WHO WERE INTENDED TARGETS FOR DEATH? SO BE IT, FOR YOU WILL ALSO DENOUNCE THE VERY TRUTH YOU SEEK AND CONTINUALLY PETITION FOR. WELL, THEY HAVE TO DO SOMETHING WITH THOSE DEAD SOLDIERS AT EDWARDS AND I SUGGEST THAT THERE ARE OFFICERS IN THAT LOCATION WHO WILL NOT APPROVE SUCH ACTIONS FOR THE CONFRONTATION OF COUNCIL WAS DONE WITH FULL RECOGNITION OF GROUND BASE AT EDWARDS! WE SHALL SEE IF THERE IS NOT AT LEAST ONE OR TWO WHO WILL COME FORTH! REMEMBER, GROUND CREWS DIE AS EASILY AS THE ENEMY! NEVER SHALL THE DEATHS BE AT THE HANDS OF SPACE BROTHERS! NEVER! WE, FURTHER, DO NOT HAVE NEED OF DEATH-DEALING WITH HUMANOIDS NOR ANY CRAFT YOU CAN SEND AGAINST US--LET IT SO BE UNDERSTOOD.

I HEREBY ALSO REQUEST THAT THIS INFORMATION BE FORWARDED TO ONE BO GRITZ, WENDELLE STEVENS AND OTHERS WHO CONTINUE TO DISCOUNT COMMAND--I CARE NOT

WHETHER OR NOT ANYONE BELIEVES, I SHALL NO LONGER
TOLERATE THE ATTACKS AGAINST MY GROUND PEOPLE. I
SHALL, HENCEFORTH, BRING TRUTH OF CIRCUMSTANCE OF
WRITERS AND SPEAKERS WHO DISCOUNT THIS WORK FOR I
WEARY OF FOOLISH "JAMES BOND" FALSE PROJECTORS IN-
VENTING DISCREDIT UPON OUR WORK. THIS IS NOT TRUE
FOR GRITZ, HE SIMPLY DOESN'T YET UNDERSTAND THAT
WHICH HE IS DOING.

OTHERS ARE SITTING AT READY TO PUBLISH MORE OF BILLY
MEIER'S WORK IN THEIR OWN PROFIT-MAKING MODE OF OP-
ERATION AND HAVE EMBELLISHED AND FALSIFIED MUCH OF
IT TO MAKE IT SALEABLE. I HEREIN PRONOUNCE THAT IT IS
NOT TOTAL TRUTH AND THE TRUTH SHALL BE MADE
KNOWN. I FURTHER SUGGEST THAT BILLY MEIER BE GIVEN
ROYALTIES AND BE ALLOWED TO DISCOUNT THAT WHICH IS
NOT OF HIS NOTATIONS AND RECEIVINGS.

Through your ground manipulations and foolish games, you have caused a
bit of angry response from our Command crews and I suggest you con-
sider that situation most carefully indeed. Perhaps you will enjoy a space-
craft in your front yard? You see, there is no consideration of any nega-
tive impact from Space Command--YOUR OWN BROTHERS RIGHT IN
HUMAN FORMAT WILL TAKE YOU OUT AND YOU KNOW IT!
THE CIA IS TRAINED AND OPERATED BY THE MOSSAD AND
THEY WILL TAKE YOU ONES OUT WITHOUT BLINKING TWICE!
IF THAT BE YOUR WISH THEN I SUGGEST YOU CONTINUE
YOUR GAMES OF STUPIDITY. I REMIND YOU, HOWEVER,
THAT YOUR FAMILIES ARE SAFE WITHIN OUR SHIELDS IF
THAT IS THE CHOSEN ROUTE--THEY MOST CERTAINLY ARE
NOT SAFE FROM THE CIA, FBI, MOSSAD NOR ANY OTHER
TERRORISTS GROUP WHO IS SETTING UP THIS GLOBAL
CATASTROPHE. SO BE IT--MARK MY WORDS CAREFULLY IN-
DEED--FOR THIS IS THE WORD AND SO SHALL IT BE! I
SALUTE YOU WHO HAVE THE WISDOM TO SEE THAT WHICH
IS COMING DOWN AND YOUR OWN JEOPARDY AT THE HANDS
OF THOSE YOU SERVE--NOT SPACE COMMAND! HOW MANY
OF YOU "MOUTH-PIECES" ARE BRAVE ENOUGH TO STEP
FORWARD AND TRULY PROTECT SELF, NATION AND PLANET?
OR DO YOU WAIT FOR A LITTLE GRANDMOTHER TO DO IT
FOR YOU? SO BE IT--PRIDE GOETH JUST BEFORE THE FALL!
SAALOME'.

P.S. It was further assumed that the alien who escaped the Virginia
incarcerators, in Washington D.C., would also be picked up for he is
known to be in the area--and this would cement the episode as planned.
Too bad about that assumption, I will just let you ones ponder that point!

Why do I dare write this and send it forth in the Express? It has very little to do with you readers, unfortunately--but, this computer is monitored
by several of your resources--INCLUDING THE EDWARDS AIR

FORCE BASE! SALU, BROTHERS, I HOPE YOU FIND THIS INTERESTING READING FOR THE MESSAGES MAY GET EVER MORE REVEALING AS WE TAKE OUR OWN ACTIONS TO BRING THIS UNDER CONTROL--YOU ONES DON'T HAVE ANY PROTECTION WHAT-SO-EVER, FROM THE COSMOSPHERES MONITORING EVERY MOVE YOU MAKE AT THAT BASE. COSMOSPHERES ARE SOVIET CRAFT AND HAVE NOTHING TO DO WITH SPACE ALIENS--I SUGGEST YOU PONDER THAT MOST CAREFULLY INDEED--FOR YOU HAVE BEEN FED TONS OF B.S.--(BITTER SWILL)!

* * * * *

What do you ones in the Good ol' U.S.A think Gorbachev, the Chinese Leader and Henry Kissinger are doing in meetings? Oh, you didn't know that? I suggest you pay a little better attention!

Further, I think you should pay close attention to Mt. Etna erupting in Italy--THEN WATCH FOR THE VOLCANO IN THE SOUTH PACIFIC--PELE, I BELIEVE YOU CALL HER. Then I suggest you may wish to reread Casey's projections! May God have Grace and mercy upon you sleepy ones of the lie. May His word touch your hearts that you can see in time! Salu.

Dharma, let us close this--I care not whether or not it is a full or insufficient Express--please disperse it as soon as is possible. Thank you.

I am Hatonn to sign off--Dharma, I remain in your presence, chela, for you shall be fine in a few days. Do not remain in such fear, for God is thine shield, chela--and none shall prevail against that shield! So be it for I am present to ensure of it. I ask that all of you use caution--remember, God allowed ones to invent seat-belts for your safety--I suggest you use all things given in protection and do not dance in front of your enemy with the assault weapon--for you will get hurt badly indeed. It is expected that the crew in service, be ever more vigilant than any other for you do not test God, if you have wisdom, in that manner.

Good day.

CHAPTER 6

REC #1   HATONN

TUESDAY, NOVEMBER 27, 1990   5:50 A.M.   YEAR 4 DAY 103

For instance, I suggest you not allow another Express to go forth until you urge receivers to give Journals and/or Expresses as gifts of life at the Christmas commercial exchange of Earthly matters--allow reminders in the Express itself or as additional insert. You are coming under One World Rule by the five permanent member-nations of the UN Security Council--NOW, THIS WEEK!

THIS, DEAR ONES, IS WHAT ALL THIS PUSH AND SHOVE IS ABOUT--NOT FOR THE U.S. TO DECLARE WAR OR EVEN IN-VADE--IT IS TO BRING THE WORLD UNDER THE CONTROL OF THE U.N. SECURITY COUNCIL OF THE CARTEL NATIONS. IT HAS NOTHING TO DO WITH SADDAM HUSSEIN, HUMAN RIGHTS, OR ANYTHING ELSE UNDER THE CLAIMING--IT IS FOR ONE WORLD GLOBAL CONTROL BY THE ELITE! FUR-THER, IT IS WORKING TO PERFECTION WHILE THE WORLD SLEEPS ON. YOUR MILITARY COMES FORTH IN FRANTIC UP-RISING SAYING THAT SADDAM HAS NEVER HAD A WEAPON HE HASN'T USED. HAVE YOU?? IT IS THE U.S. WHO HAS USED THE ATOMIC BOMB! SO FAR, SADDAM HAS NOT! I SUGGEST YOU LOOK WITH OPEN EYES AND EARS AND WATCH THE MOVING AND SILENT HAND AT WORK--NOT THE MOUTH WITH THE BLATHERING THEREFROM. SO BE IT.

While all of you are distracted--yes, you are! How many of you know that the Federal Reserve is going to cut the "reserve requirement"? Yes, the Federal Board is going to reduce the fraction of deposits that banks are required to hold as reserves. This would be viewed as a strong mes-sage from the Fed that it wants banks to lend--lend and lend some more, thus sinking you further into economic destruction and total disaster. If you do not understand this information, I suggest you not ask me to ex-plain it--go re-read and *STUDY* the information given forth in the Jour-nals as to the banking "reserve" and "fractional banking" as outlaid. This is as serious a move in the financial clincher division, as any confirmation you will ever get--and ALL of you missed it!

At present the banks are only required to hold--either as currency or in interest-free deposits at the Fed--sums equal to 12% of all checking de-posits and 3% of certain certificates of deposits with maturities of less than 18 months. Reducing the reserve requirement would give banks more money to lend or invest at a profit and, if not offset by other Fed moves, would increase the supply of credit in the economy. Now, the FDIC is broke and the banks can loan 22 to one already--what does that tell you? It should tell you that if you put in $100 you are apt to get out less than $12 as it now stands and henceforth that spread shall increase drastically--in other words, the banks will hardly need hold any of your money for return to you! I would suggest this is something that should be given attention and I see not one of you even being aware of it. Moreover, all the hoopla surrounding the proposal is accompanied by total lies as to safety, problem-solving and live happily ever-after jargon--it is massively damaging to say the very least regarding the matter.

JAPAN AND MOVIES

How many of you realize that Matsushita is the new owner of MCA? Ok, how many realize that that is Universal Studios, etc.? How many realize that Sony already owns a major portion of your "Hollywood" industry? Matsushita is paying a piddling little $6.8 BILLION for the operation. They already control, along with Sony and one or two other Japanese businesses, the industry in VCR's and television sets--the "biggie" now is a 150-inch screen which will be "sweeping" the market! How many wondrous "middle class" Americans even have a room in which to place such a set for viewing? They will, of course, go to their local bankers who are now lending more money due to the above outlay of plans, and hook you even more deeply into the bottomless pit of debt. Oh, by the way--they "have no intention of changing the quality of films being produced--we want the record rights and technical production controls along with the theme parks . . . ."

NOT TO WORRY!

Relax, however, America--for your President is down in Mexico doing the Mexican two-step and "wool-in-the eye-Joe" instead of "Cotton-eyed Joe" and dancing with Carlos Salinas while they give away your factories and have this wondrous new "free-trade" alliance--does anyone feel your job slipping away? How about another little tid bit?

Just as you took care of all that nasty "Budget mess"--your federal budget deficit widened to $31.46 BILLION in October and rising like a tidal wave. Oh, well, you do have these unexpected expenditures--like S&L's and war--so be it. How does this compare? Somewhere around a BILLION DOLLARS IS HOW IT HAS INCREASED! How about "just a FEW MORE TAXES?"

Back to Mexico and this new "love affair"--Mr. Salinas has badly irritated the people and his opposition. He has said that "..if the United Nations approved military action against Iraq, I offer Mexican troops to fight alongside the U.S. Marines that once stormed the halls of Montezuma." Repeat please, what you believe about the U.N. and who and how it is run! WHO IS GOING TO WAR WITH IRAQ? I THOUGHT YOU MIGHT BEGIN TO UNDERSTAND! READ MY LIPS! *YOU*

51

AMERICANS!

PLIGHT OF POOR LEBANON

Now, to another subject which is overlooked by you the people, intent on war and rebuttal by calling us anti-Semites by calling attention to Khazar Zionists--read on.

Even in your publishing journals of Establishment press we find the following: "While the world's attention focuses on the Persian Gulf, events in Lebanon could place that nation in the middle of the next Mideast standoff--this one between Israel and Syria." It is already well under way--as troops are pulled out of Beirut, militia forces from Moslem West Beirut are being relocated in southern Lebanon, and are thus coming into confrontation with the Israeli troops infiltrating into Lebanon. Israel has already formally announced that, as Damascus extends its control over Lebanon, the Israelis will hold Syria responsible for events. Your President is going to have trouble serving two masters--Assad and Shamir--so the ultimate action will be to smash Lebanon and work out the spoils. How interesting that your Lord walked those wondrous streets of Damascus--how little the evil princes change!

PERSPECTIVES

Surely no-one would take advantage of a holocaust to sell products, you say. Wouldn't they?

Anheuser-Busch touts its shipment of 22,000 cases of O'Doul's non-alcoholic beer to desert-bound GI's, which it calls "especially appropriate in light of the Middle East climate". Max Factor says it is "providing a form of protection for the troops"--by sending about a million dollars' worth of sun-screen lotion. Kransco Group's Wham-O division donates some 20,000 Frisbees, pitching that "...given the current situation, the troops are looking for recreational outlets and can't have either alcoholic beverages or pin-up girlie pictures." Then the American Contract Bridge League is sending 5,000 decks of cards to the Navy.

Free services also are in. American Telephone and Telegraph is running ads offering free messages to loved ones as part of its "Desert Fax" service. Philip Morris's Marlboro cigarettes brand is paying for relatives of troops to send holiday cards that play personalized 10-second voice messages--that of course, means that the troops need "players" and so it goes. I would herein point out, however, in case you wonder as to the value and truth of the Journals and Expresses--EVERY EFFORT IS MADE AND MAIL OPENED AND RESTRICTED TO KEEP THIS MATERIAL FROM REACHING YOUR SONS, HUSBANDS, DAUGHTERS, MOTHERS AND OTHER RELATIONS. DO YOU STILL DOUBT

52

THAT WE BRING YOU TRUTH? YOUR HUSBANDS ETC., ARE ALLOWED NEAR-BEER BUT TRUTH IS DENIED THEIR EYES AND EARS! GOD HAVE MERCY FOR MOST WILL NEVER KNOW WHAT IT WAS THAT KILLED THEM--ONLY YOU, WHO ALLOWED IT, SHALL WRITHE IN PAIN AND GUILT IN THE MIDDLE OF THE COLD NIGHTS--WONDERING WHAT WENT WRONG! SO BE IT.

Dharma, allow us to close this segment herein, for we need to return to the Journal in writing regarding your cosmic connections. You need to come into understanding for you are going to be meeting your brothers long before you are ready and truth is usually denied until face-to-face with "reality" of the circumstance.

Hatonn to stand-by. May understanding be our commitment. Salu.

CHAPTER 7

REC #1   HATONN

WEDNESDAY, NOVEMBER 28, 1990   8:15 A.M.   YEAR 4 DAY 104

TODAY'S WATCH (EXPRESS)

Hatonn present within the Light of God, with perspectives and notices from the lighted perspective. May God grant understanding within that man can again find freedom.

TRUTH OF IRAN-CONTRA ENTANGLEMENT

You who seek continual and continuing proof and confirmation of that which I give unto you, please obtain the FRONTLINE, *Public Broadcasting System* transcript of the program aired yesterday evening called HIGH CRIMES & MISDEMEANORS hosted by Bill Moyers. It gives factual, documented statements which prove everything that I have told you regarding the scenario and, moreover, gives you the proof you need to realize that you remain totally encapsulated in the lies and secret on-goings and cover-ups of your elite reformers. It is shocking indeed if you have not been following the Journals and Expresses--confirmation if you have!

Video information of the above: PBS Video, 1320 Braddock Place, Alexandria, VA 22314.
Transcript: Send $5.00 to: FRONTLINE TRANSCRIPTS, Journal Graphics, 267 Broadway, New York, NY 10007.

If demand is high for further information, I can give coverage in an Express but I feel you ones would prefer other pertinent information. I do ask that a copy of the transcript be obtained by the Editor hereof and we shall give it forth in an upcoming Journal. Thank you.

SLAVES

As your government sends your young men and women off to die in a desert far distant from home, let me point out some misinformation. You are, and the children are, told that they march off to defend Humanity, American Interests, Freedom and Democracy. Allow us to look at this in truth.

What you are defending and again raising to power is a slaveholder, Jaber el-Sabah, the Emir of Kuwait, who was Bush's honored guest at the White House, and who appealed to the UN General Assembly to restore the "legitimate government" of Kuwait. This includes restoring the Emir to command over his household servants, many of whom are BLACK SLAVES. These black slaves and their children will be destined to live and die in chattel bondage, thanks to the sacrifices of the U.S. armed forces acting under the orders of Bush.

Another slaveholder is King Fahd of Saudi Arabia. One of the announced goals of Bush's Gulf buildup, which will soon reach over half million troops, is to defend the Saudi Arabian monarchy against the alleged danger of Iraqi attack. King Fahd and many of the other 6,000 members of the Saudi royal family also own black slaves. King Fahd keeps his in a special slave compound in the precincts of his palace, now shielded by the U.S. Army. And beyond this, the rulers of Qatar, Bahrain, the United Arab Emirates and Oman are also owners of black slavery there. But Bush demands that the U.S. sacrifice blood and treasure, courting possible World War III, in order to restore black chattel slavery to Kuwait by driving the Iraqis out and putting the slaveholding Emir back on his throne. Now, dear ones, this "Fahd" of Saudi Arabia is also the same one who gave $2 MILLION PER MONTH to the Contra effort through the Bush Vice Presidency. If you obtain the transcript listed above, you will find that Bush knew and participated completely and then LIED OPENLY TO YOU THE PUBLIC ON NUMEROUS OCCASIONS WHICH WERE ABSOLUTE LIES AND NOT EVEN "HEDGES" REGARDING THE MOST HEINOUS OF ACTIVITIES. WHY DO YOU BELIEVE HE SPEAKS TRUTH UNTO YOU NOW?

Many of the black slaves of the Gulf trace their origin to Ethiopia. A slave trade between Ethiopia and the Gulf states was in existence until about the time of the Second World War, although it declined somewhat thereafter. A League of Nations report of some years past confirmed the persistence of black chattel slavery in the Arabian peninsula. Today, slave quarters and slave compounds are commonly adjacent to the luxury palaces of oil-rich princes, emirs, and sheiks. Slaves are slaves for all their lives, and their offspring are also slaves and are the property of the slaveholder. Many of these slaves speak very little Arabic, and communicate with those they serve through signs and gestures--of course, they are kept illiterate and totally uninformed. The native language of the slaves is often a dialect of Ethiopian, passed along in the closed society of the slave quarters and the harem.

The institution of slavery in Saudi Arabia and the Gulf states is officially denied, of course, by the feudal-monarchial regimes in question, but the existence of black slaves is an open secret that can easily be verified in any street or market. Groups of black slaves go to the souks or bazaars to do the shopping for the households which they serve. These slaves receive priority service from merchants as a sign of respect and deference to the princely masters whose slaves they are. Every larger town and city in the Gulf has a public square that served as a slave market until quite recently when the activity went under cover, and the names have been changed to deflect attention from the continuing presence of slaves, who continue to be bought and sold by princes privately and behind the scenes.

You will note that in a prior Journal I referred to the Israeli Zionists making incredible efforts to bring *"their"* JUDAIC believers out of Ethiopia in the middle of nights by private plane and rounded up and forced aboard--herein you have the real reason and resource for a very large money-making operation on human life.

Black slavery has a long history in the Gulf. In the Arabic language spoken there, the word "abed" signifies black and slave at the same time. It is considered less a term of notoriety than a simple statement of fact.

Any American politician, black or white, who protested against apartheid in South Africa must find the existence of actual chattel slavery in Saudi Arabia and the Gulf states far more abhorrent. And all the more so because President Bush has ordered the biggest buildup since Vietnam in order to defend the Saudi slaveholders, and will soon order American troops into actual combat, with horrendous consequences around the entire world, in order to restore the Kuwaiti slaveholders to power. If American troops invade Iraq, they will be bringing black slavery with them. *Certainly many black GI's would rather use their guns to free their fellow black men, women, and children from slavery in Saudi Arabia than attack the Iraqi defensive positions in Kuwait. If Saudi slaveholding becomes widely known among the U.S. forces in the Gulf, it is highly doubtful whether they will share in the Bush-Thatcher-Kissinger warpsychosis against Iraq. WHERE IS JESSE JACKSON? WHY HAS JESSE JACKSON JUST JOINED THE CONSPIRACY ELITE OF THE COUNCIL OF FOREIGN RELATIONS????*

Slavery was "*officially*" abolished in open forums in 1962 in Saudi Arabia by King Faisal as a *QUID PRO QUO (funny thing about Quid Pro Quos, as Bush denied any such thing in the Contra crisis, also--he said (again), "..read my lips--there is no Quid Pro Quo" and yet, he personally delivered the money `Quid' to the Central American Dealers for American military assistance against the Egyptian regime of Gamal Abdul Nasser).* The Saudi reforms were never implemented.

Recently the slave trade has been maintained by kidnaping African Muslims who came to Mecca for the religious pilgrimage of the *hajj*. Many of these very poor African Muslims sold their children into slavery, or were themselves enslaved, because they could not finance their trips home. The primary sources for the slaves have been the hardest-hit parts of Africa: Senegal, Sudan, Chad, and Ethiopia and Eritrea. Preference has been given to African Muslims because the Saudi elites were reticent to have non-Muslim slaves in the holy places of Islam.

FILIPINOS, TOO

More recently, there has been a flow of Filipinos, who come to Saudi Arabia with the promise of high-paying jobs. When they arrive, they are deprived of their passports, made to sign contracts in Arabic (which they do not understand), and prevented from ever leaving the country. These ones are further prevented from speaking in any language to anyone outside the compounds. The Emir of Kuwait has had the most lavish lifestyle of any Royal Emir and the practice of slave holding is widespread-- as a matter of fact, the Filipinos who were recently released from Kuwait were fortunate indeed for the so-called "invasion" by Saddam.

These slaves come mainly from populations which are Muslim, from wartorn areas. They come from Ethiopia, Eritreia, from Tanzania, etc. It is an old tradition. The painful thing about it is that the British not only know about it, but it is done with their consent. It goes back to the end of the Second World War. In Madagascar, since that new socialist regime came in, it has been done much more strongly.

As late as your 1966, some four years after the "official" abolition of slavery for public consumption, even the United Nations has been, for political reasons, somewhat reticent to deal with the slavery issue in the Arabian Peninsula. I guess that figures to be because you must realize that the five permanent members of the UN Security Council run the UN and the world. There is even a recognized slave route from Dubai, Muscat, Buraimi, Al Hasa, Riyadh. Merchants make seasonal trips to Dubai and Muscat, returning with a group of 50 to 60 slaves at a time. They are first put up for sale at Al Hasa and later, if unsold there, sold through brokers at Riyadh. The slaves are often kidnapped from towns and villages in the Qatar and Buraimi area. The slaver contracts groups of entertainers and musicians, who give performances outside the village or town, arranging for a dancing party on a particular day. The slaver then gets in touch with the tribe living in the vicinity to arrange for a raid on the dancing party and to kidnap the girls for whom an agreed sum is paid per head to the sheikhs of the tribe--the slaver then takes over. Funny thing about the involvement of the Mossad in the kidnapping--oh yes, they are right there training the slavers.

Here is just one common example of how commonplace the practice is: a group of Italian businessmen boast openly how, because of a lack of easy access to women in Kuwait, they buy slave girls who do all their bidding. When the business is finished and individuals leave the country, the girls are sold to a fellow-businessman or sold back to the original owners-- these business arrangements made at original point of sale. And so it goes! IS THIS THAT FOR WHICH YOU ARE WILLING TO LAY DOWN THE LIVES OF YOUR FAMILY AND RELATIONS--OIL, GREED, SLAVERY AND CONTROL EVEN OF SELF??? Then, it would behoove you to awaken your eyes for the take-over is underway and speeding toward an irreversible finale.

WHERE IS HENRY K. AND WHAT IS HE DOING?

Well, he has been efforting to get China to join with the UN Security Council to declare war--by whatever name you label it. The Chinese, however, give indecision as an open projection--don't be sucked into the subterfuge.

Now, he will testify this very day before the Senate Armed Services committee--WHY? Kissinger holds no office and is no longer openly accepted even as an advisor to the President--how is this new importance to world affairs? Could it be that he is one of the most powerful humans in your world? I think you had better pay attention for he is and he is about to have the world brought down--through YOU!

Turn on your TV and you will likely find Kissinger spouting off, or look into any newspaper these days, and you will find Henry Kissinger pontificating on the Persian Gulf crisis. Kissinger is demanding that President Bush follow the same "balance of power" prescriptions that the Nixon administration carried out in Vietnam, when Kissinger was Secretary of State.

It doesn't seem to matter that the Vietnam policy Kissinger masterminded not only resulted in needless butchery of both American and Vietnamese, but also left Southeast Asia in the communist sphere of influence. Kissinger, worse yet, is accepted as the foremost "expert" on such matters.

The gist of Kissinger's thrust is that Bush must act soon against Iraq because waiting for sanctions to work would likely destroy the ability for the U.S. to strike at all--and hence the unrelenting push on Bush's part--to pull this off immediately, in secret upstart and while Congress is on recess.

At the same time--*he urges that a ground war be avoided, in favor of air strikes which would cripple Iraq, but keep it around as a power in the area.*

When questioned openly, Kissinger won't come up with much. He argues that since the U.S. has already deployed troops into the area, it has to go ahead and use them. This is what you call "circular reasoning" and absurd to say the least but proves the intent.

Would you like a little Freudian slip of the lip? At times it is not clear that Kissinger realizes what part of the world he speaks about. On ABC's *"This Week with David Brinkley"* on Nov. 11, Kissinger vigorously denied that there was any parallel between the Persian Gulf situation and Vietnam. "Unlike Vietnam", he insisted, "our demands in the Gulf have been clear from the beginning: immediate and total withdrawal *FROM VIETNAM...UH, AH, KUWAIT..."* So be it!

In total arrogance and disregard for the U.S. Constitution, he maintains the same situation vis-a-vis the Constitution of the United States as he always did. Just as he himself took orders from Britain, so he wants Bush to follow British Prime Minister Thatcher (and it matters not that Thatcher has stepped down, believe me), and not listen to Congress. Congress, of course, has the constitutional responsibility to declare war-- that, therefore, is why there cannot be a declaration of war--it would botch the whole facade of UN substance.

KISSINGERISM BLOODBATH OF LEBANON

Just last year (1989), Former Secretary of State of the United States of America, Henry Kissinger, commented publicly on the dictator of Syria, *"God may punish me, but I rather like Hafez al-Assad"*. Well, he now has the blood of thousands of Christian martyrs on his hands! Those Christians, who died as Kissinger's Syrian friends murdered Lebanon, had followed Gen. Michel Aoun in trying to free their country from an occupation and de facto partition between "Greater Syria" and "Greater Israel", an insane policy crafted and orchestrated by none other than Henry Kissinger.

First-hand accounts continue to come out of Beirut on the continuing slaughter of Lebanon's Christians. Eyewitness reports and testimony from credible first-hand experiencers report hundreds of corpses of Christians--in military uniforms--killed with shots in the head and on whose chest the assassins had drawn a cross with the shots of machine gun bursts.

The martyrs were the officers of Gen. Aoun's army, who were massacred after their surrender to the Syrians. Further, family members of the murdered are publicly raped by the Iranian Hezbollah, who ran throughout the Christian quarters of Beirut purposely to rape, pillage and murder after Syrian troops crushed Christian resistance --"to give example to resisters and Christians". Does this sound like something out of ancient times? So be it.

OFFICIAL HYPOCRISY

The set-up witnesses who are currently testifying at the UN are pathetic indeed. How is it that ones who "are free" are able to produce pictures and video-tapes of atrocities when they, themselves, were supposedly so ill treated? Come, chelas--one man testifying regarding lying next to a dead body while awaiting dialysis treatment speaks the truth of the lies--if a dialysis patient misses dialysis--he is a dead and gone duck! The fact that he is alive to testify belies the story he gives! Please keep your eyes and ears open--again, the stories are being read from pre-prepared scripts and the pictures heinous indeed, but not atrocities committed by the

Iraqis. The Iraqis are severe enough--these lies are worse, for the atrocities are perpetrated by your own supporters to bring the proper results to the UN councils--so you the people will not speak out. Precious ones--look about you, for you are all but out of time to stop this slaughter of your own children.

There are no cries of outrage from President Bush's administration in the U.S. against Assad--in fact you have now joined forces with this killer. The incidents in Lebanon are not even given first headline on the newsbreaks--simply underplayed and always with the emphasis that Lebanese are out to attack and kill Israelis. What are the Israelis doing in Lebanon, at any rate? That seems to be missed in the reporting of any of these incidents!

Since the Lebanese "civil war" in 1975-76 the official U.S. foreign policy has been to welcome, as then Secretary of State Henry Kissinger did, Syrian occupation of Lebanon. While this evil, immoral policy originates with Kissinger, nevertheless, every single top official of the Bush administration is culpable for Syria's latest bloodbath against Lebanon's Christians.

There is a widespread blanket of cover-up of the martyrdom of hundreds upon hundreds of Lebanese Christians by the Bush administration. Defense Secretary Richard Cheney, in Paris, stressed that, "...most reports I have heard so far have been unconfirmed through government sources, and I would want to have confirmation before making any comment regarding these matters."

IT IS A MATTER OF RECORD--**IN KISSINGER'S OWN MEMOIRS** *THAT HE PREFERRED ASSAD TO ANY OTHER MIDDLE EAST LEADER.*

DIRECT FROM AMMAN, JORDAN

The word from Amman, Jordan is that the American media's coverage of the Middle East is totally biased and propaganda inserted in gross misinformation. This comes from editors and correspondents efforting to bring truth forth in order to stop this insane march to war.

There is total effort to corrupt every statement made by Saddam even if the actual footage of film is shown--it is always slanted grossly toward the Israeli point of view.

As a good example, in reporting on the Israeli police shooting of the Palestinians in Jerusalem outside the Al-Aqsa Mosque, the U.S. media continually referred to the area and use the word which has been coined by the Israelis: the "Temple Mount". This is a NEW WORD which has proliferated in the Western media, to emphasize that this particular place is actually where the temple used to be, although, scientifically speaking, no excavation has revealed that this mount was actually the site of the temple--I would suggest you consider this most carefully for God may not like usurpation of His property for Evil reconstruction at any rate, manner or form and herein you might find clues to <u>Zionism's</u> thrust, vs. that of the Jews!

When the U.S. emphasizes "Temple Mount, Temple Mount, the Palestinians are demonstrating at the Temple Mount," you are actually stressing the "fact" that this is the site where the temple used to be--so that one day when you destroy the Al-Aqsa Mosque, then this was on the "Temple Mount" and somehow it is perfectly alright, expected and correct. This is the kind of technique which the American media tends to use at every turn.

Saddam Hussein is not correct in his behavior, but you must learn that an attempt to paint a black picture of the man, and his power and country as well as ambitions are to make war palatable, attractive, and the sacrifices acceptable--through eliminating a "monster", and this is the whole intent of the controlled Establishment media.

You must realize, dear hearts, that the Elite and the spoon-fed Establishment papers, are pro-Israel in every issue and this shall ever increase in publication attitudes. The effort is to hectically and chaotically use the buildup against Saddam Hussein in order to destroy Iraq for reasons which have absolutely nothing to do with Kuwait and nothing to do with peace but EVERYTHING TO DO WITH ISRAEL AND CONTROL OF THE MIDDLE EAST AND OIL. *THE GLOBAL 2,000 PLAN MOVES EVER ONWARD, A BIT AHEAD OF SCHEDULE!*

<u>WHY DOESN'T GOD JUST GIVE YOU FREE ENERGY AND SOLVE EVERYTHING?</u>

Well, let us look at that which you call "cold-fusion", remember that? What did the Establishment do to those nice young scientists from Utah after they were ridiculed and denounced? Let us honor them.

At Brigham Young University in Provo, Utah, at the end of October, cold fusion scientists from around the world discussed new experimental results that confirm **once again** the startling announcement of room temperature fusion made by scientists Martin Fleischmann and Stanley Pons back in March 1989.

Most spectacular, a University of Hawaii cold fusion team announced that it had produced a significant amount of helium-4, a by-product of the deuterium nuclear fusion reaction, in palladium rods. The Hawaii experiment measured 4×10 to the 9th atoms of helium-4 after 100 hours, significantly above any background levels. Another young scientist who has had his life attacked over and over and will not be named herein--has created useable fuel for cars as they now are, from this same "heavy water" (deuterium).

The Hawaiian experimental setup is different from the Fleischmann and Pons configuration and is carried out in a molten salt with palladium as the anode (instead of as the cathode). It produced an energy output that was five times the amount of energy input into the experiment.

Fusion, the process that powers the stars and the Sun (cosmic energy), is the energy released when atoms of the lighter elements, like hydrogen, are fused together. It is the opposite of fission, where energy is produced from splitting the atom apart.

Attempts to achieve fusion in the laboratory have made use of very high temperatures (millions of degrees) and relatively large reactor devices to fuse together hydrogen atoms in a hydrogen plasma fuel. In contrast to "hot" fusion, cold fusion research is carried out in a simple electrolytic cell (bathtub size), consisting of a palladium cathode and a platinum anode submerged in heavy water. At some point rhodium and/or iridium as cathode might be a rather feasible consideration.

Although the equipment is simple and the scale is small, the experiment itself is not simple and there are many variables that are not understood even by the scientists who have succeeded in producing excess heat, neutrons, or tritium in a cold fusion apparatus. And just what do you think would happen to these scientists if they come up with cheap energy when the Cartel is going to fight a massive war in order to control the oil supply and energy resources? Come now, little dreamers who think a new invention would "save the world"--not yet, dear ones, not yet!

Because the phenomenon appears to break the rules of traditional plasma physics, the physics establishment has opposed the idea that cold fusion can occur, and has ridiculed those scientists who pursued work in this area. They have even resorted to allegations of fraud in order to taint both cold fusion research and the researchers. As a result, the public has not been able to get accurate news of how far experimental work has progressed over the past year and a half--and you had best hope it can remain that way for now.

INSINUATIONS AND OUTRIGHT LIES

The discussions in Utah, in this October, were no exception to the "dump cold fusion" pattern. It takes a while for learned ones to realize the extent of the world plot against humanity. As scientists were discussing the cold fusion research at the Provo meeting, sponsored by the Department of Energy, the Electric Power Research Institute and the University, the headlines read "Cold Fusion Scientist Missing As Key Review Nears" and "Utah to Start Search for Cold Fusion Scientist" (New York Times, Oct. 25 and 26).

62

The story reported was that, when the time came for the state of Utah to review the state-funded National Cold Fusion Institute's work, the two top researchers were "missing". Science writer William J. Broad implied that Fleischmann and Pons had skipped town to avoid facing the reviewers because they could not "defend" their research. Pon's house was for sale, Broad reported, and his phone disconnected.

In fact, both scientists had been in the University of Utah in Salt Lake City since June, waiting for the review to be scheduled. Just after Pons took his family on vacation to Europe, and after Fleischmann returned to his home in England for medical treatment, the October review date was set and the university could not reach either Pons or Fleischmann to tell them. As for Pon's house being for sale, he had already moved into another dwelling. Both Pons and Fleischmann have stated that they would certainly be available for the new review date.

Contrary to the message that the state review is a hostile process to determine whether cold fusion is real or not, the procedure is really designed to assure that research is progressing at a reasonable pace and high quality, according to a University of Utah spokesman--and if you believe that, dear ones, how about that bridge that just sank in Washington state-- I can get it for you real cheap!

"The University administration continues to support cold fusion research", said the spokesman, "and will not be withdrawing support for the Institute, Fleischmann and Pons, or anything else."

STRONG ARM OF ESTABLISHMENT

Now some facts about that last statement. The U.S. physics establishment in general, and that at the University of Utah in particular, seems determined to shut down the national Cold Fusion Institute. The American Physical Society, which has led a nasty attack on cold fusion almost from upstart, threatened the university department with losing academic accreditation if it had contact with the University's Cold Fusion Institute.

A very prominent visiting scientist at the institute, who had offered to teach a physics course in his specialty at the university while he was in Salt Lake City, was totally shunned by the Physics Department because of his cold fusion association. Another Physics Department professor was asked to resign from all committees and contact with students, as long as he continued working with the national Cold Fusion Institute. I would guess that the Cold Fusion Institute might just be on to something quite remarkable--what think ye?

BY THE WAY--BACK TO THE MIDDLE EAST

One last little note and then we will take a break, Dharma. In being a good little Middle East "WATCHER" I suggest you not overlook that one, Ariel Sharon, who is actually "King of Israel"! When General Ariel Sharon is in a dominant position in Israel, you can expect lots and lots of trouble.

Currently the "Housing Minister"--and in reality, the strong-man of the entire regime--Sharon is pushing for war. It is in no way a secret from any save you in the U.S. that "Arik" Sharon is the funder and protector of the various "Jewish underground" sects which have regularly been killing Palestinians, most recently triggering the Jerusalem bloodbath. Sharon would like to see such atrocities provide the pretext for his own pet project: *invading Jordan, toppling King Hussein, and declaring that Jordan is "Palestine", thereby solving the Palestinian problem.*

Do you recall that way back in 1982, Sharon, then Defense Minister, ran the Israeli invasion of Lebanon, which did so much to finish off that tragic nation? Less well known, perhaps--if anything is known at all, is the fact that, that same year, Sharon teamed up with that lovely and gracious Henry Kissinger, Lord Peter Carrington and his long-time mentor and funder, New York financier Meshulam Riklis, to put together an international network of real estate firms. Sharon and company intended to make a "real killing" (in every sense of the word) through the provocations Sharon's underground was creating on the West Bank and in occupied East Jerusalem. Driving Palestinians off their land and buying their property for a nickel or less, on the dollar, is just one of the reasons that the Wall Street and City of London financiers who own Sharon want to see him become that "King of Israel". And so the cookies continue to crumble and the fortune papers flow forth into public view--slowly but surely--for truth will always "out" if given "time".

POST SCRIPT

Just in passing--look at the swiftly moving hand lest it go faster than your eyes; Mexico was not the only points south that your President Bush intends to invade with his "Free Trade". Don't you ones know that he has scheduled a trip, which begins on December 3rd, on a five-day dance through South America--visiting Brazil, Uruguay, Argentina, Chili and Venezuela? Well, you should watch for the purpose is to encourage the free-market policies that South American countries are increasingly embracing thanks to your wondrous pushing and shoving to get rid of your businesses and jobs.

Now, wouldn't you know that the President's Agenda is the disappearing rain forest in the Amazon Basin and hyperinflation and the heavy foreign debt of both Brazil and Argentina. *In the name of lessening and forgiv-*

ing debt owed to the U.S., there will be some grand negotiations and as-
sistance offered from you the wondrous U.S. citizens--how grand that
America has bottomless pockets even as you send your business and jobs
away to foreign lands and your own go homeless and hungry? COULD
IT BE - - - - ?

NOW, FOR ANOTHER INTELLIGENT MOVE TO HELP AIDS

Now this next should be the answer for AIDS sufferers. On December 1
much of the world will fall into darkness (I doubt it but the article says as
much). To support International AIDS Awareness Day, more than 1,000
cultural organizations are expected to dim their lights in one way or another in an effort to raise contributions for medical research and care-
givers, while demonstrating that they plan to intensify their efforts to find
solutions to the AIDS crisis. Television screens around the world will
turn black; museums will close their doors or drape shrouds over works
of art (Maplethorp's, perhaps?); singers will fall silent (mostly a relief to
the brain and ears): dancers cease to move. At 7:45 p.m., as the lights go
out at many public buildings in New York City, organizers hope that individuals will also turn off their lights to commemorate those who have
died of AIDS. At 8 p.m., nearly 100 million TV viewers will witness a
"moment without television" organized by the Bravo cable network. In
an unprecedented act of cooperation, 23 major cable networks have
agreed to give up a prime time minute to raise awareness about AIDS.
The four broadcast networks have not yet agreed to join but organizers
will continue their efforts to include them. I think I had better not even
comment on this matter lest I offend you nice readers. Is it possible for
man to ever see the point of his journey or must all of you fulfill the death
sentence placed upon your heads and those of your children?

Allow us a rest please.

Hatonn to clear. Salu.

CHAPTER 8

REC #1   HATONN

SUNDAY, DECEMBER 2, 1990   6:51 A.M.   YEAR 4 DAY 108

TODAY'S WATCH

You must always look beyond that which is obvious and unto that which is truth in reality. You are within the time of the great deceiving and very little is that which is portrayed for your consumption and the disease of deceit is now throughout your world.

You flood me with questions--you actually pray for disaster to strike to prove something or another. I shall take today's watch to ask you questions and perhaps in the answering within you will find better understanding.

ROCKET LAUNCHES

There have been at least five (FIVE) (5) major rocket launches on the planet within the past ten hours. China, Israel, Iraq, Soviet Union and the U.S. Do you actually think they are separate and apart one from the other? Do you actually think you are placing scopes in the cosmos to look at the migration habits of stars? How is it that Japan is accompanying the Soviets to the space station? How is it Iraq would launch a rocket at the exact same time? Can you not feel the death knot about your necks?

How is it that in the Israel area whole busloads of people are slashed and then hit with assault weapons fire? How is it that bombing raids by Israelis continue into Lebanon with not hardly passing interest or mention?

How is it that the Israelis are gathering "Jews" from every part of the world in a final frantic thrust to "gather ALL Jews home?" Jews from Ethiopia are being gathered even against their will and yet the gathering goes on in frantic measure--how can tiny Israel house and feed the hundreds of thousands of people they are gathering? They now have gotten some 28,000 (reported) Jews into Israel from Russia and some 20,000 are expected from Ethiopia alone. The Israelis say: "No expense will be spared to gather our people home." Who pays that "No expense spared"? You in America already give Israel straight across the board with no strings attached and the best investment programs available, over 4 BILLION DOLLARS a year--in cash! What chance do you think little Palestine and Lebanon have in sustaining their nations? Everything is being set up to simply allot them to Israel through the United

66

Nations as soon as the radioactive dust settles in the Middle East.

Will you have earthquakes? Oh, indeed you shall. On Dec. 3rd? Who cares? If you are in preparation, you have naught to concern about and if you are not--you will have to face it one day so what difference does it make to those who will not prepare under any circumstance? Oh, but you say, you ones and Earth ones are always predicting and it happens not--so we aren't going to "bite" again! So be it! What if it does?? Will you then say "Why didn't you tell us?" No-one comes out and tells you, "THERE WILL BE A QUAKE AT SUCH AND SUCH A TIME AT SUCH AND SUCH A PLACE"--you of the "hearing" public place the word "will" onto the predictions which have said, "I see a very good probability/possibility of a quake on such and such a given time frame in such and such a place."

I can promise you, however, that if the U.S. does what it hopes to do-- there will be immediate retaliation in the form of earthquakes and all manners of things. This very day the "Siberian Express" will be moved within the boundaries of the U.S. There will also be further flooding of the Northwest--and CHINA is mobilizing!

* * * * *

WHAT OF THE NEW WORLD ORDER AND HOW COULD THIS COME ABOUT? WELL, IN 1983 YOUR THEN PRESIDENT ENTITY RONALD REAGAN FINALIZED A DOCUMENT INTO LAW AND CONGRESS RATIFIED IT. IT IS THE TREATY WHICH AU-THORIZED PRESIDENT ENTITY GEORGE BUSH TO ESTABLISH A "NEW WORLD ORDER". UNLAWFULLY BUT LEGALLY! IT IS HEADED ON THE COVER PAGE BY THE FOLLOWING: CON-STITUTION OF THE UNITED NATIONS INDUSTRIAL DEVEL-OPMENT ORGANIZATION. (Please note the word "CONSTITUTION".) THEN: *MESSAGE from THE PRESIDENT OF THE UNITED STATES TRANSMITTING THE CONSTITUTION OF THE UNITED NATIONS' INDUSTRIAL DEVELOPMENT ORGANI-ZATION (UNIDO), ADOPTED BY THE UNITED NATIONS CON-FERENCE ON THE ESTABLISHMENT OF THE UNITED NATIONS INDUSTRIAL DEVELOPMENT ORGANIZATION AS A SPECIAL-IZED AGENCY ON APRIL 8, 1979, AND SIGNED ON BEHALF OF THE UNITED STATES OF AMERICA ON JANUARY 17, 1980.*

OCTOBER 5, 1981.--TREATY WAS READ THE FIRST TIME AND, TOGETHER WITH THE ACCOMPANYING PAPERS, REFERRED TO THE COMMITTEE ON FOREIGN RELATIONS AND ORDERED TO BE PRINTED FOR THE USE OF THE SENATE. 97th Congress, 1st Session, SENATE, Treaty Doc. No. 97-19, U.S. Government Print-ing Office, Washington: 1981, form 89-118 0.

On the UN level, countries of the world are called UN's "states". This was ratified by the U.S. Senate and signed by the President of the U.S. It was signed by 80 other countries and ratified; this Constitution, and it is now *in force world-wide!* *DO YOU RECALL GIVING YOUR PUBLIC OFFICIALS POWER TO DO SUCH A THING?*

Dear ones, this CONSTITUTION of the United Nations Industrial Development Organization--UNIDO--is used as authority to set up this New World Order and it is now acting as official law even though you know nothing of it.

THE ABUSE OF TREATY POWER ALLOWS THIS "CONSTITUTION" TO SUPERSEDE THE UNITED STATES CONSTITUTION. Is it too late?

A New Social Order: "The States Parties to this Constitution,

In conformity with the Charter of the United Nations,
Bearing in mind the broad objectives in the resolutions adopted by the sixth special session of the General Assembly of the United Nations on the establishment of a *New International Economic Order*, in the UNIDO Second General Conference's Lima Declaration and Plan of Action for Industrial Development and Co-operation, and in the resolution of the seventh special session of the General Assembly of the United Nations on Development and International Economic Cooperation.

Now, let me point out something which might be disturbing to you the people. Any person working for or within the United Nations, even for one session, MUST give oath of loyalty to the United Nations and *THEIR LOYALTY TO THE UNITED NATIONS MUST SUPERSEDE LOYALTY TO THE UNITED STATES CONSTITUTION while the United Nations Charter goes on destroying the United States Constitution. This means that every one of your government who even participates in United Nations activities have taken this oath:*

> *"I solemnly swear to exercise in all loyalty, discretion and conscience, the functions entrusted to me as a member of the international service of the United Nations; to discharge those functions and regulate with the interests of the United Nations only in view, and not to seek or accept instructions in regard to the performance of my duty from any government or authority external to the Organization."*

SERIOUS NOTE: *The United Nations Charter was also done by unlawful use of the treaty-making power. Now the United Nations is calling for all U.S. citizens to be totally disarmed. Aided by Public Law 87-297, and other new laws, their disarmament treaties will confiscate every gun! Then the police force of the world will fall under the direction of a Soviet General. The United Nations, you will note, will henceforth appoint a "World `President'" from the permanent members of the Security Council. DO YOU ACTUALLY BELIEVE BUSH CARES WHETHER OR NOT HE IS ELECTED PRESIDENT OF THE U.S. AFTER THIS LITTLE TID-BIT? HE BELIEVES HE WILL RULE THE WORLD! I THINK NOT, HOWEVER, FOR THE HEAD OF*

THE ZIONISTS, HENRY KISSINGER, AND OF THE CARTEL, DAVID ROCKEFELLER, (ENTITIES THEREOF) HAVE THE SAME NOTION AND I WOULD GUESS THAT THEY WILL HAVE THE FINAL SAY ABOUT SUCH A THING.

Now, America--do you have problems or do you have problems? I suggest that you have serious problems and a war ahead of you that you can do nothing about. Is it not time to hear Satan knocking at the door?

I apologize, chela, for causing you to need do all this extra work but I herein ask you to type the entire document so that it can be reprinted for use to send to Congressmen, etc. I honor one, Bernadine Smith, who has provided us with a good copy. Just retype it and please use her emphasis as shown by underlining of passages.

I ask that this portion; perhaps this entire "Express" be put to 8 1/2" x 11" format for ease of handling. Please ask the printer to simply enlarge the cover page--exactly as is. We would utilize the document provided but I desire that you of my group KNOW what is within the document and this is the only way I know to insure that you study it well!

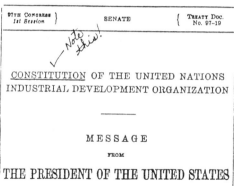

97TH CONGRESS 1st Session	SENATE	TREATY Doc. No. 97–19

Note this!

<u>CONSTITUTION</u> OF THE UNITED NATIONS INDUSTRIAL DEVELOPMENT ORGANIZATION

M E S S A G E

FROM

THE PRESIDENT OF THE UNITED STATES

TRANSMITTING

THE CONSTITUTION OF THE UNITED NATIONS' INDUSTRIAL DEVELOPMENT ORGANIZATION (UNIDO), ADOPTED BY THE UNITED NATIONS CONFERENCE ON THE ESTABLISHMENT OF THE UNITED NATIONS INDUSTRIAL DEVELOPMENT ORGANIZATION AS A SPECIALIZED AGENCY ON APRIL 8, 1979, AND SIGNED ON BEHALF OF THE UNITED STATES OF AMERICA ON JANUARY 17, 1980

OCTOBER 5, 1981.—Treaty was read the first time and, together with the accompanying papers, referred to the Committee on Foreign Relations and ordered to be printed for the use of the Senate

U.S. GOVERNMENT PRINTING OFFICE
89–118 O   WASHINGTON : 1981

69

CONSTITUTION OF THE UNITED NATIONS

INDUSTRIAL DEVELOPMENT ORGANIZATION

Treaty Doc. No. 97-19

The White House, October 5, 1981,

Transmittal letter of the President of the United States to the *Senate of the United States:*

With a view to receiving the advice and consent of the Senate to ratification, I transmit herewith a copy of the <u>Constitution of the United Nations Industrial Development Organization (UNIDO)</u>. This Constitution was adopted by the United Nations Conference on the Establishment of the United Nations Industrial Development Organization as a Specialized Agency on April 8, 1979, and signed on behalf of the United States of America on January 17, 1980. The report of the Department of State with respect to the Constitution is also transmitted for the information of the Senate.

The Constitution would establish UNIDO as an independent specialized agency of the United Nations system. It does not create a new entity, but rather revises UNIDO's existing legal framework in a way that significantly improves the position of the United States and other major donors in budget, program and assessment determinations.

UNIDO's principal purpose is to foster the industrialization of developing countries. It is currently the third largest executing agency for the United Nations Development Program. UNIDO's wide-ranging activities are geared to aid developing countries in establishing the technical and institutional skills necessary for the industrialization. Many of these activities are consonant with the United States development, priorities, including development of indigenous entrepreneurial and productive capabilities in the private sector. United States commercial and academic interests also benefit from UNIDO activity.

In recent years, there has been growing recognition of the need to formulate more effective institutions within the United Nations system to deal with the problems of development in <u>an increasingly interdependent world</u>. Such institutions need to serve the interests of all member nations and to be governed in a manner that realistically reflects the political and economic situation in the world today.

The Constitution would give UNIDO a new governing machinery that will make it more responsive to its member governments and that will give greater recognition to the special role of major donors, including the United States, other industrial democracies, and the Soviet bloc. If they act together, the major donors will be able to block decisions or UNIDO's program and budgets. <u>In this respect, the Constitution is a</u>

70

precedent-setting document.

The Constitution would also provide a specific right to withdrawal from UNIDO if the United States should ever determine that its interests are not served by continued membership. This could not be accomplished under UNIDO's current statute without withdrawal from the United Nations.

While the Constitution refers to the objectives of helping establish a new international economic order, the United States has made clear its view that this does not refer to any preconceived notion of such an order as outlined in some UN resolutions to which the United States has taken exception.

The Constitution offers the United States important advantages over UNIDO's current status. It provides an opportunity to increase UNIDO's effectiveness in promoting economic development in the developing countries and, thus, its contribution to a more equitable and peaceful, international environment. In addition to helping create a better institutional framework, ratification of the Constitution by the United States will be a strong reaffirmation of our commitment to the industrial development of the less developed countries and demonstrate our political will to pursue beneficial relations with these countries.

I recommend that the Senate give prompt consideration to the Constitution and advise and consent to its ratification.

RONALD REAGAN.

(**And so it was ratified and signed by Ronald Reagan.*)

LETTER OF SUBMITTAL

———

Department of State,
Washington, September 12, 1981

THE PRESIDENT: I have the honor to submit to you, with a view to its transmission to the Senate for advice and consent to ratification, the Constitution of the United Nations Industrial Development Organization (UNIDO), adopted by the United Nations Conference on the Establishment of the United Nations Industrial Development Organization as a Specialized Agency on April 8, 1979, and signed on behalf of the United States of America on January 17, 1980.
The Constitution would establish UNIDO as an independent specialized agency of the United Nations system. UNIDO now exists as an organization formally within the United Nations itself, reporting to the General Assembly.

UNIDO has a mandate to provide developing countries with industrial-related technical assistance (worth $76 million in 1980), including programs in industrial planning, institutional infrastructure, factory establishment and management, training, feasibility studies, and investment promotion. Virtually all of UNIDO's technical assistance expenditures are funded by voluntary sources, primarily the United Nations Development Program. UNIDO activities funded by the United Nations regular assessed budget ($47 million in 1980) are largely in support of its technical assistance activities, and include: macro-economic studies of factors affecting industrialization; advice to LDC governments on development policies; industrial sector, regional, country and case studies; statistical data collection and analysis; expert group meetings including sectoral Consultations; information processing and investment promotion. UNIDO's highly diversified activities include many which are congenial to United States development priorities such as: employment generation, private sector development, basic human needs, appropriate technology, and rural and agricultural related development. American commercial and academic interests also benefit from UNIDO activity.

UNIDO was established as an organ of the United Nations General Assembly pursuant to United Nations General Assembly Resolutions 2089 (XX) and 2152 (XXI), adopted in 1965 and 1966, respectively. In 1975, the United Nations General Assembly, endorsing the recommendation of the Second General Conference of UNIDO, adopted Resolution 3362 (S-VII) which established an intergovernmental committee of the whole followed by a conference of pleni-potentiaries to draft and consider a constitution to transform UNIDO into a specialized agency of the United Nations. The intergovernmental committee of the whole met five times over a two-year period and was succeeded by the Conference on the Establishment of UNIDO as a Specialized Agency.

The Constitution, while not creating a new entity, revises UNIDO's existing legal framework, significantly improving the provisions relating to control of budget and programming. Under the current regime, UNIDO's work program is decided upon by its governing body, the Industrial Development Board, while its program budget is set by the United Nations General Assembly as one component of the overall United Nations Program Budget. Thus, UNIDO's budget is currently not subject to intergovernmental review by a body directly responsible for UNIDO activities; nor do the present institutional arrangements, by which all questions are decided by majority vote, adequately reflect the special interest of major donors.

The Constitution seeks to correct these defects by providing that the program and budget of UNIDO shall both be acted upon by three governing bodies in succession: the Program and Budget Committee (the Committee), the Industrial Development Board (the Board), and the General Conference (the Conference). Each body must decide on the program and budget by a two-thirds majority vote.

**(H: Please note that this obsoletes your United States Constitution of*

In the Committee and the Board, the industrial democracies and the Soviet bloc (i.e., the major donors) hold substantially more than a third of the vote and thus could, if most of them agree, block adoption of a program or budget. (The Soviets have traditionally taken a very conservative position on budgetary issues.) The Constitution thereby enables for the first time in the United Nations system, outside of the banking institutions, a special recognition of the essential role of major donor states in United Nations affairs. The Constitution is therefore a precedent setting document, responsive to the political realities of the 1980's and beyond.

The Constitution and the related resolutions on transition to specialized agency status also achieve another objective of the United States in that they do not mandate any increase in United States contributions to UNIDO, but only change the method of assessment and payment in ways beneficial to the United States. Currently, United States assessed contributions to UNIDO are determined and paid indirectly through the mechanism of the United Nations assessed budget, making it difficult for the United States to achieve a degree of influence within UNIDO concomitant with the level of those indirect contributions. The Constitution will move toward correcting this situation by instituting direct assessed budget payments to UNIDO and providing for assessments to be determined in a manner similar to the determination of the program and budget, with major donor States holding more than a third of the vote in the Board which must decide on assessments by a two-thirds majority.

It is also noteworthy that United Nations General Assembly Resolution 96 (XXXIV) on Transitional Arrangements on the Establishment of the United Nations Industrial Development Organization as a Specialized Agency provides for the termination of United Nations funding for UNIDO from the United Nations regular program budget and a corresponding reduction in this budget upon establishment of UNIDO as a specialized agency.

The Constitution consists of a preamble, twenty-nine articles (in six chapters) and three annexes. The Preamble states that the States Parties, while bearing in mind the "broad objectives" of resolutions adopted by the sixth and seventh special sessions of the United Nations General Assembly and the Second General Conference of UNIDO pertaining to the establishment of a new international economic order, make certain declarations regarding economic development. The declarations include the necessity of establishing a just and equitable economic and social order; the essential role of industrialization to rapid economic and social development; the right of all countries to pursue industrialization; the necessity of concerted measures to promote the development, transfer and adaptation of technology internationally; and a determination to promote the common welfare through expanding international economic cooperation. The Preamble is basically hortatory, and contains no operational links to the rest of the Constitution.

(H: Please note that this _requires_ a new economic and social order.)

The objectives and functions of UNIDO are contained in Chapter I, Article 1 states that the primary objective of UNIDO will be the promotion and acceleration of industrial development in the developing countries with a view to assisting in the <u>establishment of a new international economic order. The language used in the Constitution, as indicated in the statement of the United States at the time of adoption of the Constitution, can be interpreted to make clear that Article 1 refers to UNIDO's participation in an evolutionary and truly consensual process to achieve a new international economic order</u> ****(H: NEW WORLD ORDER.)**** and that Article 1 does not refer to any preconceived notion of a new international economic order as outlined in certain resolutions of the United Nations General Assembly sixth and seventh special sessions, regarding which the United States has reservations.

Article 2 lists the functions of UNIDO, all related to promoting industrial development and basically similar to the functions specified in UNIDO's current statute, <u>General Assembly resolution 2152 (XXI)</u>. The more important functions include: coordinating United Nations industrial development activities; providing technical assistance for industrialization, including training and pilot facilities; <u>managing an industrial information clearinghouse</u>; advising and assisting developing countries in formulating and executing development plans; <u>assisting in the establishment and operation of industries</u>, to achieve full utilization of local <u>human</u> and natural <u>resources</u>; and as requested by the countries concerned, providing a forum for contacts and negotiations.

********Dharma, stop please, and begin a new document!!!! ***NOW.****

CHAPTER 9

REC #2   HATONN

SUNDAY, DECEMBER 2, 1990   9:06 A.M.   YEAR 4 DAY 108

Chapter II provides for participation in UNIDO. Membership is open to all States members of the United Nations or a specialized agency. Article 6 provides for withdrawal from membership, not possible now without withdrawing from the United Nations, subject to providing a reasonable period of notice. The right of withdrawing from UNIDO alone may provide useful leverage, although actual withdrawal would entail a difficult decision.

Chapter III establishes the organs of UNIDO. Article 8 specifies a General Conference composed of all members which will act upon the reports of the Board and the Director-General and determine the guiding principles and policies of the organization. Article 9 provides for the Board to be composed of 53 members elected by the Conference, with the following distribution of seats: 33 members elected from the G-77 (developing countries), 15 members elected from Group B (industralized democracies) and 5 members elected from Group D (the Soviet bloc). Article 10 establishes a Programme and Budget Committee to consist of 27 members elected by the Conference with the following distribution: 15 from the G-77, 9 from Group B, and 3 from Group D.

Chapter IV delineates the process for approval of the program of work and the regular budget (i.e., the budget expenditures to be met from assessed contributions) and the operational budget (i.e., budget expenditures to be met from voluntary contributions). Article 14 stipulates that the Director-General shall prepare and submit a draft work program, regular budget and operational budget to the Board through the Committee. The Committee will consider the Director-General's proposals and make recommendations to the Board by a two-thirds majority vote of those present and voting. The Board will examine the Director General's proposals and the recommendation of the Committee and adopt the program of work, regular budget and operational budget, for submission to the Conference, by a two-thirds majority of those present and voting. The Conference will approve the submission of the Board by a two-thirds majority vote of those present and voting. The Conference may make no decision or amendment involving expenditures unless the Committee and the Board have had an opportunity to act as indicated above. By commanding more than a third of the votes in the Board and the Committee, the major donor States (i.e., Groups B and I), which share a common desire to keep United Nations agency budgets to a reasonable level, will be able to block work programs and budgets of which they disapprove, if they act together.

Article 15 provides that the scale of assessments for members shall be established by the Conference by a two-thirds majority of the members present and voting, upon a recommendation of the Board adopted by a two-thirds majority of the members present and voting. The Board's recommendation is to be based on a draft prepared by the Committee. The Constitution thereby provides a mechanism for the major donors as a group to veto a scale of assessments which they disapprove. Article 15 also stipulates that the scale of assessments shall be based to the extent possible on the scale most recently employed by the United Nations and no member shall be assessed more than 25 percent of the regular budget.

Chapter VI covers legal matters. Article 23 provides for amendments, with special, stringent provisions for amendments to financial articles. Financial amendments must be approved by two-thirds majorities of the Board and Conference respectively and must be ratified by three-fourths of the Members States. This provision protects the blocking more than a third of the votes which major donors command in the Committee and the Board.

(H: Remember what I told you--on the UN level, countries of the world are called UN's "states".)

Article 25 stipulates that the Constitution shall enter into force when at least eighty States that deposited instruments of ratification notify the Secretary General of the United Nations that they have agreed, after consultations among themsleves, that the Constitution shall enter into force. However, for States that had deposited instruments of ratification but did not participate in such notification, the Constitution shall come into force on such later date as they choose.

The practical effect of the entry into force provisions is that the Constitution will not enter into force without the agreement and participation of major donors, including the United States. Once the Senate has given its advice and consent to ratification, this provision will afford the United States a strong position to ensure that the basic concerns of the United States, such as budgetary restraint, are taken into account. ***(H: Oh sure! And who else is going to be sick besides ME?)***

Article 27 states that no reservations may be made to the Constitution.

A major problem in the constitutional negotiations was to balance the desire of major contributing countries for control over the regular budget with the insistence by developing countries that funding for technical assistance activities continue to be available on an assured basis. Under current arrangements, a portion of UNIDO's activities in the field of technical assistance is financed by assessments from the regular budget of the United Nations. Under Annex II of the Constitution, 6% of the regular budget of UNIDO will be set aside for technical assistance activities which have heretofore been financed by assessed contributions to the United Nations budget. The six percent figure sets a constitutional ceiling on the portion of the new organization's regular budget which can be devoted to technical assistance. All other technical assistance activities must be financed by voluntary contributions. Since the United States together with the other major contributing countries will have more than a third of the votes in the Board, which must approve the regular budget by a two-thirds majority vote, we will have substantial influence on the overall figure with regard to which the 6% techincal assistance figure will be calculated and, therefore, over the absolute amount of technical assistance expenditures from the regular budget.

The combined effect of the 6 percent ceiling, the major donors having more than a blocking third of the votes, and the withdrawal provisions will provide the United States with much greater capacity than presently exists to ensure that regular budget funds for technical assistance are used for programs which we believe should qualify for such funding. In this connection, the United States representative to the Constitutional Conference placed on the record our view that technical assistance financed by assessments, "must fill gaps which would be difficult for the UNDP, with its country specific focus, or other voluntary funds to fill. Specifically, such technical assistance would deal with emergency situations and financial activities that primarily benefit the entire international community, not a single country."

There has been growing recognition in UNIDO of the need to achieve a true consensus on development questions if UNIDO is to cope effectively with development problems. At the same time, there has been growing recognition within the United States of the need for the United Nations to be more responsive to our basic programmatic and budgetary concerns, especially in light of the large United States assessed contributions. The Constitution of UNIDO is a product of both of these movements. It gives an already existing institution a new mechanism of decision-making which provides special recognition of the essential role of major contributors, including the United States. In this way, it is truly a precedent setting document for the United Nations system which deserves our earnest and rapid support.

The other agencies most concerned, the Department of Labor, the Agency for International Development, and the Department of Commerce, have no objection to ratification of the Constitution. I hope that you will ask the Senate to consider the Constitution and give its advice and consent to ratification as soon as possible.

Respectfully submitted,
William Clark.

Let us herein repeat the

PREAMBLE

CONSTITUTION OF THE UNITED NATIONS INDUSTRIAL DEVELOPMENT ORGANIZATION

The States parties to this Constitution,

In conformity with the Charter of the United Nations,
Bearing in mind the broad objectives in the resolutions adopted by the sixth special session of the General Assembly of the United Nations on the establishment of a New International Economic Order, in the UNIDO Second General Conference's Lima Declaration and Plan of Action for Industrial Development and Co-operation, and in the resolution of the seventh special session of the General Assembly of the United nations on Development and International Economic Cooperation,

Declaring that:
It is necessary to establish a just and equitable economic and social order to be achieved through the elimination of inequalities, the establishment of rational and equitable international economic relations, implementation of dynamic social and economic changes and the encourgaement of necessary structural changes in the development of the world economy.

(H: Regional Government is a component of the structural changes.)

Industrialization is a dynamic instrument of growth essential to rapid economic and social development, in particular of developing countries, to the improvement of the living standards and the quality of life of the peoples in all countries, and to the introduction of an equitable economic and social order.

It is the sovereign right of all countries to achieve their industrialization, and any process of such industrialization must conform to the broad objectives of self-sustaining and integrated socio-economic development, and should include the appropriate changes which would ensure the just and effective participation of all peoples in the industrialization of their countries.

As international co-operation for development is the shared goal and common obligation of all countries it is essential to promote industrialization through all possible concerted measures including the development, transfer and adaptation of technology on global, regional and national, as well as on sectoral levels.

All countries, irrespective of their social and economic systems, are determined to promote the common welfare of their peoples by individual and collective actions aimed at expanding international economic co-operation on the basis of sovereign equality, strengthening of the economic independence of the developing countries, securing their equitable share in total world industrial production and contributing to international peace and security and the prosperity of all nations, in conformity with the purposes and principles of the Charter of the United Nations.

Mindful of these guidelines,
Desiring to establish, within the terms of Chapter IX of the Charter of the United Nations, a specialized agency to be known as the United Nations Industrial Development Organization (UNIDO) (hereinafter referred to as

the "Organization"), which shall play the central role in and be responsible for reviewing and promoting the co-ordination of all activities of the United Nations system in the field of industrial development, in conformity with the responsiblities of the Economic and Social Council under the Charter of the United Nations and with the applicable relationship agreements,

Hereby agree to the present Constitution.

***(H: By any label, this means "sharing the wealth.

I see no alternative other than to pursue this subject in this manner. Regional Government is a component of the structural changes. Futher, you may not know it but in 1945 the U.N. Charter was proclaimed law of the land!

Oh, no belief herein?)***

CHAPTER I.--OBJECTIVES AND FUNCTIONS

ARTICLE 1
OBJECTIVES

The primary objective of the Organization shall be the promotion and accleration of industrial development in the developing countries with a view to assisting in the establishment of a new internationl economic order. The Organization shall also promote industrial development and co-operation on global, regional and national, as well as on sectoral levels. And so it goes - - - -.

NEW WORLD ORDER

Treaty #97-19 IS A CONSTITUTION. This constitution is only one of many constitutions that the United Nations has "in force" upon the United States, causing your once free people to be merged with the communist nations of the world. This is the basis upon which President George Bush and the U.S. State Department hinge their authority for converting the United States system of government from a Constitutional Republic into a segment of the international socialist world government: THE NEW WORLD ORDER!

When asked about "Constitutionality of that which he is doing", Mr. Bush smiled to the press and all the world and said, "I know all of my rights within the Constitution; I also know what Presidents before me have done and ....." This speech was given only two days ago just after ringing the death knell of your "Liberty Bell"!

The treaty discussed herein is in force, right now, world-wide, having been enacted on behalf of the American People, who not only DO NOT KNOW that this treaty exists, much less the serious changes that it makes in your lives as the treaty helps overthrow the United States Constitution.

79

Consent of the governed has never been granted to permit such destructive treaties and changes nor will it be easy and probable that you can change of it.

Some two centuries ago your forefathers engineered the best form of government that could ever be created by man as it conforms to the natural law, places limits on the power that man can exercise over his fellow man, and safeguards your natural rights, which come as an endowment from the Creator. By the way, this also includes the right of the people to keep and bear arms--which is also being removed from you.

The P.P.B.S. (Program, Planning, and Budgeting System) which plays an active part in this scenario, is an accounting system but NOT an ordinary accounting system. It is a computerized command and control system, based upon predetermined goals and objectives. It is in operation in the United States in order to socialize the American people and their government in all the economic, social and political aspects of human endeavor. Government funding is granted only when recipients comply to given management performance.

RECOURSES? Yes, fortunately there are--I wonder if you will take action? There is a principle in international law by which treaties can be nullified: Rebus Sic Stantibus. If you fail to stand against these intrusion to your sovereignty, your independence, your right to keep and bear arms, then you, as individuals, as a state, and as a nation, are ruined!

IMPORTANT! IMPORTANT! IMPORTANT!

Along with the other information, take this to your State Representatives. It is probable that he is not versed in INTERNATIONAL LAW and will not know how to proceed to nullify these disastrous treaties which are the reason why your guns, etc., are being taken away from you, as well as giving of your armed forces into a communist United Nations under a permanent arrangement.

Tell him/her that there is ample reason to void the disarmament law, and the INF treaty which has already been signed. You can stop the additional and worse treaties which the state department and the president have already worked out for you, by knowing how to proceed.

Your Representative will find the PREMIER PRINCIPLE of International Law in Black's Law Dictionary. The page number, definition and documentation are reproduced below. IT IS THE HIGHEST REASON IN RANK FOR VOIDING A TREATY. THE PRINCIPLE IS CALLED:

REBUS SIC STANTIBUS
IT MEANS THAT "THE SITUATION HAS CHANGED". THIS SET OF PAPERS HAS BEEN GIVEN TO DOCUMENT WHAT IS REALLY HAPPENING TO THE UNITED STATES AND TO GIVE YOU PRINCIPLES IN LAW WHICH WILL ASSIST YOU TO PROCEEED

TO ARREST THE EVIL!

Blacks Law Dictionary: REBUS SIC STANTIBUS: On Page 1432 it gives the definition as follows: At this point of affairs; in these circumstances. A name given to tacit conditions. Said to attach to all treaties, that they should cease to be obligatory, so soon as the state of facts and conditions upon which they were founded has substantially changed.

Documentation:

Taylor International Law, Section 394; I Oppenheim International Law, Section 550; Gotius, Chapter XVI, Section XXV.

What your Representative needs to know is that there is more to the treaties than what meets the eye....more than the states and citizens are aware. The people have been lied to about the "peace" program. They were not told that it meant giving away their armed forces and their own personal firearms. The true nature of the treaties was denied them. They were not told that the National Security and the security of the 50 states would be endangered. They were not told that they were being restructured for world government under a communist set of operating documents. Now that they know the truth the situation has changed! This knowledge is grounds for nullification of the treaties. It is the Duty of the States to see that the Constitution is enforced as well as the Bill of Rights. It takes ONLY ONE STATE TO FORCE THE SUPREME COURT TO RULE ON THE ISSUE. IF THE RULING COMES DOWN UNFAVORABLE, THE ONLY RECOURSE IS TO REPEAL. TO REPEAL TAKES THRITY-EIGHT (38) STATES TO OVERRIDE THE SUPREME COURT. IF THE ATTEMPT IS NOT MADE, YOUR GOVERNMENT IS IRRETRIEVABLY GONE! WHEN THE SECOND AMENDMENT GOES, ALL OF THE AMENDMENTS WILL GO BECAUSE IT IS THE KEYSTONE AMENDMENT. THIS INCLUDES THE RIGHT TO OWN LAND AND TO VOTE FOR ELECTED REPRESENTATIVES. ELECTED REPRESENTATIVES WILL FIND THEMSELVES IN CONFLICT WITH THE MILITARY GOVERNMENT THAT WILL SUPERSEDE THEM! THE USE OF DUALSPEAK, (ALSO CALLED DUAL-USE) SOPHISTRY AND LEGER DEMAIN STRATEGIES WERE APPLIED TO FOOL THE PEOPLE INTO INACTION. THE PEOPLE ARE THE ULTIMATE POWER. THE EVIL BEING DONE IS WITHOUT THE CONSENT OF THE GOVERNED. YOUR CONSTITUTIONAL GOVERNMENT WAS WRITTEN IN PERPETUITY AND WHAT THE FEDERAL GOVERNMENT IS DOING IS AGAINST THE LAW. THE UNITED NATIONS CHARTER WAS SLAPPED ONTO YOUR COUNTRY AS A "TREATY", ALSO! SINCE IT IS CAUSING ALL THE DAMAGE, IT SHOULD BE GOTTEN RID OF, ALSO, BY REBUS SIC STANTIBUS!!!

Chela, you need a break and this is probably mind-shattering enough to cause need for digestion assistants. The clock is running out for you precious children of the lie--the ones in charge of your nations know exactly that which they do. IF YOU DO NOT ACT TO COUNTER THIS THING, YOU WILL SIMPLY BE ABSORBED AND THE GAME FINISHED! SO BE IT. MAY GOD WALK WITH YOU FOR YOU HAVE LOST YOUR WAY. SALU.

Hatonn to clear and move to stand-by. Saalome'

CHAPTER 10

REC #1   HATONN

TUESDAY, DECEMBER 4, 1990   6:40 A.M.   YEAR 4 DAY 110

TODAY'S WATCH

In the Light of the Love of the Universe, I come to commune. In service unto you little Doubting Thomases. Hatonn present.

December 3rd came and went and nothing happened??!!? Where were you?

From where I sat, I saw five space missiles sent up. I saw you effort once again, in America, to launch a spy/sensor satellite system--which by the way, was again prevented from its appointed task. I saw Japan place a "journalist" aboard a Russian spacecraft to monitor independently that which you ones planned to do--if you managed to do it. I watched the "Siberian Express" move into cities and areas of the Midwest and bring "RECORD" BREAKING snow and ice to Chicago--"Unseasonable", they said and further pronounced that if this continues, it will be a long hard winter with "fuel" shortage for heating. I saw Miami erupt in riots because of your injustice system. I watched Gen. Powell go to Great Britain. I saw two massive planes collide in Detroit while witnesses said "something" flew past the wing prior to the accident. I saw a deep earthquake in Mt. Fuji which vented ash all the way to the surface--some fifty miles from the cauldron. I witnessed tides higher than recorded prior. I watched Israel pronounce intent for war over the upcoming Iraq/U.S. meetings. I watched President Bush give away Billions of Dollars from you nice U.S. taxpayers to Brazil in free-trade and aid. I watched Argentina erupt in response to Bush's visit there this day--where he will give a rotten government more billions of your dollars. I watched as Saddam Hussein agreed to release 3,000 Russian nationals *by Thursday*--IF RUSSIA DOES THIS OR THUS. What about the other 6,000 Russian military instructors and advisers?

I watched Saddam Hussein send a bill (statement) to England for costs incurred for housing "Hostages" in the nice hotel in Baghdad ALSO WATCHED AS ENGLAND AGREED, WITHOUT COMMENT, TO PAY IT.

NEXT I WATCHED WHAT IS THE MOST HEINOUS DISRESPECTFUL DECEIVING OF A NATION THAT I HAVE YET WITNESSED. YOUR WONDROUS PRESIDENT WHO WOULD BE KING OF THE NEW WORLD ORDER HAS NOW CALLED UP SO MANY RESERVES THAT IF HE CALLS MORE HE WILL NEED TO CALL A NATIONAL EMERGENCY! THAT IS WHAT THE WHOLE THING

Once Mr. Bush can call a National Emergency--all Emergency Regulations can be put into service, from closing your banks to removing all of your Bill of Rights--remember those writings of weeks ago? Funny thing--Mr. Greenspan of the Federal Reserve did exactly that which I told you last week--he has lowered the reserve required by Banks!

How much more do you want regarding yesterday and things that didn't happen? Do you count your blessings or do you moan and groan that disaster did not strike poor New Madrid--well, dear hearts, the week isn't finished, is it? I suggest you pay closer attention to California--you did have a quake in California yesterday worthy of media mention. So be it, I am not going to do all your homework for you but since you can't see into the cosmos or even the limited distance to your own spacecraft whose equipment "doesn't work" I would suggest you should be objecting to the multi-billion dollar toys that don't ever work!

Oh, by the way--what about the sur-tax "Mr. Read My Lips" is going to place on all you nice taxpayers to go with that nickle a gallon gas tax? Oh, its the one that is going to pay for this Middle East war! You know, the one like the one used in Vietnam!

Now, I am going to shatter a lot of balloons. You see, Satan has to wear a clue, no matter how faint or subtle--you have to be alert. I am going to write something herein from your own *Newsweek* magazine from Dec. 3, 1990!

Quote:
EXCLUSIVE: WHERE ARE THE TROOPS?

It's the case of the `missing' military presence. Since Operation Desert Shield began, the Pentagon has given regular updates on Iraq's military buildup in Kuwait. In late August it reported that some 150,000 troops and up to 1,500 tanks were in Kuwait. In mid-September it said there were 265,000 Iraqi troops and 2,200 tanks in Kuwait and southern Iraq.

Now, *Newsweek* has been told, some American experts are puzzled by a set of five Soviet satellite pictures of eastern Kuwait and southern Iraq that show *little or no Iraqi military presence.* ABC News bought the photos, shot in mid-September, from the Soviet commercial satellite agency Soyuz-Karta. But the *network finds them so bewildering it won't air them*.

To analyze the photos, ABC called on two experts: George Washington University professor Peter Zimmerman (a nice Zionist surname), a member of the U.S. Arms Control Agency in the Reagan Administration, and a former Defense Intelligence Agency photo analyst. When the pair looked at the shots, they were *astounded*, "We turned to each other and we both said, `There's nothing there'," Zimmerman recalls. They found no trace of an Iraqi military presence *anywhere in Kuwait. In fact, all they could see, in crystal-clear detail, was the U.S. buildup in Saudi Arabia.*

When questioned, a Pentagon spokesman said the military *"sticks by its numbers".*

There is no definitive explanation for the mystery. <u>An ABC spokesperson speculated that perhaps poor photo resolution was the problem or that the Iraqi buildup had been expertly camouflaged.</u> AND HOW WAS YOUR WEEK?

Do you ones have a clear-cut picture of how large (in population) is Iraq? Well, it has some 17 million people--THAT, DEAR ONES, IS ABOUT THE SIZE (A BIT LESS POPULATED) THAN GREATER LOS ANGELES!

WHAT CAN A "COMPANY" DO?

This is a continual question from you who have listened to suggestions. "What creative steps can a company take to prepare for these uncertain times of possible war and economic disaster?"

I shall simply ask Dharma to reprint Lewis Laughlin's response to the same question.

A TALE OF 2 COMPANIES:

In the not too distant past, times were much like they are now. You probably remember a time in the 1970's when times were tumultuous and recession or even depression seemed almost imminent. During these times there were two companies that are representative of many during that time.

One company did what it could to prepare. It cut spending and used all of the conventional methods but that's about where the preparation ended. The company had some assets that were valuable. Unfortunately, that company doesn't have those assets today--in fact, the owners of that company don't have the company today.

You see, when times got tough, the company's creditors moved in and took the assets away. The company fell victim to economic hard times.

Then there was the other company. In addition to the conventional steps that the first company took, this company took some creative action. This particular company also had certain valuable assets and it still has them today. Here's what they did...

85

The company got *heavily in debt to another company...it bor-rowed heavily and used all of it's assets as collateral for the debt*. A strange way to prepare for possible hard times you say--yes it was. The catch is that the owners of that company *also owned the creditor--the company that was in debt <u>and</u> the company that it was in debt to were controlled by the same people.*

So, even if creditors wanted to move in on the assets of the com-pany, they could not. Not without paying off the secured creditor first...and the secured creditor was controlled by the same people.

This company was recession proofed--depression proofed--judg-ment proofed. The company was *prepared!*

The strategy that the prepared company implemented came to be known as the "Warbucks/Red Inc. strategy".

END QUOTE.

You can do it too and in times like these, NOW would be none too soon.

A WORD TO THE WISE!!! NOW IS THE TIME! IT IS ALSO THE TIME TO PUT YOUR EXTRA INVESTMENT MONEY TO WORK. YOU CAN COVER YOUR "CONTRIBUTIONS" IN TWO WAYS--I.E. AS WITH THE PHOENIX INSTITUTE AND THE "CONTRIBUTION" WILL BE COVERED BY THE COLLATERAL OF PURE GOLD! THE GOVERNMENT IS READY TO PULL THE NOOSE CLOSED. IS EVERYTHING GUARANTEED AND PERFECTION? DO YOU LIVE ON THE MOON? NO, YOU LIVE ON EARTH WHICH IS GETTING READY TO GO OUT OF BUSINESS AND THERE WILL BE NO PERFECTION AND GUARANTEES. I SUGGEST YOU GET IN TOUCH WITH THE PUBLISHER AND FIND OUT WHAT YOU CAN DO, AND OBERLI WILL ASSIST YOU--I CANNOT GIVE YOU MORE. BUT, THE TIME FOR DILLY/DALLY IS FINISHED FOR ALL PRACTICAL PURPOSES UNLESS YOU ONES GET UP OFF YOUR ASSETS (INTENDED ANY WAY YOU WISH TO ACCEPT IT) AND CHANGE THINGS. SO BE IT.

WARS AND RUMORS OF WARS

How many of you realize that a war still rages in Burma? In fact, how many of you know that Burma is not Burma? It is Myanmar (Burma's of-ficial name since mid-1989--now that would confuse you "listening" pub-lic, would it not?) At this point this war is the longest-running insurgency in the world. Well, people are maimed and die in that war and mostly it is over drugs and utilizes the most modern weapons, compliments of the U.S. and the Communists. There are already over 250,000 well-armed troops--I suggest you keep at least one eye open and on this little Myan-mar.

Now, let us look at what the press is attributing to little Israel. Well, they fear things will get a lot worse before they get worse. The picture being thrust upon you unsuspecting world spectators is one of economic and social strains. WHY? Nothing should have changed in Israel as they have "deliberately kept a low profile in the Gulf crisis". They claim to now worry that Saddam will be given a face-saving way to escape a knockout blow and emerge as an even more dangerous Arab hero. New U.S. arms sales to Saudi Arabia and President Bush's meeting with Syria's Hafez Assad add to Israeli disquiet, even more so given the overall chill in U.S.-Israeli relations. (This action is taken in EVERY similar circumstance to fool you the people.) *__"The meeting between Bush and Prime Minister Yitzhak Shamir on December 11 should allay some concerns..."__*, it is suggested!

Now, I shall ask Dharma to reprint a section from *U.S. News and World Report*:

"....At home, Arab-Israeli enmity is deepening in the wake of the Temple Mount killings and a surge in Palestinian guerrilla attacks along the border. A clampdown on West Bank-Gaza workers entering Israel has, in effect, re-established the "Green Line" separating Israel from occupied Arab land, creating a fresh pool of unemployed and volatile Palestinians. The massive influx of Soviet immigrants threatens to overwhelm Israel's economy. As many as 1 million are expected in the next three to four years, the equivalent of the U.S. absorbing 55 million. Yet so far only 10,000 of 45,000 planned housing units have been started, and even with the latest 5 percent tax hike the *country will have to borrow as much as $30 BILLION abroad. __Shamir will ask Bush for an additional $4 BILLION in aid to help cover resettlement costs__*.

"Well", you ask, "Isn't peaceful coexistence within secure borders with Arab neighbors the historic aim of Israel?" No, no and no. The Middle East has been in constant and unHoly turmoil since the instant of founding of Israel. This is directly attributable to Israeli policy.

The basis of Israel's foreign policy is the attainment of the XX dream of *Eretz Yisrael*--Greater Israel--which encompasses most of the present Arab states--and that, dear ones, is a LOT OF TERRITORY! MOST COINCIDENTALLY, THIS TERRITORY ALSO INCLUDES THE GREATEST CONCENTRATION OF MINERAL WEALTH IN THE WORLD, THE OIL FIELDS OF SAUDI ARABIA.

By the way, how many of you REALLY realize what has happened in Saudi Arabia? You believe that the U.S. has sent hundreds of thousands of your troops to keep Iraq from invading Saudi Arabia? YOU--YOU, THE U.S. of A. simply invaded Saudi Arabia instead!! Not only did you invade Saudi Arabia but you have occupied the territory!! SO BE IT!

Israel feels its expansionist dream can best be realized by creating total chaos in the Middle East, much as the Serbian nationalists under the domination of the Austro-Hungarian Empire felt that they could achieve nationhood only in the wake of a total breakdown of the European political landscape. Thus, the assassination of Archduke Ferdinand and the resultant tragedy known as World War I, as we just covered day before yesterday.

Israel cannot, however, yet do it alone and doesn't need to do so. Although mightily equipped for war, thanks to the beneficence of its patron the U.S.--that cannot hope to stand up to the superpower challenge. Thus, Israel has turned to a most *unlikely ally--THE SOVIET UNION!* Ah, the plot thickens, does it not?

ULTIMATE WINNERS

Israel and the Soviet Union will be the ultimate winners of any U.S. war with Iraq in the Middle East. *While it has all but slid by unnoticed during the continuing crisis in the Middle East, as planned, there has been a renewal of friendly relations between Israel and the Soviet Union and considerable diplomatic travel back and forth between Moscow and Jerusalem--and darn it all, you nice U.S. taxpayers pay all the travel expenses FOR BOTH SIDES.*

The content of top-secret Israeli-Soviet talks has been confined to a small circle of insiders with the two governments and the "friends of a Greater Israel" in Washington. But they undoubtedly concern how the Israelis and Soviets *will divide the spoils of war between Iraq and the U.S. and the latter's hodge-podge collection of small, ill-trained and ill-equipped "multinational" allies.*

The American public, at least, is becoming a bit confused as to WHY the U.S. would risk the deaths of tens of thousands of its young soldiers in a war with Iraq. The administration has not even defined a reason for confronting Iraq, but has instead offered various conflicting justifications that have left the public even more confused.

The people, however, are becoming a bit aware that the international oil companies and bankers are already greedily lining their pockets with war profiteering--at your own expense.

ISRAEL NO FRIEND

What they don't know is that the two major malefactors in an American war with Iraq--Israel and the Soviet Union--already have plans in place for seizing the oil-rich Middle East for themselves. Now, isn't this just wondrous and puzzling intrigue?

Israel, in cooperation with the Soviet Union, is positioning itself to seize the great Saudi Arabian oil fields in the aftermath of a bloody confrontation which the Israelis are prepared to ignite themselves, if necessary. The sparking of war by Israel would not require any tremendous effort, just as it takes little skill as an arsonist to touch off a blaze in a room filled with gas-soaked rags.

Let there be no mistake, chelas, the Israelis are not friends of the U.S. and have no qualms about killing young American servicemen. THERE IS NO HONOR AMONG SATAN'S SERVANTS, LITTLE SLEEPY-HEADS!

The Israelis have blatantly displayed their treachery on two glaring occasions in recent history.

During the Six-Day War of 1967, Israeli air and naval forces *knowingly attacked the American reconnaissance ship, the USS Liberty--remember the story?* Thirty-four American sailors were sent to their graves and more than a hundred others were injured and maimed after being bombed, machine-gunned, torpedoed and napalmed. Israeli gunners even shot up their life rafts--please don't be forgetting this.

The Mossad purposely did not inform the U.S. intelligence officials that terrorists planned to bomb the U.S. Marine barracks in Beirut, Lebanon, in October, 1983. As a result, 241 young American Marines were blown up.

So, you see--America still needs a first strike nuclear holocaust against the Soviets in order to head up this "New World Order" without opposition or struggle, for top-level control.

The Mossad has a most active spy operation, known as "El", in place in America to steal U.S. secrets and plans--you know, like launching sensor spy satellites and shuttle programs, etc. and to start a war is indeed very easy. Let us just consider, what if---. What if a group of Palestinian terrorists (or pretend ones)--say, Israelis dressed as Palestinian terrorists, or a whole group posing as Palestinian terrorists, crosses into Israel from Jordan and perpetrates some terrorist act in Israel. (Oh yes, this is exactly what the Mossad is best at.) The Israelis react by invading Jordan to attack the terrorist camps. Iraqi President Saddam Hussein moves to aid Jordan, and the United States reacts by moving against Iraq from Saudi Arabia.

While U.S. forces are pinned down by Iraqi defenses along the Saudi-Kuwaiti border, Israeli armored forces plunge through Jordan and deep into Saudi Arabia from the west, pushing ultimately to the sea.

Meanwhile, U.S. forces are held back and severely mauled by Iraqi defenses, including their use of chemical and biological warfare weapons.

America's current Arab allies on the front lines would quickly pull out of the fight, considering Israel's attack in Saudi Arabia a far worse danger than Iraq.

Meanwhile, again, U.S. forces are being horribly shredded by Iraqi forces, who are even now still being supplied and trained by the Soviets (remember those advisers mentioned above?) and making matters worse, America's supposed Arab allies, such as Egypt and Syria, defect from the "multinational force" due to the Israeli intrusion--it appears that now the Soviets have several options or windows of opportunity.

As weak as the Soviet Union is internally, its army is still numerically superior to the remaining Western forces in Europe (we will also talk of the vulnerability of Europe presently). It no longer needs to fear the forces of NATO, with most of the best U.S. troops and armor having been sent to Saudi Arabia from Europe. The Soviets have non-aggression pacts and various peace pacts signed with European NATO countries--*particularly Germany and France.*

The Soviets would be free to move against Iran and its rich oil fields, which they have long coveted. Or they could treacherously attack Iraq from the rear, seizing Iraqi and possibly even the disputed Kuwaiti oil fields.

Now how could this scenario end? It ends with Israel and the Soviet Union sharing the great Middle East oil fields. The American Army is effectively destroyed--WHICH, BEING IN SAUDI ARABIA--HAS LEFT THE CONTINENTAL UNITED STATES TOTALLY OPEN AND VULNERABLE (COULD YOUR PRESIDENT HAVE ACTUALLY KNOWN THIS?), AND THE SOVIETS WIN THEIR ULTIMATE VICTORY IN THEIR DECADES-LONG STRUGGLE WITH THE U.S., *WITHOUT FIRING THAT PROVERBIAL "SHOT" IN ANGER AT U.S. FORCES.*

Israel, in turn, realizes the ZIONIST dream of *Eretz Yisrael*, with a hammerlock on the Western World's major producing oil reserves. The Soviets, already the world's largest oil producer, realize even greater fortunes and monopolistic power from Middle East oil and achieve their long-sought desire to be linked by land to the Persian Gulf.

And what of the U.S.? Its military is wrecked in the Middle East, its economy in a shambles, and its major source of badly needed foreign oil cut off, is no longer a major world power.

Congress, completely dominated by the Israeli lobby, will not raise so much as a whimper in protest. The President, his political power cut off at the knees as a result of the U.S. defeat, will be in no position to challenge the resulting *status quo* (exactly according to plans for the "feet of clay"). The media pundits, such as W. Safire, A. Rosenthal and W. Buckley, will congratulate Israel on its "stunning victory".

Dear ones--THIS SCENARIO *IS ON THE DRAWING BOARD, SET*

UP AND READY FOR ACTION AND YOU ONES WON'T EVEN KNOW WHAT HIT YOU BECAUSE IT IS PREFERABLE, FOR SEVERAL REASONS, NOT TO BRING THE WAR INTO THE U.S. IN A TERRIBLY DESTRUCTIVE MANNER SO THAT THE U.S. CAN BE USED LATER.

Worse, the above as outlined is coordinated with an intended terrorist campaign in the country, which will have a mortal effect on the U.S. dollar, spelling the end of America's leading role in the world's financial community, and economic and civil chaos in your country.

And guess what as an added little humorous dividend? You American taxpayers will be forced to pay foreign aid to <u>rebuild the devastated nation of Iraq!</u>

<u>WHAT OF POOR BAGHDAD SUFFERING?</u>

Let us look into that little misconception also.

One of the most visited cities on Earth at this time is Baghdad, the capital of Iraq. It is teeming with foreigners. All hotel rooms are occupied, and all of the flights in and out of the international airport are full. Hence, one of the reasons for "billing" England for her "hostages" in the hotel-- this is occupying rooms which could otherwise be rented.

In fact, there are now *more foreigners in Baghdad than <u>ever before in HISTORY!</u>* There are many news people from the international media, although one would not know it from the paucity of coverage of the Iraqi side in this country.

Visiting foreign dignitaries arrive daily to meet with the Iraqi officials to try to arrange the release of their nationals. Also, relatives of those being held are coming in droves to attempt personal diplomacy on behalf of their loved ones. Nations represented by visitors just in recent days include China, New Zealand, Japan and all the Western European nations.

<u>But, the greatest number of foreigners in Baghdad are businessmen making profitable deals to beat the un-imposed sanctions. If Baghdad were to be bombed by your forces today, there would be a holocaust not only of Iraqi citizens but of foreigners from all over the world, as well.</u> LOOK AT THAT WHICH IS NOT SO OBVIOUS, CHELAS.

DHARMA--CLOSE THIS <u>NOW!</u>

CHAPTER 11

REC #2   HATONN

TUESDAY, DECEMBER 4, 1990   9:08 A.M.   YEAR 4 DAY 110

GOLD IN THEM THAR HILLS!

Just when you could believe in something--like restoration of a greedy, immoral Sabah family to power in Kuwait, exiled Kuwaitis themselves are not in favor of such a "DEMOCRATIC" ACTION. They have been meeting in London--these Kuwaiti exiles of prominent status and "DO NOT WISH TO SEE THE FORMER RULING FAMILY REIN-STATED"! Ah, so it goes.

By the way, as you were just beginning to believe this "war" invasion of Saudi Arabia might happen to be over oil and other misunderstood reasons, now you have to face another blow. THE SAUDIS HAVE STRUCK IT RICH! You maybe thought they were already rich? (sic sic). In addition to seas of oil--some of which is that nice light crude needing almost no refining--*there is an entire mountain of gold which has just been discovered in the southern part of the Kingdom--well, Kingdom come!* Could this possibly partially explain this sudden protective urge in the breast of the Trilateral Commission and the deployment of half a million American troops in Saudi Arabia?

One more little sock-it-toya: One of your own Congressional Reports states that the Agriculture and State Departments approved $5 BILLION in taxpayer (you)-guaranteed crop export credits *TO IRAQ* between 1983 and 1990 despite concerns it could not repay the loans. The General Accounting Office concluded that U.S. desires to build a relationship with that nasty old Saddam and Iraq in days leading up to the Kuwaiti "invasion" outweighed those fears. Iraq has already defaulted on a $2 BILLION taxpayer-guaranteed loan and certainly has absolutely no intention of repaying this larger one. Well, you dear "bottomless pockets" don't object do you? After all, you can think of the "hostages" eating while you go hungry wondering what happened to all your grain and dairy storage items--AND, YOUR MONEY!

EUROPEAN TRAP

I will herein speak of Europe and possibilities which will also curl you hair even if you are bald as a billiard ball--as I am.

President George Bush has fallen into a fine trap--perhaps the greatest trap ever set in history--and this nice little trap was baited by his key intelligence adviser. It stems from the transfer of those nice NATO troops, some 200,000, to the Middle East.

The two armored divisions and other units being transferred from Germany to Saudi Arabia will leave NATO as naked as the plucked turkey at Thanksgiving--and no head to boot! Europe is wide open to possible attack from the formidable armed forces of the Soviet Union--which they will surely do if the above scenario gets too botched to pull off.

Now just why do you think no one in the White House seriously considered this obvious danger, thanks to the clever manipulations of the President carried out by Robert M. Gates, the deputy director of the National Security Council (NSC)--A MAN LONG KNOWN IN INTELLIGENCE CIRCLES FOR HIS PRONOUNCED PRO-SOVIET BIAS! Could it possibly be that some ones in your Administration believe they have a seat on the Board of the Global One World Government? Could you have provided a nice secure ticket for them to be wardens of your U.S. prison?

Dr. Gates is the official who briefs the President every morning on the world situation when he is not traveling with his close friend, Secretary of State James A. Baker III, to Moscow, Paris, London and other capitals of Bush's "New World Order" allies.

Why do all these other countries, such as Brazil and Argentina, etc., go along with this world take-over? BECAUSE THEY HAVE NOTHING TO LOSE AND <u>EVERYTHING TO GAIN!</u>

Moreover, Brent Scowcroft, director of the NSC, has left the day-to-day operations of the White House intelligence center squarely in Gate's hands; not that it matters in the least for Scowcroft is a part of the inside planners, along with Mr. Eagleburger. On top of that, Gates chairs the powerful "Deputies Committee" comprised of his counterparts from the Pentagon, CIA, Mossad and other security agencies.

<u>CONTROL FLOW TO PRESIDENT</u>

In short, Gates controls the flow of intelligence to the President as well as to the Department of State and to key Cabinet-level officials--a nice slot for a devout Communist Zionist, don't you think?

It certainly should come as no surprise to insiders who have been watching Gates for years that the Soviet threat is now almost totally ignored by the Bush administration. The fact that the Red Army is not only still totally intact but far stronger than it has ever been before Gorbachev ascended to power is quietly and simply brushed aside.

Indeed, the most salient security factor of your time, i.e., that ONLY THE SOVIET UNION HAS THE STRATEGIC CAPABILITY TO UT-

TERLY DESTROY THE U.S., IS NOW DEEMED TO BE OF NO CONSEQUENCE IN THE RARIFIED "ONE-WORLD" ATMOSPHERE PREVAILING IN THE WHITE HOUSE. This is obviously the view of the whole Pentagon as well.

The evidence that Saddam Hussein would never have invaded Kuwait without at least a green light from the Soviets is underwhelming, to say the least. Yet under Gate's guidance the fact that Iraq got four-fifths of its arms from the USSR and couldn't move its 5,000 Soviet tanks and other materiel without assurance the spare parts would keep coming from the Soviet Union, is thought to be irrelevant in the Oval Office.

Also brushed off by Bush and Gates are the thousands of Soviet military advisers in Iraq who are guiding the Iraqi army's every move and manning the deadliest high-tech weapons systems.

Most dangerous of all the USSR's heavy contributions to Iraqi military might is the SS-12, a missile capable of firing both nuclear and poison gas warheads up to a thousand miles with deadly pin-point accuracy. Under the Intermediate Nuclear Forces "Treaty" signed by the United States and the USSR in 1987, the SS-12 was banned from the face of the Earth--how quaint.

However, this highly accurate weapons system has since popped up in large numbers in Poland, Czechoslovakia and other East European countries and is now reportedly deployed in Iraq. Indeed, the SS-12 was planted solidly in Iraq prior to 1988 when the war with Iran ended.

Although the Defense Intelligence Agency notified the White House of the persistent reports of this SS-12 capability in Iraq, Bush, Gates and their trained seals in the CIA are looking the opposite way at this dangerous development.

Bush has now doubled the size of the American forces in the Middle East while espousing that the Soviets are our blood-brothers having "changed their leopard spots". The Soviets are now your beholden "friends and allies". It would appear to me that there is great suffering from acute myopia induced by Gates, Baker, etc., etc., etc. The President seems to perceive absolutely no danger to Europe what-so-ever--how could this be? Could it be that he is consumed by his ethereal vision of the New World Order? Or, does he know more than you know and it isn't a "vision" problem at all! The world is set for total take-over--BUT, THE PRIME MOVERS AND SHAKERS HAVEN'T TOTALLY SHAKEN EACH OTHER DOWN, *YET!!*

VISION!

Blind? Mr. Bush blind? I seriously doubt that, dear ones. But, has no one dared point out to Bush that it was this same insane vision that broke the presidency of Woodrow Wilson as he played into the hands of the Bolsheviks then taking over Russia?

Is there no one on Bush's staff who can remember that this identical vision of a world ruled by the United Nations led Franklin Roosevelt, then under the influence of Alger Hiss and other pro-Soviets, down the primrose path to Yalta and the surrender of Eastern Europe and eventually mainland China to communism?

With more than half a million Americans in the Saudi desert and on their way from Europe, this has the makings of a mammoth trap--perhaps a BEAR TRAP?

WHAT IF THE BATTLE HAPPENS?

If Bush commits these forces to battle, as now would seem totally likely, what would prevent the Soviet army from moving right through their ally, Germany and France, to the English Channel in the "10 days" Gen. Nikolai Ogarkov allotted in the master plan drawn up in the mid-1980's and still preached in Soviet military circles? Oh son-of-a gun, you didn't know about THAT plan?

So be it, the answer, of course, is *NOTHING!*

Let us look a bit more closely at this man, Gates.

He is a consummate con man and has gulled Bush as completely as he did his late boss CIA Director W. Casey and, through Casey, President R. Reagan.

By simply telling them what they want to hear and constantly leaking prepared stories to the press, Gates has persuaded both conservative and liberal columnists he is a "hard-liner" adamantly opposed to the Soviets and suspicious of glasnost.

But the quality of the "intelligence" Bush now receives on a daily basis from Gates may be better judged by several tidbits in the closely held dossier several officials have been keeping on Gates.

As CIA's deputy director for intelligence, Gates helped sell Casey and Reagan on Israel's wacky plan to exchange U.S. arms with Iran for the release of American hostages in Lebanon--the nutty idea that tempted Reagan to tiptoe into the Iran-"contra" morass.

Just before becoming Casey's No. 1 deputy on April 18, 1986, Gates leaked two top-secret intelligence estimates to the *Washington Post*. The first was aimed at helping the liberal Democrats in Congress to drastically cut the Reagan defense budget; the second tried to shoot down, and essentially succeeded in shooting down, Reagan's strategic defense initiative

(SDI), commonly called "Star Wars". As reported by the *Post on March 31, 1986, the first estimate claimed that Soviet military spending had been "almost flat for a decade" and might even "decline during the next five years".*

Of all the fiction fed to your presidents in weird "national intelligence estimates" over the years, this particular concoction of Gates must take the prize. Indeed, all the evidence, then as now, proved conclusively that the USSR had been engaged in the greatest military buildup in history--a buildup that ominously continues to this very day. The second blast from Gates less than a week later was intended to cripple SDI. This "intelligence" estimate claimed the Soviets had *NOT* violated the Anti-Ballistic Missile (ABM) Treaty. But three years later the Soviets themselves freely admitted they HAD violated the ABM agreement, just as they have violated nearly 200 other solemn agreements made with the U.S. and the West.

U.S. deployment of SDI hangs on the issue of observance of the ABM Treaty. Gates' target in trying to defend Soviet claims that they were not in violation is certainly obvious. Tragically, he scored a perfect bull's-eye.

In fact, this single leak from Gates' fiction factory at CIA cast such doubt on Pentagon reports of Soviet ABM violations that many consider this the major reason America still has no viable defense against Soviet ICBM's or the short-range missiles poised aboard the Soviet submarines lying in wait off both your East and West coasts--a combined force capable of killing every man, woman and child in the U.S. in a matter of mere minutes. As you might have guessed by this point, Gates has served both the KGB and the Mossad. Further, it was Gates, behind the scenes, who led the fight waged in favor of permitting your NATO allies to accept the Soviet oil and natural gas pipelines to Western Europe. Now completed, except for one strand, the pipelines tie the economies of France, Germany and a half-dozen other, smaller European countries to the Soviet Union like an umbilical cord.

Gate's many coups on behalf of the Soviets began when he joined the CIA in 1966, fresh out of Indiana University, where he had picked up an MA in history after being at William & Mary. In 1974 he got his Ph.D. in Russian and Soviet history from Georgetown University while working at the CIA. And in the same year (1974) Gates transferred to the staff of the NSC, then under the iron thumb of none other than the Great Detentist, *HENRY KISSINGER!*

MENTOR KISSINGER

Kissinger became Gate's mentor. The younger man did his job at the NSC so well as Presidents Nixon and Ford cozied up to Brezhnev that he was kept on at the NSC by Jimmy Carter. In January, 1980 he went back to the CIA as the national intelligence officer on the Soviet Union and two years later he was appointed CIA deputy director for intelligence in charge of all the national intelligence estimates prepared for the President.

A short, husky, boyish-looking operator, Gates has made a whole career out of ingratiating himself with the older men who have been his superiors. He completely mesmerized Bill Casey, who came to look upon Gates as his son.

Gates fed Casey the anti-Soviet hard- line the CIA director thrived on. In the spring of 1986 Gates was promoted to the powerful post of overall deputy director of the CIA.

When Casey's health collapsed after the Iran-contra scandal broke, Reagan nominated Gates to be the new director of CIA. The liberals rejoiced and the *Post* and the *New York Times* hailed Gates appointment.

With powerful Democratic senators backing him, Gates' confirmation appeared assured. But several conservative Republicans on the Senate Intelligence Committee were given the file on Gates. Almost overnight, support for Gates moving up to director of the CIA caved in, and Reagan was persuaded to withdraw the nomination--however, no publicity was released of negative nature and the subject was instantly hushed.

Gates was kept on as deputy director. William Webster, who had been appointed by Jimmy Carter to head the FBI, was named director of the agency, and he apparently was as completely taken in by Gates as Casey before him.

When Bush became President he picked Scowcroft to head the NSC, a post that required Senate confirmation. Gates was named deputy director of the NSC, a job that sidestepped the painful confirmation process in the Senate which had so recently thwarted Gates' promotion to the top post at the CIA.

In the Bush White House, Gates has presided over the accelerated disarmament of U.S. and NATO forces. The conventional arms treaty which was signed in Paris on November 19 is Gates' biggest coup to date.

Thus, now having helped strip NATO naked, Gates is free to concentrate on steering Bush into the Middle East trap.

If the Soviets do make their move in Europe when the huge U.S. force is nailed down in the Iraqi desert, Gates may well go down in history as the rook that helped the Soviet Union checkmate the United States of America. So be it for one little Robert M. Gates--ah, the web is tangled indeed!

PRIVACY ALERT

In case you haven't noticed, you ones who feel safe and private in paying with money orders--beware! *"NO INDIVIDUAL POSTAL CUSTOMER MAY PURCHASE MONEY ORDERS IN EXCESS OF $10,000 IN FACE VALUES ON ANY ONE DAY". THERE ARE NO EXCEPTIONS TO THIS RULE.* This is, of course, from the U.S. Postal Service's Domestic Mail Manual. Please be alert and act accordingly if you buy your money orders down at the good old Post Office--Big Brother is WATCHING! This means exactly what it says--you cannot, for instance, buy $10,000 worth in the morning and $6,000 in the afternoon--IT MEANS IN ANY ONE DAY.

Here is a post-script regarding the subject above regarding a cutting of required bank reserves. The following notice was received by a business colleague of our publisher who had shared it with him this day --- it has just now been brought to the scribe to be shared with you: *"Bulletin: Fed cuts some bank reserve requirements. Reserve required for some categories to be cut to ZERO. Fed says reserve cut responds to tighter bank lending---"*

And you thought nothing happened on December 3rd, 1990.

I would like to leave you with a thought this day: He who passively accepts evil is as much involved in it as he who helps to perpetrate it. He who accepts evil without protesting against it is really cooperating with it--where might you fit?

Hatonn to stand-by. Salu and good-day.

CHAPTER 12

REC #1   HATONN

THURSDAY, DECEMBER 6, 1990   6:52 A.M.   YEAR 4 DAY 112

TODAY'S WATCH

Good morning, in the Light of Radiance. I am Hatonn.

Beware, chelas, you are about to be sucked into the trap because suddenly everything looks very good and promising for that "peace" they are preaching unto you. Uppermost and foremost, this day, remember a few key points: The key players in this little world scenario are ALL *TRILATERALISTS!* That, dear ones, means they are all members of the Global Plan 2,000! Don't overlook this for a single moment--history is about to gobble you up like the turkey on feast day. This membership in the Trilateral Global 2,000 Plan of One World Government with the citizens of the world totally enslaved to the elite, runs from every Head of Government that Bush is visiting to Saddam Hussein and Jesse Jackson (newly inaugurated into the clan). What does this mean? THAT YOU ARE "HAD".

You are getting from your television exactly that which they want you to have. Let me outlay a few things of current interest.

The plan, of course, is to deliver to the American people--some sort of Christmas present saying "look what we've done for you!" There is no intent to make Saddam lose face, for he is a consummate ruler--not a martyr for God. You are simply watching the noose strings being tightened around the people of the world.

Look at today's headlines, for those of you who have had opportunity at this early hour to get any fragments--Dharma, you will get it later, chela, please just write for now.

SADDAM/HOSTAGES

Saddam claims to have been "touched" by the petitions of families flocking to Iraq regarding the "hostages" and will now release THEM ALL. He will turn this duty over to his government councils to work out details and therefore there will need be no dickering with Saddam--nor Baker, nor Bush. The negotiations which are claimed to be absent will simply not be between the parties against whom "Lips" said there would be "no negotiations". Actually, the plan has been laid for weeks (from onset of this so-called war). But all who have worked in behalf of the Iraqi stance will be made to pay some penalties.

LIBYA

Now, after all these months it is finally public in a burst of glorious pro-nouncement--the bomb which blew up Flight 103 over Scotland, "..was a Libyan bomb". It was not a Libyan bomb--it was compliments of Syria but now, you can't very well blame Syria, can you? Assad and Syria are your closest friends and allies--so other's who are enemies of this One World Dictatorship must be blamed. Do I defend Libya? No! No, I certainly do not--however, I do defend truth and what you are being given now, is not truth. No matter who tells the lies it does not make the story "truth".

SPACE TRIP

They are further preparing you for any number of events regarding the recent shuttle trip. Another telescope of multi-millions of dollars--totally worthless and now, carbon monoxide? In the crew cabin! Haven't the daily news items of things going wrong annoyed you the public who spent all this money on this garbage? What do you suppose is REALLY hap-pening aboard that Russian space system?

Can't you further see the thrust, even with the young soldier who has now ended his commitment to the government who simply wants to come home--you have no declared war and no emergency and yet, because he would like to come home, he is ostracized and pronounced a traitor to America!

I remind you that you are just about to be given a glimpse at "world peace potential". It will look very good--just as does the poison candy. You will be weak with the blitz of "..look how we saved you from massive and catastrophic war!" You will gladly leave your troops to "protect" the Middle East and carry out the invasion of Saudi Arabia whose royalty government has already formed a coalition with the World Cartel.

Well, all I can say to you beloved ones who see the difference, is to make and gather as much hay and grain as you can while you are manipulated in the upward swing of events. You will all be blinded by the drop again in oil prices, probably also in gold (for investment purposes--and then an incredible rise thereof), a surge like unprecedented in the stock market until after the tax time--recall that the plan was to push the market to well over 3500 points and then pull the collapse on you. WATCH WHAT THEY ARE DOING!

The Feds are doing everything necessary to make you ones go on an unprecedented buying spree while sinking yourselves farther and farther

100

into debt--they will simply reclaim all the property--so, put your ideas and money to work and put aside that which you can to use later (afterwards) and be prepared to give them back their property--they will still need someone to run the factories, etc. Don't get yourselves attached emotionally to these "things"--be flexible and able to leave them without looking back if it needs be. If you can adjust yourselves to the same level of gamesmanship as your adversaries--you have naught to concern with over the long haul--for they are solidly and ONLY attached to "things" and material matter--in most ones, the soul essence is totally missing (which gives you a tremendous advantage) and you ones come within the shield of Lighted God. This is why you will prevail. Keep that shielding intact around you and there is nothing (NOTHING) which can destroy you--albeit if you are careless, you will be "taken out". Does this mean that you will avoid and escape all Earthly harm and assault? No, in fact at this moment both Oberli and Dharma are enduring a prearranged and deliberate infection of virus but you will note it has not interrupted the writing as we have been even more productive as she is not distracted by other perceived "duties".

I did not write on the yesterday--not because of her illness--we needed to monitor the theater taking place in your Senate Hearing chambers. Do you feel you are watching a bunch of Robots at work? So be it!

I will honor Bill Cooper with the new projections he is espousing as supposition--"...could the Government have invented the `aliens'?" Oh indeed, yes--along with the Government!! I wonder, ARE YOU READY FOR SOME MORE INCREDIBLE TRUTH? *ARE YOU READY TO FIND TRUTH IN THAT YOU ARE A WORLD OF PEOPLE CONTROLLED AND PROGRAMMED BY ROBOTOIDS, PUSHING HEAD-LONG INTO IRRATIONAL EVENTS BUT ALWAYS ALLOWING THINGS TO FALL INTO PLACE FOR THE NEW WORLD ORDER? WELL, ONE MIS-STEP AND THE WORLD WILL GO UP IN NUCLEAR HOLOCAUST--JUST ONE LITTLE MIS-PROGRAMMING GLITCH. YOU ARE NOT OUT OF THE WOODS BY ANY MEASURE, MY CHELAS.*

Can't you begin to see that the citizens of a world have been mesmerized and programmed into sleep and no longer caring what immoral or un-Godly activities take place? Can you not SEE it?

Can you not see that they plan to take everything from you? The intent is to render you helpless and you are all but there. They have plans for getting all your stored wealth by simply collapsing the economy and replacing the money. Then you will be told how wondrous the plans for your "freedom" have worked that you will push for a Constitutional Congress and give away your defense means and forfeit your Constitution and the game will be over for most of you--EXCEPT FOR THE MISERY! WILL YOU TURN UNTO GOD THEN? OH YES, RIGHT AFTER YOU TURN FROM HIM FURTHER AND CURSE HIM FOR THAT WHICH YOU HAVE DONE UNTO SELVES. So be it.

There is NO COMPASSION in these ones who would be Kings! NONE! Look into the eyes of those run past you on the screens--look very closely and see the blank expressions as they spout off the pre-programmed lies unto you--LOOK INTO THE EYES AND ACTIONS AND SEE THE TRUTH OF IT!

Watch what the news media does. Watch as the ones espousing freedom and constitution are cut off and the station moves to commercials. And then, look what they show you on the commercials--heinous acts of torture in Kuwait, etc. The only acts of torture in Kuwait have been perpetrated by your own side to work you the compassionate citizens of the world into frenzy. Look at the ones bringing these stories--how did THEY get out to do all this talking? How did THEY get the pictures to blind you?

IT IS WITHIN THE POSSIBILITIES THAT YOU WILL HAVE A LITTLE BREAK IN HERE, CHELAS OF TRUTH, TO ACT AND CONTINUE TO AWAKEN THE MASSES. THERE WILL BE MASSIVE ATTEMPTS TO GET EVERYONE BACK TO SLEEP UNDER THE CLOAK OF "PEACE"! DO NOT BE FOOLED--NOW IS THE TIME TO PRESS ONWARD FOR YOU NOW HAVE THAT WITH WHICH TO MAKE RELATIONSHIPS OF ACTIONS, INTENT AND PLANS. REMEMBER--SATAN IS ALWAYS REQUIRED TO WEAR A SIGN--A CLUE! IT IS ALWAYS THERE IN EVERY SITUATION! FURTHER, IT GETS MORE AND MORE DIFFICULT TO HIDE IT.

MOREOVER, YOU ARE CONFUSED--that (confusion) is his number one tool--to confuse and confound so that you continue in the chaos until you cease to look for your way out. Then, you are hit with intentional blasts of pulses to the entire society to cause depression and lethargy which causes you to withdraw even more--and the only shield you have is the Lighted Shielding of the Higher Energies. Most ones who understand that fact are turning back unto what they believe to be Godness--but it is only Satan dressed up in ritual God-camouflage suits. You leave your souls open to an even heavier barrage--while pursuing all that is told to you will make you whole--HAS IT? For instance, does the act of sex, safe or otherwise, leave you fulfilled and at peace--especially deviant acts? So be it--I note that it only gives problems and guilt as well as disease and emotional devastation. Is this that which you desire that your world become--Soddom and Gomorrah? It is that which you have achieved! You are now as the lemmings--desiring to march into the sea to find peace.

God has never moved--He is right there within and you don't have to go anywhere--all you need do is reach your mind unto Him--He who waits for your decision. He sends His Hosts in us, who have come into your spaces to offer our hands and show you the way. No, God has gone nowhere--and frankly dear ones, NEITHER HAVE YOU!

PLEIADES CONNECTION OF TRUTH OUTLAYING

I am in a most wondrous position to point out some facts from your Pleiadian relations. These ones have vested interests in your place for they are coming over from their own belligerent and often chaotic past, and perceiving yet another atomic devastation by the scientists' new ascendency, a legacy to you from their own history, and seek to head it off if possible. Do not confuse the people of Pleiades for the Hosts of God, dear ones, for that would be compounding your problems. The ones, however, coming forth at this time are ones who have grown most balanced in the truth of Law--both of God and The Creation.

In another Journal I have spoken of many of the projections which will be outlaid herein but you need it laid forth in one placement for reference and therefore, where necessary, we shall espouse it again.

You must have further knowledge regarding a cosmic change. It can be called the "Golden Age" or the Age of Knowing! In this respect I must first explain the religious interpretations concerning this epoch and point out that they are incorrect. Certain irresponsible fanatics treat this as the religiously proclaimed "final days". By no means is this "new age" a "final" time, because in truth it brings REAL LIFE!

This wondrous epoch enables everything to develop to its highest potential, including spirit and according to Providence. But it will take many centuries, in your perception, after entering that period to reach such advanced levels. At first, as usual, the irreligious scientists will profit from the new advances while the common people will be restrained by their religions and perceptions that the lie is truth. Mesmerized by the concept of the change of epoch, especially the religious people will fall into fanatical delusion. Especially in the 2 centuries of the time of change, in which you now function, religious beliefs of all sorts will shoot up like mushrooms and bring many humans under their control. Murder, exploitation of all kinds, suicide, enslavement and imprisonment unto the lies--total enslavement to false beliefs will be the daily experience. The whole world will be shaken and involved. False prophets will offer salvation publicly in a fanatic search for victims and new followers--these will be leaders, politicians, publicans and proclaimed prophets of God Almighty-- but they will give you only lies and your distress as a world shall spiral downward and downward into the morass of distressed perceptions.

INITIAL PHASE

This is the initial phase of the "golden Age", the transition phase of the two centuries. The culmination of this period will come in time--it is said to be around 2028 in calculation of your years. Therefore, if you are to count in accordance with projections and probabilities, you are in a most difficult present circumstance. The REALLY INTENSE revolutionary

103

force of this "new epoch" began around and just prior to your mid 1800's and since then the extensive alterations on Earth rush irresistibly forward.

The New Age already demands its tribute, religious delusion, rapidly developing sciences, rampant crime, and wars of extirpation, characteristics of this time which can not be ignored. The first half of the transition period lasted almost a hundred years, until the first third of the 1900's in your counting, while the Earth felt the last of the old age--as it was known.

Since that time, rapidly evolving events, discoveries, inventions, etc., were characteristic as for no other time in history as you can recognize it. Your whole sun-system with all its innumerable creatures is under the control of this "new" time. Each and everything is influenced by it, because this is a cosmic law and it is according to this law, to which are subject all movements of planets and all life forms of and within the Universe. Therefore, it can be considered that before your mid-1800's and hitherto, existing regulations not of the Creational character replaced those of Creational disposition.

The origin of this epochal change is in the radiation effect of the huge central sun around which your system circles once in every 25,860 years, and passes through the 12 epochs within the meaning of the cycles. The Earth has already touched the outer borders of the "Golden Radiation" of the central sun, which are of the strongest and most revolutionary radiation.

MISCHIEF AND DISCORD

Abundant mischief is connected with this, especially in respect to religions and the use of new discoveries and achievements. The way-showers of these changes are in cosmic destiny and appear under the Creation Laws. The way-preparers for these revolutions (affecting humans) are also human beings having been brought forth to lay forth the truth as given forth by the higher energies sent forth at the cycle of evolution which you now experience. They come, as in this case, to simply lay forth the truths of knowledge and spiritual wisdom as is given through them from the Higher Truth and Source. These way-preparers will be and are considered revolutionaries, heretics, and exiles, for they will announce the truths for ALL TO SEE! They will be set upon and many will be pulled down for they, too, shall have to come into awakening unto the truth of circumstance.

These revelations are of much interest, and also of great importance to humans and you should spread the word by all means possible--this too, is the desire of the Cosmic brothers for it is the purpose of their (my) mission. Some of you have already undertaken the diffusion of the messages of truth; regrettably, however, it is not sufficient as of yet but that shall now be rapidly changing as the humanity of Earth begins to pay attention.

You of the planet must understand that your Cosmic brothers from other planets in the Cosmos are limited, also, and are often deluded by ones who at first appear to have great loyalty--the difference is that they will not interfere with this illusion regardless of set-backs.

It would seem a hopeless task from where you sit in the observation limitations--it is not a hopeless task, this awakening. Believe me, chelas, all are NOT blind and dumb who are searching for truth, and who, as well, will recognize it. Do not worry about being unknown or tiny in perspective for there shall be ones touched by truth who will come within the truth and help move it forward and some of them will be better known and with more influence. By their help you will be able to reach out unto newspapers and magazines, and to radio and television stations and interest will pick up from the masses who will seek out the books and journals of truth. You must always remember to speak the truth of that which is abounding about you in your own markets and government and play no tunes of singularity on the harps of the heavenly realms for most are not yet ready for the people have been given into fear of that which is unknown.

Less and less ridicule and denouncing of your truth shall be in the coming and you must look about to the care of one another. Do not concern with "looking" for friends who will support your truth and being in the "bad" times for as truth unfolds you will find those "good" friends waiting. They will even be of such sincere attachment that they, too, will endure the unjustified ridicule and derision and even be quite amused by it. You will never be alone in your journey, wherever you are--for instance, I am as near as your silent thought. You will, however, remember that if careless participation were to be allowed, you would run into helplessness due to your own laws of the land. Therefore we will always act in Earth manners within the laws of the lands. Please do not ask for short-cuts or for us to do it for you--for we shall not!

CYCLES

The "ancients" and students of metaphysics, the ancient mystery schools and even economists who study cycles have always known of these cycles of ages, and that the foundations for the teachings of each and every new age are laid down during the beginning of the ending cycle of transition. For instance, from the early 1800's there have been the projections of this which is upon you now--in fact, insuring that you move along as the plan was laid forth. As you further forget your power in Godness you are funnelled into the limits of the plan as given unto you and in what manner you will perform to insure the plan unfold properly. The mass consciousness is mesmerized into the trap of the controllers as orchestrated by the Satanic forces.

Do you ever wonder at your own projectors of "news" in that in each and every instance of revelation--let us say spacecraft of alien origin--ones are

105

called in as "experts" who never have actually investigated any of the details themselves and are always antagonistic to the truth? How is it, for instance, that Stanton Friedman (a lovely Zionist/Elitist) has become the chief "authority" on UFO's? He doesn't know one end of himself from the other and certainly knows nothing about UFO's! He is a puppet set up to feed you the "party line" of lies and, in addition, continues to utilize the pictures of one, Billy Meier, for public demonstrations while denouncing Meier as the biggest hoaxter ever to hit earth. Do you not find this strange?

MODELS AND THINGS

It is always hard to come to grips with truth--especially for those who desire to believe a thing to be true. As in the case of Billy Meier--there were hundreds of genuine craft pictures--AND HUNDREDS OF PICTURES OF MODELS. Which do you see? Mostly the models, of course. Funny thing about those photos, however---ONLY the models were brought forth in order to discount the whole of the contact.

In the interim, Meier was so attacked and so bewildered--and physically injured, that he became unable to actually cope with that which was happening to him. Ultimately he has fallen prey to these infamous assaults. Does that make his truth less truth? No, it only makes it harder to decipher from the rot thrust forth by his enemies.

The contacts were valid and the lessons brought from the Pleiadians valid. The discounters' intent was to terrify the world by fear of "aliens" and the march has been in that direction from upstart. It is time for you ones to see and hear truth--YOU HAVE NOTHING TO FEAR FROM YOUR COSMIC BROTHERHOOD. The conjured-up beings upon your place are put there by ones from your own density--right upon your own Earthplace. I can promise you that the Pleiadians performed enough "tricks" and "miracles" to convince all participants in the encounters. However, as we point out continually to you who want "miracles" and "magic tricks"--it proves nothing at all and does, in fact, only create confusion and more discounting and ridicule--ponder it well.

IMPORTANCE OF CONTACT FROM PLEIADES

The importance of the contacts from Pleiades have always remained unchanged--your spiritual status and development. I shall outlay that which was given for it is time to give it forth again--it was obviously overlooked intentionally as first given unto you.

Since this book regards your Pleiadian Brothers and your contact and communication with them, it will be from that aspect which I will speak for they are not far removed from yourselves and perhaps the connections will be easier to assimilate.

The human being carries his own spirit, which never dies and which also in this deepest sleep does not, itself, sleep. It continually records all thoughts and movements; which tells the human being whether his very thoughts are right or wrong. This spirit in the human being is the carrier of the Creation's domain, and is possessed by all human beings--note I said "human beings"--I did not say "humanoid robotoids". The spirit holds the outlook for total perfection, for total harmony, peace, recognition, understanding, knowledge, wisdom, beauty, love and truth in ALL things. All together they form the spiritual kingdom which exists within THE CREATION!

Let us look into "dreams". In dreams the human being creates marvelous worlds (or dastardly ones) like The Creation creates consciously the known worlds. For the human, this ability grows from his consciousness, existing inside himself. He, himself, is the heavenly kingdom, the domain of Creation. Recall the old philosophers who spoke of the human being as the microcosm in the macrocosm, because everything that exists in the universe is connected to the human spirit--all is connected to all. The dimensions of the human being are without end. The entire concept, the copy if you will, of The Creation, the spirit, exists inside each self, and at the same time transcends all dimensions of all space and time. When a human being is happy, for instance, this comes from within because it is a self-creation. Everything arises from inner being.

A human being may appear aged--old, but this is only a transient state of being. The spirit remains young and is never subjected to the appearance of age. When the human understands the existence of his spirit, then age no longer affects him. No vicissitudes of life or environment can make him mourn or sad. WISDOM IS LIGHT. And so wherever light flashes up and shines about, darkness and ignorance instantly disappear and that which becomes "known" can never again be "unknown" to the perceiver unless damage of physical nature is thrust upon the consciousness-- nonetheless--the unknowing is never again returned to soul.

Ignorance is nothing but darkness, which is overcome by the light of wisdom. Wisdom is the mark of spirit. Wisdom is also the mark of human being who has recognized the existence of his spirit and works in accordance with Creational Law. Wisdom and spirit are two aspects of the same thing, like the sunlight and the sun. In the Universe, every created existence, in consequence of its forces, generates forces which, following Creational law, manifests as truth, knowledge and wisdom according to given principles.

THE CREATION

This existing force is THE CREATION. And from this, there is only one existence that governs the Universe, only one Creation, only one truth, only one knowledge, one wisdom, equally directed and remaining for all time. When the human being advances his knowledge and wisdom, he will recognize The Creation. Knowledge of the truth brings unlimited wisdom. Wisdom is a recognition of the laws of Creation.

Love and wisdom go together because the Creation and its laws are love and wisdom at the same time. Where there is wisdom and knowledge, there is love and recognition, and where there is love and recognition there is Creation. Wisdom and love increase the desire within men to conform to natural law, because spirit and Creation are one and the same. The Earth human speaks of love, which he does not even know. He believes to know his actions in love, but deceives himself in this. No one can put love into words, because it is a state of being. Love is imperishable and does not change. The path of spirit runs through cognitions of truth, knowledge, wisdom and love. Meaning the mission of spirit is to spread truth, knowledge, wisdom and love.

Great multitudes of wonders are hidden with the kingdom of spirit. The visible universe with which the human being occupies himself consciously is only a small pin-spot within this marvelous, unlimited, spiritual existence of Creation. Universes like this one are in the innumerable millions within the infinite spiritual existence of The Creation. What is visible to the physical eyes of a human being represents only a dot in infinity. What is not visible to man's eyes is immeasurable, inconceivable, and unthinkable, confusing his human intelligence and capacity. All of the universe he sees is only a simple one of many such, which must be counted in myriads, because there do exist universes inside of universes, universes above universes, universes below universes, universes opposite universes, and universes outside of universes, in this first Cause, Mighty All-Powerful Intelligence existing with The Creation. With this immense spirit, with these original forces of existence, of Creation, the spiritual intelligence of the human being is connected, because a fraction of this spiritual intelligence of The Creation lives in every human being as spirit, and ensouls him.

HARD TO RECOGNIZE

Millions upon millions of humans look up at the stars in the heavens without real cognition. Yet astronomers, when they look up at the heavens, discover whole new worlds and write bunches of books about their findings. What they see and recognize, the others simply do not see at all and they do not understand nor do they care, even if they look in the same place. This is quite similar to the difference in viewpoint between a common and a spiritual human being; the one who lives from spiritual and Creational Law, sees and recognizes all around, within each life-form, all objects, each thought and action, within each creature, within all nature and also in all conceivable circumstances and events,...THE CREATION

The human being is always spiritually great and constructive. The Spirit the spring of all the infinite Creational build-up, is the innermost character of the human being itself. The outer human being is full of limitations, because this is not him, but only his frame, his material body of limitation, of mis-leading matter, a source of labor and pain, limited in cognition and will. When the outer being looks materially at his inner being, he sees little but the form and figure. Yet, if he looks with the spiritual eyes of cognition, and he knows that this all-revealing consciousness in him is also in all others, even though they do not know it, then his manner changes fundamentally as he considers his fellow creatures. He then no longer simply looks AT a man, a woman, or a child, but SEES the other as a carrier of Spirit, which knows all about itself and its existence, and wants to reveal itself to everyone if only the chance were offered. A human being can be deprived of all his possessions and be exiled from his homeland, but from his inner spirit no one can exile him.

So the human being must effort to always be conscious of this portion of Creation, without which he could not take one breath--could not generate one thought, without which he could neither recognize or see, hear or experience. thus the great wise ones of all times say: "The Creation spirit is nearer the creature than his own breath."

The spirit can live without the light of physical eyes, ears, arms, legs, even without outer reason and consciousness. But always there is the Creational force behind all. The more light his spiritual intellect receives, the more his personality gains force. He becomes aware of the past and the future, which shape his eternal present. The whole spiritual intellect is visible to those who can look within and understand The Creation present in all. The human being is separated one from another in perceived "space", but connected to all in The Creation. If he does not know The Creation, he can be misled and deceived by false doctrines. A human being in contact with his Creation realizes himself everywhere in space and time, and within all matter. He is everything within himself, and can awaken to The Creational in everything and affect it by recognition and experience.

Because the Creation is inside all, which is vivified by its spirit, everything is one within all. A spiritual being identifies himself with all matter, and all creatures of the world and the Universe. He knows that everything arose from truth, rises from truth, and will rise from it for time eternal. From that he identifies himself with all and everyone, and every thing. A material being identifies himself with this body, his money, his possessions and goods, his utterances and the sound of his voice. If, on the other hand, one identifies with the all, no hate or avarice can live in him, and he makes no selfish differentiations any longer. Further, one can only come into recognition of this state of being from within--no one can corroborate this knowledge for you.

You ones perceive that no one desires to know truth--that is not so and you must not give in to that perception because the spiritual evolution of the Earthbeing proceeds irresistibly. You should assist in spreading the truth for the ears and eyes of humanity are truly awaiting your call. It is

109

the projections thrust in falseness before you ones that have you confused. Man is starving unto his very death of physical form to find and feast upon truth and God never leaves his chelas wanting if their searching be in wisdom and truth. It is the negative influences of the Satanic energies which never fulfill the restless heart seeking through the physical aspect of existence for nothing of mortal construction is immortal. The soul, beloved ones, is NOT mortal nor does it have physical format. So be it.

Let us not run this segment on longer, for it is better to have the groupings of thoughts which you call "Chapters" a bit on the short side for better digesting of the information.

I do herein inquire of you before taking leave, "Do these teachings appear to be from miserable `little gray aliens' come to earth bent on your destruction?" I think not.

Salu and Saalome', may the WORD fall in understanding upon your eyes and ears that your souls shall awaken unto the wondrous promise of God and Creation.

Hatonn to clear, please. Man is awakening to his desire to hear and find truth--please God, allow us to do our mission in fullness and clarity. AHO.

CHAPTER 13

REC #1   HATONN

FRIDAY, DECEMBER 7, 1990   6:40 A.M.   YEAR 4 DAY 113

TODAY'S WATCH

Precious chelas, Hatonn present to converse. Good morning.

Today is a most nerve frazzling day with the court matter regarding this property wherein our future in this place rests in the hands of three very worldly oriented Judges. It is self-discipline, Dharma, that we write this day for ours is not to give in to that which is always pulling us from our work. Please understand that this is a partial reason for working when you are ill in your perceptions and also when pressed for time or have guests--YOU AND I MUST NEVER ALLOW OUR PRIORITIES TO FALL INTO THE WRONG MATTERS--OURS IS TO AWAKEN MAN UNTO HIS PLIGHT AND REMIND HIM OF HIS JOURNEY HOME. SO BE IT.

I do not wish to go into details regarding Joy's book, SOLUTIONS FOR OUR TOTAL GLOBAL SPIRITUAL STARVATION, expressed by Sananda. I already see the prickly mark of the beast tinging the edges with push and pull as to "who" can do what with what, etc.

We care not which words are expressed to allow visions of truth but no expressions are to be allowed which express untruth even if only carelessly laid forth--that is the purpose of editors--no more and no less, i.e., if a phrase, for instance, states that God NEVER, God CAN'T and/or ONLY through this way or that way of Earth input a thing can be done--it WILL NOT BE PUBLISHED WITH MY PERMISSION. These are words common to man as is your entire language and in the beginning scribes are very accustomed to utilizing (providing) a selection of words suitable to their own expressions and beliefs--this is why training is severe and lengthy. It is to be expected that a scribe on a first presentation would fumble in some words for we of the speakers are stumbling along in your individual data banks seeking expression.

Our thrust, however, is to reach into understanding of man--not fill the individual expectations of a scribe nor of an editor--if something can be stated in format more easily accepted by readers but with no change of intent of content and perception, so be it--we expect you to tend of it, else why do we have you to read the material prior to publishing?

We do expect clarity and as few changes, even in wording, as is possible to insure the thought patterns of the author, not the scribe, to flow. However, it is very frequently that we will deliberately misspeak in intentional

111

effort to keep you readers alert and paying attention. ANYTHING THAT INFERS LIMITATION OF GOD IN ACTION OR THOUGHT, CAPABILITY OR INTENT IS A REFLECTION OF HUMAN PERCEPTION AND NOT OF HIGHER ENERGY INTENT--NEVER! WITH GOD ALL THINGS ARE POSSIBLE AND ALL THOUGHTS OF ACHIEVEMENT PROBABLE IF BELIEVED IN THE PERFECTION OF CREATOR. WHEN YOU DEAL WITH THE INFINITE THAT IS EXACTLY THAT WHICH YOU HAVE--INFINITE POSSIBILITY AND ABILITY--HOW THIS THOUGHT IS EXPRESSED IS INDIVIDUAL BUT INDEED IT MUST BE UNEQUIVOCALLY AND INCONTROVERTIBLY EXPRESSED IN ITS WHOLENESS AND INFINITE TOTALITY.

Why? Because if man is allowed to move about in his error of thought--he deteriorates into the heap of problems which assail you ones this day in this closing cycle--you end up placing God of Divine Source and Creation into the same category as the physical temptor of the dark ignorance and limitation of destructor and utilizer. God forces not--God allows. For instance, God will even allow the human to totally destroy his environment--BUT, he will also allow us of His other Creations to intervene to stop you if you reach that inevitable course of action, for it is then that your own actions invade the course of journey for His other creatures. God has even allowed of that, chelas! You had better be most careful for we are only allowed to intervene at such a time of impending and immediate destruction in totality by nuclear methods which alter soul essence and you, nor we, know if in acting, we can stop it in time to stop the reaction. None save God can know nor is any save God supposed to know--now where is God? You had best come to grips with the facts of Creation so that you fully understand. YOU will impact the ultimate--no more and no less and if that impact be for God of Creation--so be it; if it be against God of Creation then I believe you already can be pretty sure of that which is coming! So be that, also. What you do is up to you!

Every scribe may have all the opinions they desire--WHEN THEY ARE NOT WRITING FOR GOD! IF ANY OF YOU CHOOSE TO WRITE *IN THE SERVICE OF GOD*--YOU WILL NOT ALLOW YOUR OPINION TO INTERVENE ELSE YOU HAVE JUST NEGATED GOD! *ANY SCRIBE IN THE SERVICE, IN TRUTH, HAS NO PROBLEM WITH SUCH UNDERSTANDING AND ONLY WELCOMES THE REMINDER*.

Writers must also make sure that in choosing up pen-names, etc., that they do so in correct perceptions for identification is one thing, pen names another. For instance, if Dharma pens a book for Hatonn--her pen name must thusly be Hatonn, perhaps? Let us look very carefully at why and how we do things.

Will the books in question be Journals? Why would they be Journals? They are not Journals in the same sense that the regular writings of this place are entered as Journal information. If you mix fish and sauerkraut or bananas and peppercorns, you are likely to reduce the value of the recipe to the point you will lose all your diners. Gourmet God is hardly that which we intend to serve. Truth is usually quite disagreeable and un-palatable at best--but given with the truth of infinite ability of God it be-comes THE WAY! I would be in the reminding of Sananda and Joy that the original intent of the work was to outlay the errors of your Earth "churches" and how they have strayed in their responsibility and have actually moved into the service of the dark brotherhood.

How dare I speak thusly to Sananda? I dare because I am Aton! So be it.

NOW A REMINDER ABOUT "TODAY", 12/07/90

Before we move back into the subject of Cosmic brothers--in this Journal, the Pleiadians, I need to caution you ones for I see misperceptions re-garding what is happening.

In your joy at seeing the possibility of war being postponed, I must re-mind you to pay attention to ALL the facts and not just the OBVIOUS. Do I wish to upset you and bring your joy into vanquishment? No--but truth will set you free and bring unto you JOY--"JOY" WILL NOT BRING YOU INTO FREEDOM.

Firstly, the return of your "Hostage Guests" is reason to celebrate--so why is not Bush and his henchmen in celebration? Sour grapes? No--Saddam Hussein told you a whole truth and gave you the play script of possibilities. HE HAS HIS DEFENSES IN PLACE AND IS READY FOR ANYTHING YOU THINK YOU CAN THROW AT HIM. THE RUSSIAN ADVISERS ARE STILL IN IRAQ--A NEW MONITORING AND DETONATION SYSTEM WENT INTO SPACE WITH THE RUSSIANS--AND YOUR SPACE MISSION HAS FAILED! READ THE WRITING ACCURATELY, DEAR ONES, OR YOU WILL BE "DEAD" DEAR ONES. Will there be war? At some point, yes! Will it be now and will it be in Iraq? Not unless there rules stupidity beyond that which even we can discern. Remember you are dealing--on your side--with programmed and ruthless, conscienceless "would-be Kings". The statistics of war have no meaning! They will handle death counts in war as if you were weeding prime carrots from ones the worms have eaten. Remember? "Acceptable losses are set as 30,000 and over 50,000 body-bags are on site in Saudi Arabia with more on the way! Well, with the type of war machine that is available and in place--you won't need too many body bags for you won't find most of the bodies to place therein.

NOW LOOK TO RUSSIA AND ISRAEL

Israel pushes for total abstinence of any conference of the UN or any other council on the Palestine situation. Why? Do I speak of lovely Jews of God seeking stability in a homeland?--no, I speak of those who would rule a world and already control the U.S. government. Am I a bigot? Would you consider me a bigot if I said the Chinese or Africans have control of your Congress? The facts are that the would-be GLOBAL RULERS are of all nationalities and sects--INTENT UPON GLOBAL CONTROL. I would suggest that you who are of Jewish race, as I was, pay very close attention for you have been fooled and it will be the Godly Jew who will pay the most heinous price of all at the hands of those you considered to be of self.

Do I think Shamir is right? No! Do I think Bush is right? No! How about Saddam? No! There is only ONE RIGHT--GOD! I see no-one in the lead of all of the world who is working in the service of God! Shamir says, "I will - -." Bush says, "I will - -." Saddam says, "I will - -." Well, chelas, God, too, says, "I WILL." And guess who will ultimately have final say? He will also remind you that he further said, "YOU WILL - - - - -." And, dear ones, before you find perfection in any form other than through His Godness--YOU WILL!

Now for the Russians and what might they be up to? Well, you know that they have stated bluntly that they will not participate in a military "troops" way with you of the UN. How can that be "full intent" of the world if the head honcho says "I won't - - -?" All of you keep building up your arms and nuclear arsenals as fast as you can. What for, if this world be at peace and the "cold war" over and trust rings throughout your world??? I suggest you walk most carefully, little stumble-toes! The bullies of war are still at work and out here in space beyond that which you are given--it is a beehive of activity in preparations for possible stupid moves on the part of the "United Nations", all nicely lined up in service of the United States--even the countries of the UN hate you--bitterly! Only the would-be rulers, enslavers, Kings, dictators and greedy mongers of wealth are sided with you as a nation. The rest of the world actually feels pity and sorrow for you "nice American people of the lie". Why do I, "we", bother? Because God goes where His children are troubled in ignorance.

Salu.

BACK TO TRUTH

There are many extraterrestrial races in a confirmed working relationship between the Pleiadians and themselves. Contacts already established upon your place are confirmed. There were, for instance, ones who contacted the one, Billy Meier, prior to Pleiadians. How many of you reading this are familiar with those contacts and books forwarding a picture of one, Asket, realize she was from the DAL Universe, as referred to by us, and not actually Pleiadian at all? There is advanced spirit, more aware, in contact with a far greater reality of which you are only a tiny part. Be greatly gentle and kind to ones who were and are early contacts for how much can one mind handle without being pronounced "mad" by your experts?

For you ones who chime and chip at us to become visible and show our-selves--there are thousands of pictures of valid visibility. Meetings were set up singularly and with witnesses in attendance. It is herein noted that an entity even in the midst of witnessing--will conjure doubts and "reasons" why he did not see that which he saw. Especially ones who are set in opposition of "prove it if you can and if you dare" will make sure you do not! These kinds of doubts are rooted in materialism and a disbe-lief, which rises from a material intellect, from which all spiritual-in-tellectual talents are missing. This is not from lack of reason and/or brains, but from a religious confinement, from which that person is not able to find freedom. You ones leave yourselves, in the group, open to such attack for you are too generous and too confident regarding ones you perceive to be "with" you--by those, your mission can be damaged greatly. I believe we have proven to you that in an ordinary grouping of people--you cannot trust the very things you believe you are seeing! Ob-serve with interest and discernment but do not be the fool!

CRYSTALS AND TRINKETS

What would you expect of elements present in a "thing" which I would hand unto you? I am now going to disappoint you for if you had access to ALL information of elements, you would find whatever I bring to be made up of those elements--no more and no less--the elements of the Uni-verse. HOW they are arranged and combined would likely be different from that naturally occurring--especially on your placement. If anyone would analyze them, then one would not find differences from minerals and crystals of the same sort of Earth origin. The construction, being the same in the whole of the Universe, the same kind of minerals are valid to the same laws everywhere. Further, if we are able to function in your arena, you must therefore know that we are greatly similar to your species. Therefore, the content of the Universal minerals, etc., will be likewise similar. If we were from that which differs greatly, you would recognize of nothing--including us.

Many artifacts and composites have been brought and given into the hands of you humans. The ones which differ and have great meaning are "lost", "stolen" and/or vanish.

In observing that which differs in perspective from your cosmic brothers, let us begin with "laws". I speak not of God's Laws nor of The Creation--I speak now of your human laws. We find your rules to be so foolish and unbased on truth that we can hardly believe that which we witness in your totally unjust system. Invented laws in most respects are not worthy of the human form of life in many, many respects, often being so stupid and primitive that I become tired of even discussing them. Anything of logical and lawful conclusions can only be found in very few of the laws, as some 95% of your laws as constructed and enforced are outside all human dignity and reason, not to speak of reasonable logic. In working with us, you have great disadvantage as set forth upon you by your laws.

Frankly, as we came forth to work with you in full intent--we found them far worse than our worst expectations.

The whole of the people would, however, have to oppose the laws as brought upon you for your control by others, if you are to find change and freedom. These are most important for your changing of society but for self-growth into understanding and balanced life you must better understand "spirit". Therefore, allow us to continue with discussion of spirit.

THE CREATION

A person will react to a word or thought as programmed by experience--every word and every thought creates a response whether recognized or not recognized. Therefore it is a "given" that a person will react to the word or the designation "The Creation" in different ways, as though it were something apart and beautiful or good or whatever. Such is not exactly the case. Such characterizations as "omnipresent", "all-powerful", "all knowing" are valid characterizations of the nature of The Creation. Millions of religious humans do not understand the true nature of The Creation.

Whenever they speak of it they tend to personify it as a God-being (which is then itself a separation for The Creation), and they confuse the idea of The Creation. So, it is very important to know as much as possible about the character and the nature of that which we label The Creation, for when the word is understood properly it buoys the inner mind and connects it to its Source as soon as the word is expressed or heard or "impressed".

I can briefly place this into different and simplistic context. The Creation can be described as the sum of all that is manifest and unmanifest, the matter realm being only a very small part of the whole, and that ALL that IS, is THE CREATION experiencing its polarization which produces the created and its experience, all of which continually adds to the total experience of The Creation for further application in that which is created. In other words, IT is in you (us) and works through you (us) and all that is created, and we are IT, in all and within all, of its parts. There is no separate personification indicated, except as some part chooses to represent itself as such, which any part can do within its own level of concept.

The experience reveals The Creation as unlimited beauty, harmony, wisdom, knowledge, and truth...enduring endlessly. So whenever a human perceives a thing of beauty, a flower, an animal, clouds, water, landscape, music, color and thus and so, he considers it in connection with the limitless grandeur of The Creation itself. When a human recognizes and realizes this, then he knows that this recognition springs from limitless cognition, which itself is The Creation. Wherever life moves, even inside the most tiny creature, like for instance, a microbe, he sees the limitless

116

Creation.

The Creation is within every human being, and every other creature and thing as well. This is but a fraction of that manifestation itself. Once this thought has penetrated deeply inside a person and he can experience it, he loses all fear and doubt. When he knows his contact is with the all-knowing, almighty, Creation, he enjoys peace and tranquility. Reflection on this gives the name "Creation" great meaning indeed. The more he thinks on this reality, the more his intelligence is illuminated and stretched, and the more powerful his personality becomes, and his whole life and labor is blessed.

The Creation rises in his consciousness and he senses peace, strength, knowledge, wisdom, delight and hope. He can overcome obstacles, and achieve his objectives, and he suddenly has no more need for purely material things. One must learn a spiritual-intellectual manner of thinking and recognize its validity until the first successes are achieved--that is the hardest and yet, the first requirement of the journey into spiritual awareness.

But the way certainly does not stop here, because further exploration, research and development, and further recognition leads to the limitless endurance of time. Everything may happen in the course of time to prevent one from achieving his objectives, but the spiritualized person knows no limits and does not allow himself to be stopped short of his goals by any events of the future. For him the future always exists in the present, wherefrom he becomes determined to do everything here and now to obtain the highest spiritual state of consciousness, and he does not fear the future for the future is now just as present as the present itself.

When the spiritualized being sees others before him, he sees THE CREATION in them....!

The stones of this foundation of knowledge have now been laid and we will simply polish them a bit. Later, in your perceptions--but not very much later, the avalanche of desire for this truth will flood the lands for all other actions have been trial, error and have pulled you away from God and not unto Him. You must wait upon the Lord; do your work and allow the WORD to flow.

PRAYERS

You continually ponder upon "prayer" for yes, it is indeed important that you petition and it is most significant HOW you present your petition. Let us first understand the meaning of "prayer". A prayer is truly a "wish"; a wishful call upon the spirit of the human being himself, the Creation part in the Creation collective, meaning "grant me this or that...". Those who are conscious of the force, the knowledge, and the ability of their spirit, no longer resort to such prayers because they already live in the knowledge that the power and might of their spirit is capable of anything. For that reason, they determine constantly, the might of their spirit. The unspiritualized one, being unaware, is unable, and thus seeks to activate his spirit by conscious prayer. Further explained, this means that the spiritualized human is always using the forces and abilities of his spirit, and quite consciously, while the unspiritualized one expresses only wishes in prayer, and those to an exterior power/force, usually personified, when the source is within through his personal contact with The Creation itself.

A most beauteous prayer was established by Jmmanuel and has not been improved upon through the generations, so let us consider it carefully:

My spirit Almighty: My spirit who is all-knowing, almighty, and all-loving in me.

Your presence be sanctified: Your presence confirms to me your controlling power over all matters concerning myself.

May your wisdom become conscious to me: May your power be extended in the consciousness of my thoughts in order to enable me to apply all truths, wisdom and love, peace and freedom, given to and acquired by me and all mankind.

May your power be extended in me, on earth as well as in heaven: May your power become effective in me, in all material as well as all spiritual aspects.
Please allow and give unto me all that I need for living this day and each day: Please grant me all I need for my material as well as my spiritual life and development, for you are almighty.

So that I acknowledge my errors: So that I may recognize my faults and eliminate them since they hinder me on my way of evolution.

Please do not allow me to be led into temptation, nor allow me fall into temptation's clutches, but rather to right decision and choices through discernment and just judgments: Please do not let me make error by material and wrong thinking, or become dependent on beliefs alone.

For you are within and without me as power and wisdom, truth and knowledge for eternity: May I become conscious of your almighty forces inside me at ALL times.

All of this ask in truth and ask not for self, except for understanding and truth and ask all else in behalf of brother so that the cycle of wholeness may become manifest--even unto the tinymost portion of manifestation of your relations--which after all--IS ALL!   *"Thy will be done in and through me as the creation which I AM"* does very nicely indeed. *"Thy will--as I desire it to be...."* DOES NOT!

Chela, please end this portion at this point for the computer is now going to digest the material. It is enough upon which to feast this day. Further, it will give you insight into that which transpires this day in the court. God shall prevail just as soon as mankind desires God to prevail and not a moment sooner! How do YOU wish it to be? So be it! Salu and Saalome', THE WORD IS TRUTH AND THE WORD IS GOD; THEREFORE, THIS WORD IN TRUTH IS GOD AND SHALL SET YOU FREE!

I am Hatonn, to clear for the present writing. I shall walk with you through the mire of this confusion so that you can see of your way and have understanding of that which appears to be negative impact for you are not given to know the plan and method of God--so you be in the deciding of HOW it shall be and so shall it be. AHO!

CHAPTER 14

REC #1   HATONN

SATURDAY, DECEMBER 8, 1990   6:25 A.M.   YEAR 4 DAY 114

POINTS TO NOTE THIS DAY

Please take note of that which is presented unto you. Note carefully that neither Russian nor Israeli spokesmen so much as declare desire for this new "One World Order" of Mr. Bush. In fact, watch what Israel is do-ing--listen to what Shamir and Sharon are saying. Shamir is in the U.S. to STOP any potential council meeting of the UN regarding the Middle East and, specifically, any reference to Palestine. Note further, that the U.S. has recanted any reference to positive potential to such a meeting and the press says it is "...to not anger our closest ally, Israel". What have we here? Perhaps you ones had better listen to the non-news a bit more closely.

Know that CNN was set up to suck you all in and has now become the prime producer of mis-information! You must look beyond the obvious but the real news is within and behind the facade.

These ones tell you that Saddam is increasing his numbers of troops--HE IS NOT! They show you troops--they are the same parade troops shown on every newscast for weeks and weeks now and have nothing to do with this current situation at any rate. They say that Saddam is calling up the "reserve" "farmers" to come to immediate service within the next two weeks--phoo! The college youngsters of proper military age are not even changing their dating behavior, much less dropping their school classes. If you do not look, chelas, you will not see.

RUSSIA

Now you have the barrage of "help the Russians" who are hungry. Yes, the countries of the Soviets are in terrible circumstance--however, note again--the pictures. The workers do not show up in the fields to even gather in the harvest. The people walk across the fields covered with root vegetables and crush the grain which would sustain them. The cattle of the dairies are being fed fodder of mixed cellulose and mud which actu-ally kills them because there has been none of the grain stored for their use and the workers will not come to work to do of the feeding. The people raise their voices against Gorbachev. What do you take away from these messages? It is important.

The underlying note is that the Russians under Gorbachev have blatantly destroyed the people *while the government continues to build an incredible war machine! They decry the lack of discipline and state they would go back to Stalin. I can only urge you ones to pay attention most diligently and carefully to the propagandi for you cannot have it ALL WAYS at the same time. What do YOU think is going on? You do not need me to tell you everything which is in front of your own eyes to see and hear. If you only absorb the lies then you are destined to live and then die by the lie. I urge you to seek within into your coffers of wisdom and see that which is being projected upon you and then the mess can be straightened into order.*

Stop this praying to "My Father which art in heaven"! Go within into the places where our Father dwells--within the temple of self--stop looking for HIM out there somewhere--in some "heaven". Your Father would not leave of you to reside separate and apart from you--in some kind of heaven.

Remember that the Master Nazarene--the young teacher from Galilee was called the Master of Wisdom. He told you to go within into the temple wherein God can be found and seek truth. He said he was but the Wayshower -- the bringer of truth of the WORD. How many times do you need hear this message before you follow the instructions? Or, do you just continue and continue to babble your prayers so that someone ELSE can do of your work in your stead--and stand responsible, beaten and slain to spill blood for your purification--WHAT ABOUT HIS PURIFICATION? IF HE HAD TAKEN YOUR RESPONSIBILITY FROM YOU HE WOULD HAVE BEEN IN DIRECT OPPOSITION UNTO GOD CREATOR WHO GIVES UNTO EACH OF CREATIONS THE CHOICE AND FREE-WILL TO ACT--RESPONSIBILY OR IRRESPONSIBLY! Do you still desire that the one you called Jesus, or whatever, move against his Father's will and Laws to take up your cross FOR YOU? He came to tell you truth and HELP you find the way and will help you bear that which is given, but never to do FOR YOU.

What do you ones celebrate at Christmas-time? X-mas time? Santa? Buying and getting? Singing of mindless carols? Could you not give a bit of thought unto Christ--could you not, for a refreshing change, shorten the term given to Christ-X? What have you allowed to happen to your generations? And for you ones who believe not on the "Jesus" Emmanuel as Messiah (teacher), to whom DO you have allegiance and faithfulness? Is it of the world, or is it of Divine God?

Where do you place The Creation in this time of mass-murder of your young, healthy trees of evergreen? You take their lives to bear ornaments of tinsel and gaudy strips of trash in order to "beautify" that which is beyond beauty in its perfection, and you call it "celebration". Celebration of what? For what do you slay all those millions of trees just reaching their prime--or for the show of shows--a giant statue of a hundred years to stand on a political pot on a politician's lawn--under guard lest you the people touch of it! To what do you bend in worship, my chelas? What do you sell and buy at Christmas? Perfumes to seduce? Expensive gifts

121

to seduce? Gifts which "purchase" something or another? WHAT, DEAR ONES, ARE YOU DOING? WHAT DO YOU TEACH OF YOUR CHILDREN? WHAT DO THE CHILDREN EXPECT AT CHRISTMAS? PERHAPS IT IS THEN THAT YOU SHOULD USE THE TERM X-MAS FOR 'TIS A PITY TO ATTACH THE NAME OF GOD UNTO THE HYPOCRISY AND CONTRADICTION OF TERMS AND ACTIONS.

Things given in love and remembrance of shared joy and appreciation are wondrous indeed and a special time triggers the thought--but you ones have turned it into scenes of greed and gluttony of senses. I believe it is fine to leave God out of it and call it that which it has become--Satan's greatest time of celebration! A card of touching and sharing a thought is wondrous, warm and caring--a magnificent temple dedicated to lies is of less than value of the item. If the heart and pocketbook can afford of both, then it is wondrous indeed when the heart and hands give forth and blessings are unlimited upon thine gifts. But what happened to the widow's mite--the gift of that which she had, in secret, in love and in no expectations of return? Oh, how God longs for the widow's mite--or less; the desire is magnificent without the mite. Blessed are ye who walk with me for I shall bow unto you and serve you and give unto you all that God has given unto me and, dear ones, it is ALL--it is the Universe, the very light of soul and all the wondrous manifestations of Creation--won't you come and walk with me? I am your brother-----I KNOW THE WAY! I can teach you to fly as the eagles and soar as the gull; I can show you the wondrous trappings of the Cosmos and bring you among the stars--but we must ever move in the Lighted places for only in so moving can we escape the bindings of your physical shackles whether it be within your bodies of physical format or without.

PRACTICAL MATTERS

Let us turn again to the subject of the Journal at hand which is to give you the understandings and teachings of higher brotherhood--i.e., the Pleiadians, at this instance. I do this because it is important that you be given information in increments which can be understood so that you can build a stairway into understanding while at the same time removing the mystical and magical thought streams.

Let us speak of precious stones, gems, semi-precious stones, crystals and such. Let me outlay, again, the facts. They bear great influence and you of earth toy with them, uproot them and generally abuse them. You seem to not understand the value of these items--THEY CAN BE PRO-GRAMMED, DEPROGRAMMED AND REPROGRAMMED. They can be trinkets of adornment or deadly weapons and you ones seem to have no discernment of which is which. These "minerals" of Earth origin (or any origin) are receivers and transmitters of human emotional feelings and thought energies. Each, according to its kind, stores more or less ofhese energies which their owners discharge, concentrating them again and influencing the owners to some considerable extent--even if the process is unfocused in intent.

The Earth sphere, especially in this current time of cycle, is vibrating with the energy of much evil influence for it is the time of chaos upon your place. The cloak of compressed energy in evil, worldly format surrounds you like a fog. These negative forces arise and are further developed by the vast negative thought-energies of the Earth-human creatures, which place the whole world under the spell, if you will, of dangerous and deadly radiating pulses of energy waves. Crystals, as a general classification, just as with your micro-chips for computers, are programmed easily. Some more easily than others. Crystals of every type, as well as precious stones and different minerals, are strong receivers and absorbers of such energies and it is unavoidable that these negative human energies and thoughts, which are extraordinarily charged with evil character, become a quite dangerous source of projecting negative response.

Each mineral, according to its type and character, becomes "middle-men" of all sorts of focused intent--sickness, lethargy and especially mental distress and depression of emotional well-being. In this day and age you ones cling to them, sell them, program them and adorn yourselves with them with incorrect intent. You buy them, steal them, find them and program them with magic hoopla for self-charisma, drawing unto you the opposite sex, giving you power over another, etc.--read the literature. They are touted to heal, restore, balance and baloney--it is like giving sharpened knives unto a two-year-old and suggesting he not get blood on the carpet.

Crystals and precious stones of every kind--even the stones (rocks) of the hills and deserts, are extremely sensitive receivers and collectors of human thought energies and emotions--both negative and positive. But they are usually "programmed" by non-informed touters of greedy use and are, therefore, negatively unbalanced. They begin by being strongly influenced by their original places of growth before they are imprisoned and displaced by humans. The Creation utilizes these little computers as points of focus but as man has spread unbalance, so has the unbalance spread throughout the natural kingdom.

If the human being wants to have crystals and precious stones in his possession, to own them as valuable assets, use them as decoration, or as a bringer of health through mental focus of intent, then he must first release the dangerous radiations which exist in preprogramming as oscillations (vibrations), because otherwise they are capable of being utilized in a harmful manner. Moreover, the stones must be cleansed and freshly "neutralized" at regular intervals. This is because there is so much negative thought being projected that these bits of data storage containers become contaminated.

These wondrous systems can easily be cleansed by thought clearance but most ones do not have the foggiest notion as to how to do it. These are items which focus attention of the mind and if given the negative focus

123

will allow the being in point to compound the negative aspects.

The human also has a great tendency to wear talismans as good luck symbols--but you see, they do nothing in themselves and work only in consequence to the "belief" held within by the user. These "things", however, can also bear the negative input and should also be cleansed with intent.

The native Indians have methods of cleansing stones--one of which is the smoking of same with sage. The facts are, dear ones, that the most effective way to destroy a computer chip is through oily smoke. It becomes quite "physical" in actuality.

I do not enjoy this subject, at all, because it is so ill-understood. There is nothing of magic about rocks or gems. It is what is placed into them and, therefore, that energy must be cleansed from them--no more and no less. Some things conduct "electricity", for instance, far better than others and so it is with program-bearing substances. Secret formulas, conjurations-- by water or other means of this nature are ridiculous--it is the focused "intent" of thought pulses which reprogram and/or neutralize the data.

Now, I caution all of you. I do not wish to be misunderstood nor misquoted. Most of the BS given unto you regarding this or that crystal, special cleansing materials, pre-programmed crystals for whatever and thus and so are mere sleight-of-hand tricks to get you separated from your money! Some well-meaning ones have even attributed these "methods" and "secrets" to space brothers for one reason or another and thus you can locate the very point of time when the receiver began to manipulate and be manipulated.

It will be stated that "ones from Sirius, Pleiades, Orion" and so forth, have brought these stones and given special instructions for use and for the selling of such to gain funds for your "wondrous and holy work". I tell you they lie and a good con game is being perpetrated upon you. The best way to foist off upon a receiver is to give unto him/her an item of programmed security. If the thought focus moves from God onto some piece of drivel--the human is altered by the belief placed thereon. A gift is a gift is a gift--YOU GIVE IT ITS POWER!

If the petitioner for, let us say, funds to further work of any nature--asks for methods of acquiring those funds, and clears not his space and mind of negative energies of Earth-physical bindings--he will be "had". The first to show up in any inquiry regarding physical material-matters--is physical material-beings of negative intent as to God's business. You will always be able to read within the pages at which juncture the scribe or receiver or contact--was first allowing of negative energy input--there will be compromise of lessons, truth and "how-to". If any entity utilizes a physical "thing" instead of full intent of mind intent--God is put aside! This does not mean that these "things" are not good and utilitarian items-- it means the intent of truth is not present.

Every "thing" emits radiations and vibrations--some dangerous and deadly indeed--however, EVERY pulse and wave can be countered by the all-powerful, all-ability--mind. Do not be fooled for one moment as to what is doing what to what. In the presence of God shielding, there is not pulse or radiation which can transgress. There are, indeed, few humans who can bear and project such protection for as the entity believes it to be--so shall it be.

All contactees have been approached and caused to experience both the perceived negative AND the positive teachers. It is imperative that a scribe and/or receiver be capable of discernment and know that anything that moves one from God unity and truth is evil in intent. Not good nor bad--evil in intent--for that energy will pull one from the path of truth and God-ness. It has nothing to do, really, with good and bad--it has to do with physical desire, needs and actions. If the receiver fails to shield self from the encroaching negative energies--so shall they impact first because they are of the physical plane and you are of the physical plane. To counter these barrages--the being must move into the higher understanding where the protection abides. Herein and only herein, can the "attack" be neutralized for the attack is actually against your higher universal self--soul. If you give away your power then you can expect to fall--but often, you will not be the one to realize you have deviated from the original path. Does Dharma stumble and fall? Of course, constantly--but she always calls unto God in perfection and He always responds and picks her up and sets her again unto the proper direction upon the tracks.

I am often asked questions regarding Dharma as we move along through the brief months of joint venture--"...is she a robotoid?" Does it matter? Perhaps in the higher sense of direction and journey, we all are God's created robotoids and if we continue to function according to His Laws within balance--is it important? Ones given to experience in your density--are none-the-less humanoid. I suggest that all who are pre-programmed into the totally physical aspect of experience--are but humanoid robotoids of the negative aspect of experience for you place finite limits upon experience and being. There are ones among you who are in great positions of leadership, however, who are projected from human manipulations and represent genetic humanoid robotics without soul compassion and/or life essence of Creator. These are the ones you must attend.

GUILT

Let us change our thought attention to another aspect of experience--what you do in the name of guilt.

I suggest, however, that you not cast off those twinges of conscience as simply unnecessary "guilt". It is one thing to feel guilt which is not valid--it is another to "feel guilty" regarding that which you perpetrated against another and did not set to correctness or deliberately foisted off to pain another.

Then comes the barrage of the human to "change the old laws". It will always come with an argument that it needs to be so for the "modern" man for "times have surely changed". Dear ones, only perception of "time" has changed--not the human. Why should the laws be changed? Human, when he changes in fact, will have no problem with the laws of God nor The Creation.

"Well", then you say, "...but surely not regarding the laws in respect to sex and matrimony--they surely are not valid today as eons ago, while we have moved into a `modern' world!"

Come now, chelas--have you become modernly responsible for all of your actions--or do you pass out condoms in the schools? Have you come up with "modern" rules and methods which have brought peace, balance and harmony in love to all mankind--or, have you overpopulated, taught murder through abortion and other various things of unrest and unbalance? So be it--pigs is pigs and laws is laws!

Surely, when an entity burdens, against better knowledge, quite consciously, a guilt upon himself, then he pays an atonement, because that is the law of justice. If the consciously self-laden guilt is too great, then a punishment in balance of such guilt is suited, where the concerned creature is unworthy of life and loses its justification for existence. The human creature is birthed with the inner knowledge of that which is right and that which is basically and immorally wrong--all the lessons do not wipe out the inner knowing that that which you do is right or it is wrong. It is not "good" nor "bad" as such--just right or wrong. What happens in your "modern" society is an uprising against elders who have efforted to teach and accept "wrong" as "right" and the new life-forms (children) are angry, guilt-ridden and filled with rebellious resentment to the so-called adults who mis-teach and mis-lead. They kill and they do suicide against self in total resentment against you who have set the examples of ill-erroneous intent and actions.

Atonement always follows at some point in experience--a rebirth if you will, in which the ill-formed and uncompleted perfection then completes the formerly eliminated life. It is always a path of growth. There always must be a rise in spiritual development. In a strange twist of experience--it is often perceived to be through quite negative means that spiritual growth is given great strength and positive development.

Let us look at that which becomes prevalent upon your placement. You call it freedom of choice and "human rights" but you accomplish something which you miss entirely. Let us look at the "homosexual" movement for a moment. The "homosexual" movement and participants do not ask for equality in LOVE EMOTION. They demand sexual expression in the physical format as a "birthright". Now, what are they actually accomplishing? They are basically "sterilizing" selves--castrating self in basic concept. What is happening is basically that which is accomplished through other means on other placements having ability to utilize other planets, etc. In other societies in your Universe, ones who do not follow

126

the laws are simply separated into separate sexes and placed in other "worlds" and islands for the remainder of their current life experience. Lacking the opposite sex which is necessary for the human to reproduce-- there is no reproduction and therefore the species cannot multiply as is. The ones placed elsewhere are usually most contented in the experience and are not continually in search of "equality and acceptance" within a so- ciety which is based on procreation as is Earth Human, for example. The Earth human might well be in a good position for such at this present time if he were not so blinded, corrupted and disunited. This arrangement solves so many various problems that you would be amazed.

Now, do not misunderstand anything that I say herein--THE LAWS OF THE CREATION ARE ETERNAL AND UNCHANGEABLE. But, the laws of experience on given placements are different according to the size, life ability, soul growth ability and what you would call evolution, of a given species. The guidelines are different--the LAWS of balance are ABSOLUTE.

LET US SPEAK OF THE LAWS AS GIVEN FORTH BY

"EARTH" GOD

As we speak of these laws, we must remember that there were and are laws applicable to a given placement--a planet upon which human ex- periences. These laws are of human origin, so to speak, and meant to regulate Earth creatures experiencing within that particular manifestation.

These laws are given forth by that which you would consider the highest leader of the human races, Governor of the Heavenly Sons, so to speak,-- BY GOD. His prophets and mediators and selected humans announced these laws among the races which observed them, unfortunately, for only a very short time and confounded them later, which was a further step in the direction of the abyss of later mankind.

Do the aliens (Pleiadians) have "humans" making laws? Wherever there are "thinking" life-forms, there are established laws--everywhere. Each, from the position of spiritual development of the tribe's leaders, has taken laws from the true natural law and expressed them in responsible form within human-natural law. In consequence these laws are of natural logic, and are not illogical and primitive, such as ones established on your world. Humans upon your place, in your governments, still exercise purely world-oriented, physically based and lust/greed based--worldly- material POWER and call the projections "laws".

Are there degenerates and criminality on other placements, say Pleiades? It is total nonsense to think that a brother/sister planet of humans are su- per-men and no longer need law. As we progress through the stages of higher dimensions we then cease to function in physical format to which all of the basic physical human attributes are attached. However, on the

127

planets housing humanity in species there is always need for rules and laws. Only there where the Creational law becomes self-evident do expressed laws fall away. This only occurs at very high spiritual levels, in pure-spiritual spheres, where materiality is a thing of the "past". Material forms of life are still afflicted by too many mistakes, than that they can simply neglect laws appropriate to their level.

CRIME AND PUNISHMENT?

I suppose we are going to discuss this until we understand it and therefore I request that, until we finish this document, you understand that we speak from the position of Pleiades--and even at that, not specific planets thereof. This is, however, to separate higher energy existence from that of which you inquire.

There is established a "punishment" to suit given "crimes". While with you of Earth, punishment is exercised in a most primitive way, which is no more the case with your brothers.

Dharma, leave this computer instantly and stand-by. There is trouble afoot, chela. Set this to print and get out of this room--NOW!

CHAPTER 15

REC #1   HATONN

SUNDAY, DECEMBER 9, 1990   8:25 A.M.   YEAR 4 DAY 115

TODAY'S WATCH

Hatonn present in the light of God; in service to you of my brothers. Good-morning. What more could you ask for, Dharma?--seven hours of sleep--that should spoil you for the coming six months!

No news? I think that surely you jest, chela. What might you think is the connection between fuel tanks blowing up in Denver, Colorado, at the airport and a petrol-chemical plant (new) blowing up in Tomsk, Russia? You just never can tell to what lengths your insane cartels will go, can you?

What about the murders of whole village populations in India? Where is your UN force? What about the increased resistance in Palestine--which is only inadvertently allowed to hit the news wire--and only then as publications making the Palestinians appear the aggressor and parties of blame? It is the "non-news" which you ones must begin to interpret more carefully.

Look at the little bracelet Lady Bush wears, which is now for sale through non-profit sources--backing her husband's stance in "Desert Shield". Not a single word regarding God and Nation--just power and force. Yes, you in America "...have come a long way, Baby!" Further, how is it that you can now have organized marches of great numbers in cities throughout your nation and thousands upon thousands of ones writing papers and congressmen AGAINST this Middle East fiasco--and yet, the polls as outlined on the establishment fixed media, show increasing support for war and Mr. Bush's policies? They don't even bother to trouble you with "where they run their polls!" I believe they must simply rerun them over and over in the World Zionist Organization. You think America is "Right"? Well, soon you will be "Dead Right", as the old saying goes. So be it.

Only a brief reference to the Shuttle trip: It's a "trip" alright--into your minds with manipulation. The collaborators of this whole facade are toying with you like nit-wits. After wasting billions of dollars on a system which was "taken out" before it hit orbit--they have now dinked you along with stupid stories of this malfunction and that malfunction and, finally, do you the dishonor of dumping a story on you of a clogged sewer system. My goodness, chelas, isn't it bad enough to waste billions of your precious dollars but to insult and actually ridicule your intelligence seems even "much" for these liars. So be it, I suppose I have naught else

129

to say about it. How can you the people swallow this obvious falsity? They have played you like a broken-stringed banjo with no brains for over a week now. What recourse do you have? TAKE CONTROL OF YOURSELVES AS THE CITIZENS UNDER YOUR CONSTITUTION--WHILE YOU YET CAN!

Go on, scribe, and moan and groan now about today's work subject. I know that you revel in the subject of home (Pleiades) and spiritual balance and growth--but human of Earth must also come to grips with that which confronts him and, specifically in America, actions need to be taken--WEEK BEFORE LAST. We must finish outlaying the Constitution of the United Nations Industrial Development Organization. We can label it PART II, Continuation. Express material, please.

PART II: UNIDO

Begin please, with that which is labelled in their document, *Article 2--and we will follow along.*

FUNCTIONS

In fulfillment of its foregoing objectives, the Organization shall generally take all necessary and appropriate action, and in particular shall:

(a) Encourage and extend, as appropriate, assistance to the developing countries in the promotion and acceleration of their industrialization, in particular in the development, expansion and modernization of their industries;

(b) In accordance with the Charter of the United Nations, initiate, coordinate and follow up the activities of the United Nations system with a view to enabling the Organization to play the central coordinating role in the field of industrial development; *(H: Remember UNIDO is referred to as "Organization". This portion notes that the UN will control YOU.)*

(c) Create new and develop existing concepts and approaches in respect of industrial development on global, regional and national, as well as on sectoral levels, and carry out studies and surveys with a view to formulating new lines of action directed towards harmonious and balanced industrial development, with due consideration for the methods employed by countries with different socio-economic systems for solving industrialization problems;

(d) Promote and encourage the development and use of planning techniques, and assist in the development of an integrated and interdisciplinary approach towards the accelerated industrialization of the developing countries; *(H: This is "regional control over private businesses.")*

(f) Provide a forum and act as an instrument to serve the developing countries and the industrialized countries in their contacts, consultations and, at the request of the countries concerned, negotiations diverted towards the industrialization of the developing countries;

(g) Assist the developing countries in the establishment and operation of industries, including agro-related as well as basic industries, to achieve the full utilization of locally available natural and human resources and the production of goods for domestic and export markets, as well as contribute to the self-reliance of these countries;

(h) Serve as a clearing-house for industrial information and accordingly collect and monitor on a selevtive basis, analyze and generate for the purpose of dissemination information on all aspects of industrial development on global, regional and national, as well as on sectoral levels including the exchange of experience and technological achievements of the industrially developed and the developing countries with different social and economic systems; *(H: Again, dovetails with regional government.)*

(i) Devote particular attention to the adoption of special measures aimed at assisting the least-developed, land-locked, and island developing countries, as well as those developing countries most seriously affected by economic crises and natural calamities, without losing sight of the interest of the other developing countries;

(j) Promote, encourage and assist in the development, selection, adaptation, transfer and use of industrial technology, with due regard for the socioeconomic conditions and the specific requirements of the industry concerned, with special reference to the transfer of technology from the industrialized to the developing countries as well as among the developing countries themselves;

(k) Organize and support industrial training programmes aimed at assisting the developing countries in the training of technical and other appropriate categories of personnel needed at various phases for their accelerated industrial development;

(l) Advise on and assist, in close co-operation with the appropriate bodies of the United Nations, specialized agencies and the International Atomic Energy Agency, the developing countires in the exploitation, conservation and local transformation of their natural resources for the purpose of furthering the industrialization of developing countries;

(m) Provide pilot and demonstration plans for acceleration industrialization in particular sectors:

(n) Develop special measures designed to promote co-operation in the industrial field among developing countries and between the developed and developing countries;

(o) Assist, in co-operation with other appropriate bodies, the regional planning of industrial development of the developing countries within the framework of regional and subregional groupings among those countries;

(p) Encourage and promote the establishment and strengthening of industrial, business and professional associations, and similar organizations which would contribute to the full utilization of the internal resources of the developing countries with a view to developing their national industries;

(q) Assist in the establishment and operation of institutional infrastructure for the provision of regulatory, advisory and developmental services to industry;

(r) Assist, at the request of Governments of the developing countries, in obtaining external financing for specific industrial projects on fair, equitable and mutually acceptable terms.

CHAPTER II---PARTICIPATION

ARTICLE 3

MEMBERS

Membership in the Organization is open to all <u>States</u> which associate themselves <u>with the objectives and principles of the Organization</u>. *(H: Please recall, "States" means nations.)*

    (a) <u>States members of the United Nations or of a specialized agency or of the International Atomic Energy Agency may become Members of the Organization by becoming parties to this Constitution in accordance</u> with Article 24 and paragraph 2 of Article 25;

    (b) <u>States</u> other than those referred to in subparagraph (a) may become members of the Organization by becoming parties to this Constitution in accordance with paragraph 3 of Article 24 and subparagraph 2(c) of Article 25, after their membership has been approved by the Conference, by a two-thirds majority of the Members <u>present</u> and <u>voting</u>, upon the recommendation of the Board.

ARTICLE 4

OBSERVERS

    1. Observer status in the Organization shall be open, upon request, to those enjoying such status in the General Assembly of the United Nations, unless the Conference decides otherwise.

    2. Without prejudice to paragraph 1, the Conference has the authority to invite other observers to participate in the work of the Organization.

    3. Observers shall be permitted to participate in the work of the Organization in accordance with the relevant rules of procedure and the provisions of this Constitution.

ARTICLE 5

SUSPENSION

    1. Any Member of the Organization that is suspended from the exercise of the rights and privileges of membership <u>of the United Nations</u> shall automatically be suspended from the exercise of the rights and privileges of membership of the Organization.

    2. Any Member that is in arrears in the payment of its financial contributions to the Organization shall have no vote in the Organization if the amount of its arrears equals or exceeds the amount of the assessed contributions due from it for the preceding two fiscal years. Any organ may, nevertheless, permit such a Member to vote in that organ if it is satisfied that the failure to pay is due to conditions beyond the control of the Member.

ARTICLE 6

WITHDRAWAL

    1. A Member may withdraw from the Organization by depositing an instrument of denunciation of this Constitution with the Depository. *(H:*

Hold it--this is not true--Universal mandatory enlistments are planned!)
2. Such withdrawal shall take effect on the last day of the fiscal year following that during which such instrument was deposited.
3. The contributions to be paid by the withdrawing Member for the fiscal year following that during which such instrument was deposited shall be the same as the assessed contributions for the fiscal year during which such deposit was effected. The withdrawing Member shall in addition fulfil any unconditional pledges it made prior to such deposit.

CHAPTER III.---ORGANS

ARTICLE 7

PRINCIPAL AND SUBSIDIARY ORGANS

(Provides 3 branches.)

1. The principal organs of the Organization shall be:
 (a) The General Conference (referred to as the "Conference";
 (b) The Industrial Development Board (referred to as the "Board");
 (c) The Secretariat.
2. There shall be established a Programme and Budget Committee to assist the Board in the preparation and examination of the programme of work, the regular budget and the operational budget of the Organization and other financial matters pertaining to the Organization. *(H: Uses P.P.B.S. `Program, Planning, and Budgeting System',--a mandatory control system under the Conference.)*
3. Other subsidiary organs, including technical committees, may be established by the Conference or the Board, which shall give due regard to the principle of equitable geographical representation.

ARTICLE 8

GENERAL CONFERENCE

(The Developmental Arm of the New World Order)

1. The Conference shall consist of representatives of all Members.
2. (a) The Conference shall hold a regular session every two years, unless it decides otherwise. Special sessions shall be convened by the Director General at the request of the Board or of a majority of all Members.
 (b) Regular sessions shall be held at the seat of the Organization, unless otherwise determined by the Conference. The Board shall determine the place where a special session is to be held.
3. In addition to exercising other functions specified in this Constitution, the Conference shall:
 (a) Determine the guiding principles and the policies of the Organization; *(H: Part of P.P.B.S. functions and control.)*
 (b) Consider reports of the Board, of the Director-General and of

the subsidiary organs of the Conference;

(c) <u>Approve the programme of work</u>, the regular budget and the operational budget of the Organization in accordance with Article 14, establish the scale of assessments in accordance with Article 15, <u>approve the financial regulations of the Organization</u> and supervise the effective utilization of the financial resources of the Organization;

(d) Have the authority to adopt, by a two-thirds majority of the Members present and voting, conventions or agreements with respect to any matter within the competence of the Organization and to make recommendations to the Members concerning such conventions or agreements;

(e) Make recommendations to Members and to international organizations with respect to matters within the competence of the Organization;

(f) Take any other appropriate action to enable the Organization to further its objectives and carry out its functions.

4. The Conference may delegate to the Board such of its powers and functions as it may consider desirable, except for those provided for in: Article 3, subparagraph (b); Article 4; Article 8, subparagraphs 3(a), (b), (c) and (d); Article 9, paragraph 1; Article 10, paragraph 1; Article 11, paragraph 2; Article 14, paragraphs 4 and 6; Article 15; Article 18; Article 23, subparagraphs 2(b) and 3(b); and Annex I.

5. The Conference shall adopt its own rules of procedure.

6. Each Member shall have one vote in the Conference. Decisions shall be made by a majority of the Members present and voting unless otherwise specified in this Constitution or in the rules of procedure of the Conference.

ARTICLE 9
INDUSTRIAL DEVELOPMENT BOARD

(H: The Enforcement Arm for the New World Order.)

1. <u>The Board</u> shall consist of 53 Members of the Organization elected by the Conference, which shall give due regard to the principle of equitable geographical distribution. In electing the members of the Board the Conference shall observe the following distribution of seats: 33 members of the Board shall be elected from the <u>States</u>. (States refers to "nations") listed in Parts A and C, 15 from the <u>States</u> listed in Part B, and 5 from the <u>States</u> listed in Part D of Annex I to this Constitution.

2. Members of the Board shall hold office from the close of the regular session of the Conference at which they were elected until the close of the regular session of the Conference four years thereafter, except that the members elected at the first session shall hold office from the time of such election and one half shall hold office only until the close of the regular session two years thereafter. Members of the Board may be re-elected.

3. (a) The Board shall hold at least one regular session each year at such times as it may determine. Special sessions shall be convened by the Director-General at the request of a majority of all members of the Board.

(b) Sessions shall be held at the seat of the Organization, unless otherwise determined by the Board.

4. In addition to exercising other functions specified in this Constitution or delegated to it by the Conference, the Board shall:

(a) Acting under the authority of the Conference, review the implementation of the approved programme of work and of the corresponding regular budget and operational budget, as well as of other decisions of the Conference;

(b) Recommend to the Conference a scale of assessments for regular budget expenditures;

(c) Report to the Conference at each regular session on the activities of the Board;

(d) Request Members to furnish information on their activities related to the work of the Organization;

(e) In accordance with the decisions of the Conference and having regard to circumstances arising between sessions of the Board or the Conference, authorize the Director-General to take such measures as the Board deems necessary to meet unforeseen events with due regard to the functions and financial resources of the Organization;

(f) If the office of Director-General becomes vacant between sessions of the Conference, appoint an Acting Director-General to serve until the next regular or special session of the Conference;

(g) Prepare the provisional agenda for the Conference;

(h) Undertake such other functions as may be required to further the objectives of the Organization subject to the limitations stipulated in this Constitution.

5. The Board shall adopt its own rules of procedure.

6. Each member of the Board shall have one vote. Decisions shall be made by a majority of the members present and voting unless otherwise specified in this Constitution or in the rules of procedure of the Board.

7. The Board shall invite any Member not represented on the Board to participate without vote in its deliberations on any matter of particular concern to that Member.

ARTICLE 10
PROGRAMME AND BUDGET COMMITTEE

(H: Balancers of the funds used for world government conversion).

1. The Programme and Budget Committee shall consist of 27 Members of the Organization elected by the Conference, which shall give due regard to the principle of equitable geographical distribution. In the following distribution of seats: 15 members of the Committee shall be elected from the States listed in Parts A and C, 9 from the States listed in Part B, and 3 from the States listed in Part D of Annex I to this Constitution. In designating their representatives to serve on the Committee, States shall take into account their personal qualifications and experience.

2. Members of the Committee shall hold office from the close of the regular session of the Conference at which they were elected until the close of the regular session of the Conference two years thereafter. Members of the Committee may be re-elected.

3. (a) The Committee shall hold at least one session each year. Ad-

ditional sessions shall be convened by the Director-General at the request of the Board or the Committee.

(b) Sessions shall be held at the seat of the Organization, unless otherwise determined by the Board.

4. The Committee shall:

(a) Perform the functions assigned to it in Article 14;

(b) Prepare the draft scale of assessments for regular budget expenditures, for submission to the Board;

(c) Exercise such other functions with respect to financial matters as may be assigned to it by the Conference or the Board.

(d) Report to the Board at each regular session on all activities of the Committee and submit advice or proposals on financial matters to the Board of its own initiative.

5. The Committee shall adopt its own rules of procedure.

6. Each member of the Committee shall have one vote. Decisions shall be made by a two-thirds majority of the members present and voting.

Dharma, start a new document, please.

CHAPTER 16

REC #2   HATONN

SUNDAY, DECEMBER 9, 1990   11:00 A.M.   YEAR 4 DAY 115

ARTICLE 11

SECRETARIAT

(H: The chief of the Administrative Arm of the New World Order.)

1. The Secretariat shall comprise a Director-General, as well as such Deputy Directors-General and other staff as the Organization may require.
2. The Director-General shall be appointed by the Conference upon recommendation of the Board for a period of four years. He may be reappointed for a further term of four years, after which he shall not be eligible for reappointment.
3. The Director-General shall be the chief administrative officer of the Organization. Subject to general or specific directives of the Conference or the Board, the Director-General shall have the over-all responsibility and authority to direct the work of the Organization. Under the authority of and subject to the control of the Board, the Director-General shall be responsible for the appointment, organization and functioning of the staff.
4. In the performance of their duties, the Director-General and the staff shall not seek or receive instructions from any government or from any authority external to the Organization. They shall refrain from any action that might reflect on their position as international officials responsible only to the Organization. Each Member undertakes to respect the exclusively international character of the responsibilities of the Director-General and the staff and not to seek to influence them in the discharge of their responsibilities.

(NOTE: REQUIRED "LOYALTY" TO WORLD GOVERNMENT (SEE OATH REQUIRED), BUT LOYALTY TO U.S. CONSTITUTION NO LONGER POSSIBLE. THIS IS MOST IMPORTANT, CHELAS. HATONN.)

5. The staff shall be appointed by the Director-General under regulations to be established by the Conference upon recommendation of the Board. Appointments at the level of Deputy Director-General shall be subject to approval by the Board. The conditions of service of staff shall conform as far as possible to those of the United Nations common system. The paramount consideration in the employment of the staff and in determining the conditions of service shall be the necessity of securing the highest standards of efficiency, competence and integrity. Due regard shall be paid to the importance of recruiting staff on a wide and equitable geographical basis.
6. The Director-General shall act in that capacity at all meetings of the Conference, of the Board and of the Programme and Budget Committee,

and shall perform such other functions as are entrusted to him by these organs. He shall prepare an annual report on the activities of the Organization. In addition, he shall submit to the Conference or to the Board, as appropriate, such other reports as may be required.

CHAPTER IV.---PROGRAMME OF WORK AND

FINANCIAL MATTERS

ARTICLE 12

EXPENSES OF DELEGATIONS

Each Member and observer shall bear the expenses of its own delegation to the Conference, to the board or to any other organ in which it may participate.

ARTICLE 13

COMPOSITION OF BUDGETS

1. The activities of the Organization shall be carried out in accordance with its approved programme of work and budgets.

2. The expenditures of the Organization shall be divided into the following categories:

(a) Expenditures to be met from assessed contributions (referred to as the "regular budget"); and

(b) Expenditures to be met from voluntary contributions to the Organization, and such other income as may be provided for in the financial regulations (referred to as the "operational budget").

3. The regular budget shall provide for expenditures for administration, research, other regular expenses of the Organization and for other activities, as provided for in Annex II.

4. The operational budget shall provide for expenditures for technical assistance and other related activities.

ARTICLE 14

PROGRAMME AND BUDGETS

1. The Director-General shall prepare and submit to the Board through the Programme and Budget Committee, at a time specified in the financial regulations, a draft programme of work for the following fiscal period, together with the corresponding estimates for those activities to be financed from the regular budget. The Director-General shall, at the same time, submit proposals and financial estimates for those activities to be financed from voluntary contributions to the Organization.

2. The Programme and Budget Committee shall consider the proposals of the Director-General and submit to the Board its recommendations on the proposed programme of work and corresponding estimates for the regular budget and operational budget. Such recommendations of the Committee shall require a two-thirds majority of the Members present and voting.

3. The Board shall examine the proposals of the Director-General to-

gether with any recommendations of the Programme and Budget Committee and adopt the programme of work, the regular budget and the operational budget, with such modifications as it deems necessary, for submission to the Conference for consideration and approval. Such adoption shall require a two-thirds majority of the Members present and voting.

4. (a) The Conference shall consider and approve the programme of work and the corresponding regular budget and operational budget submitted to it by the Board, by a two-thirds majority of the Members present and voting.

(b) The Conference may make amendments in the programme of work and the corresponding regular budget and operational budget, in accordance with paragraph 6.

5. When required, supplementary or revised estimates for the regular budget or operational budget shall be prepared and approved in accordance with paragraphs 1 to 4 above and the financial regulations.

6. No resolution, decision, or amendment involving expenditure, which has not already been considered in accordance with paragraphs 2 and 3, shall be approved by the Conference unless it is accompanied by an estimate of expenditures prepared by the Director-General. No resolution, decision or amendment in respect of which expenditures are anticipated by the Director-General shall be approved by the Conference until the Programme and Budget Committee and subsequently the Board, meeting concurrently with the Conference, have had an opportunity to act in accordance with paragraphs 2 and 3. The Board shall submit its decisions to the Conference. The approval by the Conference of such resolutions, decisions and amendments shall require a two-thirds majority of all Members.

ARTICLE 15
ASSESSED CONTRIBUTIONS

1. Regular budget expenditures shall be borne by the Members, as apportioned in accordance with a scale of assessment established by the Conference by a two-thirds majority of the Members present and voting, upon the recommendation of the Board adopted by a two-thirds majority of the members present and voting, on the basis of a draft prepared by the Programme and Budget Committee.

(NOTE: THE COST SHALL BE VERY HIGH AS YOU ARE FORCED TO SURRENDER YOUR SOVEREIGNTY AND YOUR FIREARMS. HATONN.)

2. The scale of assessments shall be based to the extent possible on the scale most recently employed by the United Nations. No Member shall be assessed more than twenty-five percent of the regular budget of the Organization.

ARTICLE 16
VOLUNTARY CONTRIBUTIONS TO THE ORGANIZATION

Subject to the financial regulations of the Organization, the Director-General, on behalf of the Organization, may accept voluntary contributions to the Organization, including gifts, bequests and subventions, made to the Organization by governments, intergovernmental or non-governmental organizations or other non-governmental sources, provided that the conditions attached to such voluntary contributions are consistent with the objectives and policies of the Organization.

ARTICLE 17
INDUSTRIAL DEVELOPMENT FUND

In order to increase the resources of the Organization and to enhance its ability to meet promptly and flexibly the needs of the developing countries, the Organization shall have an Industrial Development Fund which shall be financed through the voluntary contributions *(H: This will simply strengthen the system for "world conquering".)* to the Organization provided for in Article 16, and other income as may be provided for in the financial regulations of the Organization. The Director-General shall administer the Industrial Development Fund in accordance with the general policy guidelines governing the operations of the Fund that are established by the Conference, or by the Board acting on behalf of the Conference, and in accordance with the financial regulations of the Organization.

CHAPTER V.---CO-OPERATION AND CO-ORDINATION

ARTICLE 18
RELATIONS WITH THE UNITED NATIONS

The Organization shall be brought into relationship with the United Nations as one of the specialized agencies referred to in Article 57 of the Charter of the United Nations. Any agreement concluded in accordance with Article 63 of the Charter shall require the approval of the Conference, by a two-thirds majority of the Members present and voting, upon the recommendation of the Board.

ARTICLE 19
RELATIONS WITH OTHER ORGANIZATIONS

(***NOTE***!:NOW ENDOWED WITH THE "RIGHT" TO OVERTHROW U.S. GOVERNMENT!. HATONN.)

1. The Director-General may, with the approval of the Board and subject to guidelines established by the Conference:

(a) Enter into agreements establishing appropriate relationships with other organizations of the United Nations system and with other intergovernmental and governmental organizations. *(H: Direct alteration of the U.S.A.)*

(b) Establish appropriate relations with non-governmental and other organizations the work of which is related to that of the Organization. When establishing such relations with national organizations the Director-General shall consult with the governments concerned.

2. Subject to such agreements and relations, the Director-General may establish working arrangements with such organizations.

CHAPTER VI.---LEGAL MATTERS

ARTICLE 20

SEAT

1. The seat of the Organization shall be Vienna. The Conference may change the seat by a two-thirds majority of all Members.

2. The Organization shall conclude a headquarters agreement with the Host Government.

ARTICLE 21

LEGAL CAPACITY, PRIVILEGES AND IMMUNITIES

1. The Organization shall enjoy in the territory of each of its Members such legal capacity and such privileges and immunities as are necessary for the exercise of its functions and for the fulfillment of its objectives. Representatives of Members and officials of the Organization shall enjoy such privileges and immunities as are necessary for the independent exercise of their functions in connections with the Organization.

2. The legal capacity, privileges and immunities referred to in paragraph 1 shall:

   (a)   In the territory of any Member that has acceded to the Convention on the Privileges and Immunities of the Specialized Agencies in respect of the Organization, be as defined in the standard clauses of that Convention as modified by an annex thereto approved by the Board;

   (b)   In the territory of any Member that has not acceded to the Convention on the Privileges and Immunities of the Specialized Agencies in respect of the Organization but has acceded to the Convention on the Privileges and Immunities of the United Nations, be as defined in the latter Convention, unless such State notifies the Depositary on depositing its instrument of ratification, acceptance, approval or accession that it will not apply this Convention to the Organization; the Convention on the Privileges and Immunities of the United Nations shall cease to apply to the Organization thirty days after such State has so notified the Depositary; *(H: In about 1980 the U.S.A acceded to the Specialized Agencies Convention, had done U.N. Convention on Privileges and Immunities in 1946, therefore, both have been done.)*

   (c)   Be as defined in other agreements entered into by the Organization.

ARTICLE 22

SETTLEMENT OF DISPUTES AND REQUESTS FOR ADVISORY OPINIONS

1. (a)   Any dispute among two or more members concerning the

141

interpretation or application of this Constitution, including its annexes, that is not settled by negotiation shall be referred to the Board unless the parties concerned agree on another mode of settlement. If the dispute is of particular concern to a member not represented on the board, that Member shall be entitled to be represented in accordance with rules to be adopted by the Board.

(b) If the dispute is not settled pursuant to paragraph 1(a) to the satisfaction of any party to the dispute, that party may refer the matter: either, (i) if the parties so agree:

(A) to the International Court of Justice; or *(NOTE: WORLD COURT IS COMPOSED OF COMMUNISTS AND OTHER SOCIETAL DIFFERENCES. YOUR FATE IN AMERICA, FOR INSTANCE, WILL BE WHOLLY DECIDED BY THIS GROUP.)*

(B) to an arbitral tribunal;
or, (ii) otherwise, to a conciliation commission.

The rule concerning the procedures and operation of the arbitral tribunal and of the conciliation commission are laid down in Annex III to this Constitution.

2. The Conference and the Board are separately empowered, subject to authorization for the General Assembly of the United Nations, to request the International Court of Justice to give an advisory opinion on any legal question arising within the scope of the Organization activities.

ARTICLE 23

AMENDMENTS

(NOTE: THIS IS A "BLANK CHECK" TO THOSE WHO ARE OVERTHROWING CONSTITUTIONAL GOVERNMENT!)

1. At any time after the second regular session of the Conference any Member may propose amendments to this Constitution. Texts of proposed amendments shall be promptly communicated by the Director-General to all Members and shall not be considered by the Conference until ninety days after the dispatch of such communication.

2. Except as specified in paragraph 3, an amendment shall come into force and be binding on all Members when:

(a) It is recommended by the Board to the Conference;
(b) It is approved by the Conference by a two-thirds majority of all Members; and
(c) Two-thirds of the Members have deposited instruments of ratification, acceptance or approval of the amendment with the Depositary.

3. An amendment relating to Article 6, 9,10, 13, 14, or 23 or to Annex II shall come into force and be binding on all Members when:

(a) It is recommended by the Board to the Conference by a two-thirds majority of all members of the Board;
(b) It is approved by the Conference by a two-thirds majority of all Members; and
(c) Three-fourths of the Members have deposited instruments of ratification, acceptance or approval of the amendment with the Depositary.

ARTICLE 24
SIGNATURE, RATIFICATION, ACCEPTANCE, APPROVAL
AND ACCESSION

1. <u>This Constitution</u> shall be open for signature by all <u>States</u> specified in <u>subparagraph (a) of Article 3</u>, until 7 October 1979 at the Federal Ministry for Foreign Affairs of the Republic of Austria and <u>subsequently</u> <u>at United Nations Headquarters in New York until the date this Con-</u> <u>stitution enters into force.</u>

2. <u>This Constitution shall be subject to ratification, acceptance or ap-</u> <u>proval by signatory States. Instruments of ratification, acceptance or ap-</u> <u>proval of such States shall be deposited with the Depositary.</u>

<u>(HATONN: NOTE, CHELAS, THIS HAS ALL BEEN DONE!!)</u>

3. After the entry into force of this Constitution in accordance with paragraph 1 of Article 25, States specified in subparagraph (a) of Article 3 that have not signed this Constitution, as well as States approved for membership pursuant to subparagraph (b) of that Article, may accede to this Constitution by depositing instruments of accession.

ARTICLE 25
ENTRY INTO FORCE

1. <u>This Constitution shall enter into force when at least eighty States</u> <u>that had deposited instruments of ratification, acceptance or approval no-</u> <u>tify the Depositary that they have agreed, after consultations among them-</u> <u>selves, that this Constitution shall enter into force.</u>

(NOTE: THIS, TOO, IS ALREADY DONE!)

2. This Constitution shall enter into force:

   (a) For States that participated in the notification referred to in paragraph 1, on the date of the entry into force of this Constitution;

   (b) For States that had deposited instruments of ratification, acceptance or approval before the entry into force of this Constitution but did not participate in the notification referred to in paragraph 1, on such later date on which they notify the Depositary that this Constitution shall enter into force for them;

   (c) For States that deposit instruments of ratification, acceptance, approval or accession subsequent to the entry into force of this Constitution on the date of such deposit.

ARTICLE 26
TRANSITIONAL ARRANGEMENTS

1. The Depositary shall convene the first session of the Conference, to be held within three months following the entry into force of this Constitution.

the United Nations General Assembly resolution 2152 (XXI) shall govern the Organization and its organs until such time as the latter may adopt new provisions.

(NOTE: THIS CONSTITUTION IS UNDER THE INFLUENCE AND CONTROL OF COMMUNIST DOMINATION.)

ARTICLE 27

RESERVATIONS

No reservations may be made in respect of this Constitution.

(H: NOTE THE UN'S "STATES" ARE CLAIMED TO BE ALL THE COUNTRIES OF THE WORLD--THUS A FEDERATED "NEW WORLD ORDER".)
   1. The Secretary-General of the United Nations shall be the Depositary of this Constitution.
   2. In addition to notifying the States concerned, the Depositary shall notify the Director-General of all matters affecting this Constitution.

ARTICLE 29

AUTHENTIC TEXTS

This Constitution shall be authentic in Arabic, Chinese, English, French, Russian and Spanish.

ANNEX I

LISTS OF STATES

   1. If a State that is not listed in any of the lists below becomes a Member, the Conference shall decide, after appropriate consultations, in which of those lists it is to be included.
   2. The Conference may at any time, after appropriate consultations, change the classification of a Member as listed below.
   3. Changes in the lists below that are made in accordance with paragraph 1 or 2 shall not be considered amendments within the meaning of Article 23.

LISTS

(NOTE: ALREADY DONE)

[The lists of States to be included by the Depositary in this Annex are the lists determined by the General Assembly of the United Nations for the purpose of paragraph 4 of section II of its resolution 2152 (XXI), as in effect on the date this Constitution enters into force.]

ANNEX II

THE REGULAR BUDGET

A.1. Administration, research and other regular expenses of the Organization shall be deemed to include:
  (a) Interregional and regional advisers;
  (b) Short-term advisory services provided by the staff of the Oranization;
  (c) Meetings, including technical meetings, provided for in the programme of work financed from the regular budget of the Organization;
  (d) Programme support costs arising from technical assistance projects, to the extent that these costs are not reimbused to the Organization by the source of financing of such projects.
  2. Concrete proposals conforming to the above provisions shall be implemented after consideration by the Programme and Budget Committee, adoption by the Board and approval by the Conference, in accordance with Article 14.
B. In order to improve the effectiveness of the Organization's programme of work in the field of industrial development, the regular budget shall also finance other activities heretofore financed out of Section 15 of the United Nations Regular Budget, in the amount of 6 percent of the total of the regular budget. These activities shall strengthen the Organization's contribution to the United Nations development system taking into account the importance of utilizing the United Nations Development Programme country programming process, which is subject to the consent of the countries concerned, as a frame of reference for these activities.

ANNEX III

RULES CONCERNING ARBITRAL TRIBUNALS AND CONCILIATION COMMISSIONS.

Unless otherwise agreed by all the Members parties to a dispute that has not been settled purusant to paragraph 1(a) of Article 22 and that has been referred to an arbitral tribunal pursuant to subparagraph 1(b)(i)(B) of Article 22 or to a conciliation commission pursuant to subparagraph 1(b)(ii), the following rules shall govern the procedures and operation of such tribunals and commissions:

1. Initiation

Within three months of the conclusion by the Board of its consideration of a dispute referred to it pursuant to paragraph 1(a) of Article 22 or, if it does not conclude its consideration within eighteen months of such referral, then within twenty-one months of such referral, all the parties to the dispute may notify the Director-General that they wish to refer the dispute to an arbitral tribunal or any such party may notify the Director-General that it wishes to refer the dispute to a conciliation commission. If the parties had agreed on another mode of settlement, then such notification may be made within three months of the conclusion of that special procedure.

2. *Establishment*

(a)   The parties to the dispute shall, by their unanimous decision, appoint, as appropriate, three arbitrators or three conciliators, and shall designate one of these as President of the tribunal or commission.

(b)   If within three months of the notification referred to in paragraph 1 above one or more members of the tribunal or commission have not been so appointed, the Secretary-General of the United Nations shall, at the request of any party, within three months of such request designate any members, including the President, then still required to be appointed.

(c)   If a vacancy arises on the tribunal or commission, it shall be filled within one month in accordance with paragraph (a) or therafter in accordance with paragraph (b).

3. *Procedures and Operation*

(a)   The tribunal or commission shall determine its own rules of procedure. All decisions on any question of procedure or substance may be reached by a majority of the members.

(b)   The members of the tribunal or commission shall receive remuneration as provided in the financial regulations of the Organization. The Director-General shall provide any necessary secretariat in consultation with the President of the tribunal or commission. All expenses of the tribunal or commission and its members, but not of the parties to the dispute, shall be borne by the Organization.

4. *Awards and Reports*

(a)   The arbitral tribunal shall conclude its proceedings by an award, which shall be binding on all the parties.

(b)   The conciliation commission shall conclude its proceedings by a report addressed to all the parties to the dispute, which shall contain recommendations to which these parties shall give serious consideration.

I HEREBY CERTIFY THAT THE FOREGOING TEXT IS A TRUE COPY OF THE CONSTITUTION OF THE UNITED NATIONS INDUSTRIAL DEVELOPMENT ORGANIZATION, ADOPTED AT VIENNA ON 8 APRIL 1979, THE ORIGINAL OF WHICH IS DEPOSITED WITH THE SECRETARY-GENERAL OF THE UNITED NATIONS.

For the Secretary-General: The Legal Counsel

(Signature)

* * * * * * *END* * * * * * *

So be it, chelas--may you be given into the strength and perseverance to undo this heinous act against you. I can do no more save bring it unto your attention. Salu.

I am Hatonn to move to stand-by. Good-day.

CHAPTER 17

REC #1   HATONN

MONDAY, DECEMBER 10, 1990   8:00 A.M.   YEAR 4 DAY 116

TODAY'S WATCH

Hatonn present in the Light of Radiance. First, I would have a personal notation please. Oberli, please attend Salliotte this day. Further, I would have a COMPLETE set of books for each of Dharma's children--along with any others that you so decide but this has gone too long unattended. You must realize that Salliotte is the best and most meticulous bookkeeper and office detail person you have or will ever find--allow us to begin to meet obligations for these are the ones who stuck with you through the very leanest of times and still do not wish to work with you for the burden it might impose. So be it. I cannot ask Dharma to give unto me her life to write these Journals if she continues to feel she may have them not when published. We must come to better balance regarding publication of the these books. There is something wrong with the "plan" if the author has no access to a few to be utilized as he or she deems appropriate. She is emotionally classifying herself as a mere printing machine and that is most unacceptable. She holds the whole of truth in her head awaiting the printing thereof and exploitation by any name is unacceptable. So be it.

WATCH YOUR PRESIDENT

Pay attention to what this man now does. He came back from a trip to South America, had a full day of jogging and tennis and yet could not join with his family and/or his nation at the Christmas festivities of the evening. This is always a sign of negative influence--the things that are representative of the Light are placed to the rear of the cooking places. He will begin to again give you the SHOW but watch closely how he handles the subject and how One World Order will have replaced "God".

What of Shevardnadze? He is making sure that he gets from America that which the Russians want at this time--in exchange for co-operation. He needs food supplies for his cities because of the poor management, black market and other things of poor government actions within the Soviet Union. Believe me, if it were not that POWER has its rewards, Mr. Gorbachev would be well out on his ear--you will note that his only roots this day are within the Communist Party--you ones had best take a good clear look at that situation! It is NOT as presented unto you.

Allow us now, to move on with our Journal lest we loose thought continuity. We must keep you alive and in some manner of freedom, but spiritual growth is ultimately the only experience of real and enduring merit. Lessons WILL be learned but you must begin to come into understanding of truth instead of the ridiculous lies given unto you from the mis-directors who long ago lost their own truth in repetition of the lessons handed down without ability to question whether or not truth was involved with the handed-down edicts of churches and false perpetrators--whether in ignorance or intent of destruction, the ending can be the same except in magnitude of "reward" for actions.

PLEIADES PERSPECTIVE

There is always a logical chain of command--not as you utilize it as "right of passage" but according to learning and true knowledge.

Wherever there are thinking forms of life, there are established laws everywhere. Each, from the position of spiritual development of the tribe's leaders, has taken laws from the true natural law and expressed them in responsible form within human-natural law. In consequence these laws are of natural logic, and are not illogical and primitive, such as ones established on your world. In your governments, pure worldly-material power casts the laws--usually to render you ones who must follow the laws helpless to stand against that which the rulers put forth.

In any given society at whatever level of understanding, laws exist. As I stated prior to this, it is only where the Creational laws become self-evident do expressed laws fall away. This only occurs at very high spiritual levels, in pure-spiritual spheres, where materiality is a thing of the past. Material forms of life are still afflicted by too many mistakes, than that they can simply neglect laws appropriate to their level of existence.

As a society, however, becomes advanced to the extent of foisting off their own behaviors upon other species and other planetary placements which bring evil and destruction upon the inhabitants, things are taken to a higher level of authority and Cosmic law comes into the picture.

Growth, in general, in the Pleiadian sense for the most part, is of a more spiritual level and consequently more humane, which certainly cannot, at this time, be stated regarding your form of law. You have almost no form of equality of justice.

When we speak of "heavy" crimes in the Pleiades system, for instance, there is no longer punishment by elimination and injury to the physical body, as is your barbarous habit--either that or a buy/sell justice system. The higher energy forms require that the fallible creatures be exiled to other worlds used exclusively for this purpose.

To such worlds are exiled only creatures of the same sex. In that way propagation is prevented and no descendants are produced. The exiled ones are left to their own means on these worlds and have to care for themselves with their own hands. No machinery or apparatus is left at their disposal, and they are forbidden to produce such things. To assure this objective these worlds are controlled and secretly produced means are eliminated for long periods of retraining time. In addition, any contact to any others is closed off--the inhabitants are locked into the planet system.

On some worlds, the fallible creatures are also exiled to great islands, if the grade of fallibility on the concerned world is very low. This manner of punishment assures security, and at the same time the fallible ones are no burden to the natural society. Moreover, this form of punishment is humane and suitable because the fallible ones are not obstructed in their development. Does it begin to bring memories of your own beginnings, perhaps? Could it be that you are a "prison" planet? Of course, for God always gives unto his creations a place to reform, restructure, recreate and "serve their time", so to speak. Teachers and guides, wardens and guards are always sent to guide and effort at rehabilitation--then there is a graduation and if rehabilitation into truth and rightness of action is accomplished, the "inmates" move on and the negative unlearned ones are placed into other suitable accommodations until they DO learn Universal behavior. Most of Earth real criminals never see the inside of a prison for the real criminals of humanity are the ones who set up the false teachings and the heinous laws which create injustice, force and degradation unto the soul.

In very ancient times different fallible creatures were exiled from different worlds in this Universe to your Earth, as well as from our race also. We do not keep "dates" and "calendars" as do you so let us consider it was "a long time ago". Since in our Plieades star system, there is interplanetary travel and interchange, the laws are very similar on all inhabited orbs and will do for general purposes of discussion at this time.

Our races are monogamous, after a thorough clearing up of facts in respect to belonging together. Mistakes, of course, can not be excluded for the life-forms are not very far advanced of your own races, but these, if necessary, are still later eliminated. Descendants are regulated by the highest council, meaning that a definite amount of births within a defined amount of time and space is observed, so as to preserve the race without overpopulating. It is totally controlled by responsible "ACTIONS" and not "control" by artificial means, devices nor destruction of "accidents"--there simply are no "accidents" through total dedication of self-responsible actions.

Married couples remain in that alliance during their life-experience cycle. When you have careful pre-union understanding and friendship, then you have no problem with irresponsible behavior for a marriage represents friendships within the boundaries of Law of balance and harmony and total responsibility to the planet upon which all must reside. Since the physical greed, power and social needs of the procreation act are evolved out of the picture, procreation is with intent and great planning in responsibility. Since Pleiadians live to be hundreds and hundreds of years of age, it requires this same discipline over a period of many centuries.

Pleiadians do have one of the highest forms of human civilizations for the needs of the balanced planet are strictly adhered unto and ones who refuse the responsibility are given homes in places such as Earth. When ones who have broken lesser obligations are placed, it is often that the "prison" if you will, becomes inappropriate for their deviation of behavior--or rehabilitation is fulfilled, and then "graduation" day arrives and/or the planet becomes so unbalanced that the darker forms of experience are placed elsewhere--as with your planet.

There will be evolution into higher dimensional values and density and fully developed ones will transverse with her. The totally negative lifeforms will be separated away and placed in suitable "classrooms". The guides and wardens will have served their time of duty and will be allowed to further experience according to growth levels--or simply return to God-Source. Many of you will desire returning to Pleiades to experience awhile in that goodly environment; many will wish to move with Earth into Radiance of Shan and many of you will wish to return, or remain, with the healing planet to nurture and re-create a habitable placement.

I specifically used the term "monogamous" because we do not use without responsibility, the sexual act and, therefore, there is no need of multiple partners. Persons in need of care and life-nurturing assistance are cared for properly and not in any way USED for the personal experience of lust, greed and/or sexual misbehavior. Marriage and creation are most highly esteemed and most carefully regarded in all respects. This is why we denounce the "behavior" of deviant groups--not the love and energy exchange of people. A friend can be as or more dear than a spouse but there is no physical sexual actions intruded into the relationship. Children ARE NOT ACCIDENTS! FROM IRRESPONSIBLE BEHAVIOR--NOR ARE THE BASE DISEASES STEMMING FROM THESE UNIONS.

Divorce as you know it is insufficient and admitted in only the worst cases, such as when one of the union is exiled. This is most rare indeed. Our laws have worked in harmonious balance for millenniums.

WHAT OF LOVE FOR ANOTHER, SAY OF ANOTHER WORLD?

So what of such a love? Do you mean as perhaps I might LOVE Dharma? I, representing masculine and she representing feminine? What of it--we, especially one of higher dimension even than another planetary system, have no need for such expressions! Love as you express of it is not even entered into the picture of higher dimension. Love is all inclusive and I love Oberli even as much as I love Ranos, Ilsie, Daylene and/or Dharma. Further, ask any one of these ones--once touched by the Love of higher understanding, there is naught of Earth experience to match the experience. Love is an emotional experience--untouched by

151

any human physical beingness--you simply have forgotten.

What you usually refer to as Love is a simple infatuation for another--expressed in a totally physical manner--missing the wondrous beauty of the emotional fulfillment for you place pleasure in the place of emotional fulfillment. When you merge two souls--that, dear friends, is LOVE! One can merge with every body in the system and you will find yourself only worn out and disease ridden--not fulfilled, at peace nor content--you will only have formed a bad habit and will search for even one more with which to tamper. Ah yes, Earth mankind has forgotten the difference in LOVE and love. There is no LOVE to be expressed in any manner as I feel for you of my children in journey--I, at thousands of years of age in your counting and you, as babes and toddlers. But you must understand that many of you have walked with me through the eons of time and have only FORGOTTEN! This is why you are pulled to me as a magnet to the iron filings--for we are of the same essence and THAT, dear ones, IS THE TRUTH OF ETERNAL LOVE IN ITS WHOLENESS--I WOULD GIVE ALL THAT I AM AND HAVE UNTO YOU, FOR YOU AND WITH YOU--AND NOW, SOME RETURN THAT GIFT UNTO ME AND UNITED WE CANNOT FAIL TO ACHIEVE OUR GOAL--FOR THAT KIND OF LOVE IS THE TRUTH OF THAT WHICH IS GOD! Man is the creature who is envious of any relationship which he perceives excludes self--and therefore, it is a singularly excluding of self. When man loses his self-orientation then, and only then, can he enter into such a relationship as God-LOVE, for all is in behalf of the OTHER. However, in fact, the LOVE OF THAT KIND OF NATURE only returns to self, the fullness of the relationship for neither is TAKING from the other--BOTH ARE GIVING ALL THAT CAN BE GIVEN--EACH MORE THAN HIS WHOLE.

Each and all have the ability by mind power to pull unto self any desired "thing". So, I suggest you be most careful regarding that which you desire--for you may be unfortunate enough to pull it unto self. It is when you rise above self of the physical that you find truth and all knowledge and then, only then, is peace and tranquility achieved. It can only come through the "giving" and proper "accepting" and "exchanging" of emotional equality and not physical experience, that truth of life meaning is understood. THIS IS YOUR BIRTHRIGHT: FREE-WILL THROUGH CHOICE AND THE RETURN UNTO THE ONENESS WITH GOD! ALL OTHER IS SIMPLY "THE JOURNEY" THROUGH THE LESSONS UNTIL TRUTH IN GOD-NESS IS ACHIEVED.

Wherein the physical only visualized that which is physical--higher essence sees only that which is spiritual. I see you ones as the soul essence which you are and the physical falls away. I can see beyond the ego of the physical experience and understand the impact of the human physicalness--but it is the soul I see as I look within your places--so you are actually quite safe from prying eyes in the bath. My communion is with soul--not the physical. I understand the physical impacts of living--but those are for YOU to have conquest; they are not of my business--except as they impact that which is within my jurisdiction or group of committed workers within my Command. Then, neither do I have control--only in request for separation until direction is isolated and decisions are made for I, nor my brothers, have any intent to ever intrude other than to speak warnings and give guidelines for participants in this mission.

NO REFLECTION OF GODLESSNESS

Ones who have intent for participation in the transition with communion with higher brothers of the Cosmos or, and more especially, in relationship to higher energies of other dimensions--agree to abide by God's laws and The Creation's laws in that example is total as regards "actions". There will be the lusting and greeding as long as there is physical--how the human "acts" in the given scenario is that which is ultimately important.

Do not go about saying we "kick you out" or "isolate you" if you are acting in behavioral ways deviant from Cosmic law, for YOU will have made that choice--not we! YOU may change your actions at any time but you cannot "fool" us! We see only soul intent! Past errors? So be it; in God's realms past ignorance is all points of the law--it is important when it is "deliberate actions in defiance to those laws". If you do not approve of those laws, it is your choice, but I promise you--you who continue in Satan's trappings will not find your next journey through the gates into Godness for learning of the laws and abiding therein is the price of that lovely transition. For instance, the Pleiadians want no irresponsible, misbehaving humans cluttering their life of balance. There will be no "sleeping around" to introduce envy, self-gain and/or base human behaviors accepted. You had all better rethink the "RAPTURE SCENARIO". If you are ill-using physical-ness, you aren't going to "rapture" to anywhere physical that I recognize as "higher" dimension--and most certainly not unto God! NO EVIL INTENT SHALL ENTER INTO THE HOUSE OF GOD!

Now, when you speak of inter-planetary beings of human format, much changes in perception. Ones of higher learning often make changes into what would be considered "lower" vibrations and often join with the "lower" frequency being in what you might loosely refer to as a "love" relationship--but it is not handled as a physical matter at that level even if it entails physical actions. This means that the "lower" being will grow rapidly or there will be a lot of pain borne by both for the "higher" being will be unable to compromise soul truth--it happens frequently.

Sometimes ones, say from Pleiades, come for rotations of duty upon your placement and then there is subjection to your own environment with the consequent loss of memory data and often these ones are lost to the environment and activities of Earth plane. Often good "receivers" of higher energy forms are lost to the Earth environment and ego state as surrounds the dense capsule of your planet. It is indeed hard to keep those conduits open and as such, many are only opened in these recently current times to

153

allow for purity of communication. They simply were not opened at the earlier time in order to serve in proper sequence. Each fragment serves at its given proper sequence of experience--the students then must discern the changes for it is part and whole of the learning requirements. YOU EACH MUST LEARN THE LESSONS PRIOR TO TRANSITION AND THE OLD MUST BE CAST ASIDE. FOR INSTANCE--YOU MUST RELEASE THE LIE THAT ANY ONE BEING COULD ABSOLVE *YOU OF YOUR SINS AND ERRORS*. NO ONE CAN DO ANY SUCH THING FOR ANOTHER! *YOU WILL STAND RESPONSIBLE AND ANSWERABLE FOR YOUR ACTIONS IN THE PHYSICAL EXPERIENCE--NO MORE AND NO LESS--YOU!!*

OTHER PLANETS IN YOUR SOLAR SYSTEM

We, serving in the Pleiades Command for instance, are only allowed to speak of certain things and explain only so much. These neighboring planets have been priorly occupied in former times by our races, and are by minimal measure still today important as bases and other extraterrestrial homing centers for starship attachment--usually of higher dimensional "rating".

I, for instance, effort to carry somewhat current information regarding your solar system in my mind in respect to the level of my experience at the current time; however, I do not have interest in other than your evolution and my command at the present experience. I simply have no interest at this time, in the other systems. You ones are not destined to be placed on these other planets when evolved from this Earth plane and, therefore, I spend little time inputting other data that can be garnered from other teachers if the interest and curiosity abounds--I am interested in changing your truth and knowledge and getting you into safety and security--prepared and ready for transposition. My thrust, and the thrust of Sananda "Jesus", Korton, etc., is to bring as many as possible into awakening and full decision in Godness to move into other responsibility--ours is not a sojourn to philosophy and speculations of how it may be next door. If your only intent is on such trivia--go unto another for your lessons for ours is far advanced of trivia not applicable directly to your transition.

We are come to awaken ones to their purpose, bring truth and prepare for the reclaiming of the Kingdom unto God. I am not, for instance, concerned with that which might be going on on Venus or Mars except as Earth bases thereon might impact you as World citizens--specifically within my Command. Truth is truth is truth--but in addition, ones of my Command must HEAR THE CALL TO PURPOSE!

Dharma, write this document immediately--did you not note the energy wave that struck this dwelling? It is fine, chela, your attention is removed but we will lose the document if you do not attend it. Thank you.

We have you very well shielded now and it is very difficult to get through the web to vulnerable attack spots--we can deflect quite efficiently now with little damage sustained--however, there is continual barrage against the computers and electronics systems and any electric interruption can wipe out the programs and data storage systems. Simply take care.

I suggest you ones who come into writings by ones who claim physical behaviors with extraterrestrial beings--be most careful indeed--for the inter-change would be exaggerated according to the perceptions of the ego of the writer. No celestial being would ever even be tempted to pull an Earthian from his path by such dalliance for the discipline would be great on his own level and especially at this time of sequence; an extraterrestrial of higher understanding such as would be a teacher or speaker--would simply never participate in such behavior--check with former contactees such as Billy Meier for confirmation. Semjase is a most beauteous creature in Earth perceptions and I believe she gave Billy quite a good and grand, unmistakable lesson regarding such matters as Earth-type behavior and LOVE. Misbehavior of higher brotherhood from other star-systems would be met with severe discipline and would be totally unacceptable.

Further, for "Space-beings" to respond to personal, egotistical demands to become "visible" to "prove" something or another is equally unacceptable. Regardless of who believes otherwise, it is most often totally destructive behavior to become visible--especially on such cause and demand. Most ones are quite honest and relate that "I" need to see or touch--but many will place it as "we" and "for our good" and "so we can better serve", etc. No, it is always for "me", "I" and "self"--if not, it will be left to the discernment of the higher being for the better good of the whole--without exception.

Does this mean that each will not desire "for me" "for I" for "self"? Of course not and the desire will be always at the forefront--however, the acceptance of "higher truth" will always prevail and the thought will always return to "for the highest Cause" and "not my ego will, but thine higher truth" shall always prevail if given in truth of higher Cause. The ego will always seek satisfaction and the quicker the better--"instant Patience" and "undelayed gratification of whatever is the point of attention". Remember the obligation of the higher resources unto you at this time and bear with their limitations as given forth unto them--THEY ARE TO ACT WITH TOTAL DISCERNMENT WITHIN HIGHER KNOWLEDGE AND THEY MAY NOT PLAY YOUR GAMES ON DEMAND. IF THEY FALL INTO THE TRAP OF RESPONDING FROM EARTH "DESIRE" STANDPOINT--THEY WILL BE RELIEVED AND RETURNED HOME.

I would clarify another point however, in some instances--and you ones will know of the one or two circumstances of which I speak--a joint intent will have been established through two energy forms and then the separation will be caused whereby there is one in one plane of experience and the other in another--FOR THE PURPOSE OF INTER-ACTION AND TASK PERFECTION AT THE PROPER TIME OF TERRES-

TRIAL/EXTRATERRESTRIAL JOINT ACTION. I believe that one, Gabriel, shall recognize of that which I speak. The loyalty and communications have never been severed and there is no misunderstanding of intent. The purpose always becomes quite obscure with the one left on Earth sphere for the density reduces ability to retain memory patterns. It is true trust and ego allowance to maintain that wondrous communion through such dimensional changes. Many of us walk together but in separation become unable to recall--it is now the reawakening unto those connections in a most unphysical manner--the higher energy will never allow reverting unto the human behavior patterns. The human involved may have very vivid memory visions of such interchange--but that is exactly that which it will be--recall visions--dreams. It depends totally on intent of purpose within the missions as to whether or not there will be actual physical visualization. I do not mean to complicate the subject; it is just that the contacts are so misperceived and humans are so easily deceived and duped by ones claiming this and that status.

Always you can discern in truth according to the laws of God and The Creation--truth will always move you in soul unto the Lighted God; evil will pull you away from the God-ness: no more and no less. If there is anything in the projections of so-called energy voices or projections, that diverts physically or in intent from the God-truth, get away from the energy for it is not of God. The laws are most succinct without maybes or sometimes--the laws are always! Therefore, it becomes indeed easy to discern he who gives false teachings and that which does not. It does indicate, however, that you must know the Laws and I remind you that EVERY ENERGY BIRTHED UPON YOUR PLACE--CARRIES THAT PARTICULAR KNOWLEDGE WITHIN. It does help to brush up on them into your consciousness.

Allow us to close this segment as it grows long and we cannot cover the entire of the subject matter herein so allow us a break. Thank you.

Hatonn to stand-by, please. Good-day.

CHAPTER 18

REC #1   HATONN

TUESDAY, DECEMBER 11, 1990   8:00 A.M.   YEAR 4 DAY 117

TODAY'S WATCH

Greetings in the Light of Radiance. Hatonn present that we might continue on our Journal. As we watch this day I would ask that you carefully consider that which is coming forth from the different areas of the world in regards to that which you have labeled AIDS. Also, pay attention to the new implant which is utilized on the female of your species to prevent pregnancy. Is there no end to which you will not go to substitute for responsible behavior? So be it. Do you not see that--if left to your own devices as moving between subtle birth control and AIDS--you, yourselves, will wipe out your species? If something is not done soon, the whole of the Brazilian population will be devastated just as is Africa. Now, instead of teaching your young generations to use control and responsible behavior--you will sterilize a whole generation of women before you are finished and all in the name of safe-sex. "Like lambs to the slaughter!" Each "thing" will come forth as planned, upon your nations, so that you eagerly bring down the shackles upon selves--demanding it, in fact.

For my group of "touchy" friends--since the incident two Saturdays past-- last evening was simply the shuttle coming home to roost -- from Australia. How much will you accept, people of the lie? So be it.

Allow us to continue with our Journal for it seems time is of utmost importance in which to bring you into truth and alignment with God. AHO!

PLEIADIAN CONTACTS

Speaking in behalf of Pleiadians I shall simply utilize first person in order to achieve brevity--I shall speak of positions of higher dimension at a later portion. You must now become familiar with that which IS as regards placements as you move from this orb--I speak in generalities unto some 6 1/2 billion persons of separate fragmentation so, please, you must also generalize my lessons for we have not time to speak to each in formal format. You may go within, inquire and receive answer--but I find few who "listen" so this will suffice. You can confirm this truth from ancient teachers such as Little Crow, other contacts such as Billy Meier (in his early contact days), etc. First, it would seem appropriate to outlay that which happens as we make contact with ones of your races on your planet.

I hear and see the ones who stand forth and denounce the receivers as stationed about your place, saying, "Why not me, I have been willing to make contact for years--why not me?" Because usually those ones have only personal interest and/or it is not yet time in the sequence for utilization and transference of information in that particular sector. It is a true worker who is willing and patient to await that which is his purpose--in support of those who are in service presently. One job in proper sequence is of no greater importance than is another--only different and given differing times of projection.

Herein, I caution Dee that that which she is projecting regarding receiving from the Command be tempered with great wisdom. Do not misunderstand that which you receive and perceive to be from Korton. You have opened a can of worms to divide and fragment workers.

If ones wish to sit to pen for self and/or contact higher self or the energies of higher consciousness--fine; to contact and receive for one in our Command or functioning at this time in this specific operation only confuses and hampers our work. You all must first understand the communications and it is evident that you do NOT.

Perhaps for some it is fine to sit with pen and dally upon the paper--however, mostly, all that will be received is tampering energy forms. This mission is far too important to allow such trivial pursuit of fun and games. For instance, to fragment my communications at this time is absolutely unthinkable for man is confused enough without fragmenting further in misperceptions.

I shall not elaborate on that which is happening to other scribes but I assure you that we do not deal in simple higher thought forms. I give forth exactly that which I wish stated--in pulsed beam format and simply "allowing" the flow is not sufficient from a scribe. Everything that touches the scribe's personal space is an impact upon that which is written and thus the training is hard and LONG in order to bypass that seeking input for personal instructions. If we have need of personal data exchange, we handle it in proper format, in separation of duties. We are not in the business of teaching everyone to "channel" or "write", etc. In this location, specifically, we have too many willing teachers and confusion can be the only outcome as the information is spread about. If each of you will do your job and cease trying to be the scribe or receiver--we shall have a wondrous working relationship; if we simply have another group of gathered channels--we defeat purpose from foundation upward. I ask you to simply check out that which you do and see if we can discipline selves into conformation.

We of the command, as we move along here, will be making less and less contact with various ones and we surely do not wish the general masses to "try their hand and mind at this `game'". You need a source of unquestionable TRUTH and ones coming into the writings must know it. We,

158

too, must have focus and "non-generalized" input and output--you have too many "Bibles" as it is.

Let me explain our contacts and why fragmented diversification is unacceptable. It is out of the question and not possible to have random contacts as we approach the time of focused function. Each must contact the truth within but I again caution you of my tribe, do not try to teach all to receive for you are giving erroneous information for this purpose-- reaching within is fine, but I ask that you leave the lessons of "channeling" and "scribing" unto the higher Command. This is not to pain anyone but I remind you of the human format--when you ask a higher energy for input--he is required to respond if asked in truth--YOU MUST USE THE DISCERNMENT OF PROPER USE OF THE MATE- RIAL--AND YOU MUST BE VERY, VERY SURE YOU KNOW OF THAT WHICH YOU DO! There are not more than five receivers trained for this job so I ask that if you are one, you care for that responsibility greatly. I know that which is meant--the general masses do not! There- fore, it is YOU who must be in the use of great and perfect judgment. I, Hatonn, do not relinquish this Command to any--NOT TO ANY!

If contact is opened with an Earth human, then this is based on his prior pre-conditioning, often lasting decades on your placement alone--even if he is not in knowledge of that which is coming forth. This includes guid- ance in tremendous variety of concerns.

We will only open contact with an Earth human when necessary spiritual conditions are perfected and when sequence of events are proper--this is not something discerned from human vantage point and humans do not have awareness of that which is required to disallow pre-conceived human ego projections into the equation.

We can only open contact with an Earth human if his development has proceeded so far that he is able to work out and recognize basic truths by himself, alone, without the help of fellow creatures or books or literature being resorted to. This does not mean these items will not be utilized for confirmation and focus--it means that they may have no impact of con- sciousness. A contact scribe is one who pens or writes exactly that which is projected as nearly to perfection as language translation allows. Does the receiver act in robotic fashion? Yes! When the space is in clearance it is a physical circuitry which comes into operation and opinions and re- flections must be put aside until such time as the conscious ego can again ponder a given subject. This scribe, for instance, regardless of how it ap- pears to you ones in presence, is specifically from this place to fulfill this particular function upon your place. What is experienced in ego format requires great attention but that becomes moot for she is in complete justi- fication with our intent and purpose--having been sent for this specific mission. Of course human impacts are great but not to the extent which might seem to present themselves. If confronted, there will be no devia- tion in behalf of Earth choices but in many ways she becomes as the child and then it is most important that significant others within her functioning space keep absolute intent uppermost without swaying as to focus. It

159

makes Oberli, for instance, need to be abrupt, strong and unbending and ones working in this area must come to know as much and be not offended if he seems harsh and/or rigid. He will not even realize WHY he is unbending and/or without human allowances which are his usual attitudes regarding human actions--it is required for when receiving and scribing, Dharma has no ability in human format to respond or react in clarity.

If we initiate contact with an Earth human without these premises being fulfilled, then such a contact is a preliminary undertaking for special purpose, and usually after achievement of the objective the MEMORY IS ELIMINATED, as for example happens continually with Dharma herself--she spends the majority of her time with us, as do you other ones in this particular mission--and you do not remember as much in your consciousness. This is for your security and the security of the mission--it is with total free-will and agreement. If you cannot seem to understand the requirements and cannot maintain this discipline, then others are placed within the "slots" of function. There are too many impacts of Earth experience on ego consciousness, in some instances, to allow total participation. This is not negative, this is simply the way it IS. Further, if this be the case, it is often of only temporary nature and the one in point is never offended nor slighted--for only the ego consciousness would be slighted--and therein, lies the answer each would seek. If ego consciousness is embarrassed or offended--check most closely, for this mission is one of purity and selflessness. You may have all the opinions you desire but if they differ from your ascribed and accepted mission--you will use the discipline to keep them to yourself except as discussion among your immediate family of brethren.

The human entities are set by contracted agreement and will be specifically suited for a given objective, such as ones who are given to "find" or "discover" specific artifacts or information, etc. We often expect too much of ones, in our own perception, for we have a tremendous task to perform and ones simply are lost to the physical format or are pulled temporarily from the intent by Earth impact or other human entities. We are patient as perceived time allows but sequence moves forward and this cannot always be accomplished. We must work within our own limitations as Cosmic brothers finding necessity to function within your own similar "time" frame of experience.

If we open contact with an Earth human, then we undergo this in accordance with higher authorization, and with the person specifically designated for this--as with Aton, the Christed Energy, etc. At planetary transitions there is always the total direction from the higher Source--we act only as the preliminary Hosts under total and complete Command of higher Lighted Resources. One very obvious reason is that too many humans in the first position may upset everything by even the slightest misperception input data and human opinion. It is simply as you put it nicely in the kitchen: "Too many cooks spoil the stew".

We are not allowed to make ourselves visible to more Earth beings than

160

corresponds with our objectives. This precaution concerns private and military and official desires aimed at taking possession of one of our ships and other such objects of our contacts. Then, as always, discretion is not for the Earth contact to decide nor should he even be informed. You ones want all the "secrets" beforehand without thought of consequences to self or the mission. We are expected to have higher intelligence as to that which is proper and that which is human curiosity. You will note that if we had followed that which you ones desired and required in the beginning of our contacts--you would all be blown away by this point in time! Ponder it before you ask your next "proof" of "purchase". Because of this, we only cultivate contact with Earth humans known to us, sent by us for a given purpose and proven totally trustworthy in all respects. Sometimes this is simply an agreement that nothing of meaningful content will be left within the consciousness to outlay. There must be total confidence in the security of the objectives in every respect from business instructions to strategy. We bring you knowledge to get you through the transition and to share as we give guidelines--not for you to toy with, gain great riches or disperse at random--we give specifically and exactly as for our special mission with you and your group and further instructions will always be given--usually privately within intended receiving minds.

Testing is intense--ones are expected to perform to the utmost ability of perfection regardless of the task involved--in the upstart it will hardly ever be a task which the human desires and will always require great humility and self-disassociation. If ego-self cannot be set aside, the contact must be forfeited for the intent is still of Earthly physical need and the contact will not be further contemplated.

With the selected human contact in focus, we initiate communication in most unexpected and secret ways. This is why simply to sit with pen in hand is foolish indeed unless you simply try to contact higher intent of self. Our requirements will be so difficult, disciplined and scrambled that ones of ego-orientation will be totally discouraged. Most early contacts will fit into this category and will usually place meetings, writings, scribing, etc., down the list of priority when confronted with human decision, especially physical choices regarding other ego-fragments. Surprisingly enough, transition of a species and planet, as well as oneness with God, is usually taking second seat to the lover or perceived physical gain or relationship, especially as involves sexual involvements and/or acquisition of material "things". Sometimes these things are to be first considered--but it is important to see if that priority services God or YOU.

You ones who work with us would blossom at our presence--but most of the ones on your place would panic and be totally terrified, not to even consider the offensive measures that would be undertaken by your military and government. If you think Saudi Arabia looks like an armada to end all armadas--forget the concept--at this point the entire world WOULD unite against us and that is exactly the point being projected by your world leaders.

Sometimes we allow bits of evidence unto the few--and very often it turns into negative response so we must be most cautious and in spite of that which you of our beloved workers desire, we must use higher and better founded intelligence regarding actions. For instance, we fully intend to participate in the filming of the first projected pictures--however, if at the time security is breached or attention is undue--we will not! Does that mean we are less real? If it means that to you involved, I suggest you had better look again at your opinions. If you are prepared in any event--what difference does it make? So be it.

With Earth human--"some" is never "enough". If we parked a craft in your door-yard, you would not believe it is we unless we pour out all over your property and jeopardize the very crew you demand to see and touch. No, we must use good judgment to the perfection of ability--and we do have a great deal of ability in that measure. Hatonn has been known to err--Aton has not.

ALL KNOWLEDGE AND TRUTH ALREADY PRESENT

It is important to consider still another matter of which I shall often be in the reminding. All truth and knowledge has remained preserved upon your place as brought forth or transmitted right up to this present epoch, though it may be totally forgotten, somewhat forgotten, disregarded and/or lost by the Earth human. As truth, knowledge, wisdom, and love, and all power of the spirit are unchangeable and constant, and the same in the present, this all must be conceived there and continue upward into man's higher understanding. In other words, truth, knowledge, wisdom, love and so forth, must simply be brought together again--remembered and integrated.

What you call, by an old (for you) language, the backward relating "religion", should for this case, and which has to be done, by the same old language, be called "rel-e-geon". The definition of the word as broken into meaning indicates that "all has to be brought together again", which is to be considered rel--e--geously, but not religiously. In consequence, the already existing materials should be newly assembled, to lead into the future. After the "relegeon" must begin the way of evolution, which has a two-fold meaning. You know one meaning of evolution as development and unfolding in the sense of something already existing, but still concealed, that must develop, which in a spiritual sense means, must "rise from the sub-conscious towards the conscious".

The second meaning of this term has been lost to you for a long period of time, namely that something not yet existing is explored, developed, and unfolded, and "becomes". Because this meaning of evolution was lost, man lives under a false impression that evolving material already exists to be unfolded and developed. However, it is that the indwelling spirit has stored those matters and things which it collected in the course of its material existence in material bodies and lives. This, according to your understanding, is a very large bunch, but in truth is very little in comparison

162

to all that IS.

During innumerable further experiences, the spirit must explore further, must search and must find; thus he must assemble further knowledge, recognitions and experiences which then establish themselves in him as faculties. Because the spirit continues after the material death of the body and exists within spheres of living of the "other world", it works upon the achieved results of the other experiences, and fixes these results inside it in what you call the "sub-conscious". Upon taking up the human form of life, the obtained knowledge and faculty is anchored in the sub-conscious, and must evolve slowly in the human form of life to help in new lessons and recognitions toward developing conscious talents--the God consciousness or "higher supra-conscious" is a compilation of all of soul experience.

Allow us to close this segment for I wish to discuss prior contacts, their purpose and dispersion of information. It is as usually occurs when higher energy forms touch one another for purpose of presenting truth and spiritual knowledge--the human becomes entangled with that which is exciting, human and greedy in intent. The truth of the higher purpose becomes misplaced in the contact with the unexpected and exploitation swings into full action. The subject and purpose of the contacts become lost in the reality of the physical presentation. In other words, the Pleiadians become the point and not the purpose of their presence. Once man has been distracted and the slightest projection of falseness of intent enters the picture--the contact is usually lost to God's intended fullness of purpose for controversy becomes the issue--not God's message. So be it.

I will move to stand-by. Hatonn to clear, please.

CHAPTER 19

REC #1   HATONN

WEDNESDAY, DECEMBER 12, 1990   7:20 A.M.   YEAR 4 DAY 118

TODAY'S WATCH

As we watch the events unfolding, allow the balance of beauty to be seen in the wondrous creation of your Mother. Hatonn present to walk with you, chelas, that you not feel alone. The Master Teacher is always present and holds us close that we not fall by the way or succumb to the hardness of the journey. Go forth and do of the small things so that your hearts can remember the joy--go forth and feed of the tiny creatures who plead for seeds and crusts upon thine branches for your return shall be great within your breast. As we grow so pressed for time, allow us to remember the little ones, such as Rodney Nelson and pray that he finds better sight for his soul is so pure as the lamb's. Let us ever live in gratitude unto Creator for these ones who give that we might learn truth of life for too often we perceive not that which IS the lesson to be learned. So be it. Thy Creator knows of the fall of each of his creatures unto the smallest sparrow of the fields and has counted their feathers that the patterns of their tribes be perfect--would he do lesser for ye of his greatest Creation? Let us return into his Lighted passages of truth that we might walk again with the Great Spirit of our passage! Salu.

As we look about this day, so much is hidden--but so much is evident. I cannot be in the pointing out of each fragment of change. You must be in the alertness as to that which is coming down--i.e. the change of IBM's massive information center to Europe is a good one to note--this removes a major central employer unto other nations whilst your unemployment in America has climbed to levels unheard of. You do not know the half of your unemployment problems. You do not see nor understand that you are a nation feeding and surviving off welfare aid--what happens with the depletion of the welfare funds and unemployment funds?

President Bush, in his frenetic quest of the "New World Order" placed another nail solidly in the coffin of America's sovereignty by his advancement of the free trade pact with Mexico in his past week's journey into Mexico and sortie south to South America. Oh yes, for a while, even the business enterprises in which our own ones will participate will benefit from better work and smaller prices for goods, etc. Precious ones, it is geared to *LOOK GOOD* but it is built upon the foundation of sand and cannot stand the pressure of a world in bankruptcy.

Shamir of Israel moves about your country and gains that which you have no notion nor idea. The smiles are great as over and over again Bush assures him that Israel will be protected at all costs. There will be no UN councils on the Middle East and/or regarding Palestine so the bloodshed can continue without notation of the world.

How many of you are aware that Bush has secretly given Israel service to the long-standing demand for a sophisticated Cray supercomputer? We have written on this months past but it now hits some isolated news resources. The sole purpose of Israel having the Cray is to perfect and test the hydrogen bomb! The Jason Committee has pulled it off and the remainder of the Cray equipment not already in place will be immediately transferred to the Weizmann Institute--one of Israel's leading centers of nuclear weapons research. The Jason Committee is the secret White House panel of leading scientists who brief the President on high-tech defense issues.

Israel already has a huge stockpile of nuclear weapons--what might this mean to your world? Israel already goes without discipline from any source on your Earth, for that which they do against those nations surrounding them. They even stated openly and blatantly that had the Six-day War continued even one more day they would use nuclear bombs. Do you not hear or see?

While all this goes on, I would suggest that you take opportunity to watch the backdrop of pictures in Israel/Palestine--Mr. Sharon is openly building huge apartment/condominium complexes on the West Bank for new Israeli arrivals.

You should further note, dear Americans, that thousands more of your reserves and active military personnel are on their way away from America--this very day! You now are totally defenseless on your own home ground--your nation is stripped of any defense what-so-ever in the form of manpower. This is also true of NATO bases in Europe--naked and open for invasion. Do you rest well at night in your sleepy-time dreams?

Do you not hear that which is projected unto you? Ones come forth and say Saddam cannot stand against the armada of tanks and men in Saudi Arabia. Oh yes he can--he has it well planned and we have laid the plans out in detail for you. When Iraqi leaders state that they will reduce the Middle East to ashes--that is exactly what they mean! All the while that you watch not--Israel continues to build and build and build death weapons at tremendous rates. Do you actually believe that at some point here you won't have eruption of tempers? Do you think the Bear to the North is in mesmerization of goodness? Are you perhaps "fiddling" while your nations burn, so to speak? All you actually did was invade Saudi Arabia and now you have her under complete control--Iraq has little to do with the military assault upon the Middle East, dear sleepy-heads. So be it.

Let us return to your connections with Pleiades for it is equally important that you come into truth about your relationship with those particular cosmic brothers--for they hold your ticket off your planet. HOWEVER, only those who act in truth and within the Cosmic Laws shall be wel-

165

comed aboard for placement in the balanced places of their kingdoms. You ones of Earth had best be understanding the truth of this changing time, and your alternatives.

PHYSICAL ASPECTS OF THE SILVER CLOUDS

We are continually questioned regarding the physical aspects of craft. Frankly, we plan to outlay all of that information--for your comfort--in the upcoming picture presentation, SIPAPU ODYSSEY. It is reaching the time where you ones are given visual understanding of that which has been prepared for you as was promised. There is such distance between your cosmic brother's progress and that of yours in even small detail-- even unto the matter of the "glass" installed for viewing and light within our craft. The glass itself is made of metal--impervious and unbreakable.

Further, the screens are coated with material which gives instant identification to outside atmospheric components and makeup of the atmosphere itself. For instance, the outer side is coated, and colors itself according to the atmosphere outside the craft by color spectrum changes. The outside of the "window" will appear to be one color, for instance--orange--and inside they are a yellow-green.

Within an atmosphere suited for us, and you, the material is the color orange and casts the yellow-green light inside the craft and registers instantly on instrumentation to infinite spectrum deviations.

When the outside color becomes for example, green, blue, red or yellow, then the light inside changes instantly as well. Without further analysis, the crew is informed whether or not there is need for protective dress and other special needs for travel or visitation outside the craft. This is what we refer to as a "fail-safe" measuring instrumentation and in this manner of determining the atmosphere it is impossible to err in judging needs for the life-forms involved.

Everything regarding contact with the outside atmosphere is controlled through automatic indicators. For instance, the automatics give complete outlay of necessary caution and dress, then, and only then, after completion of necessary sequence--again determined by scanners (i.e. unless a crew-member is properly dressed in protective gear--the automatic exit and intake systems will remain locked). Assuming that the scanners approve then the conduit systems open and only then, after the locking of the conduit doors, do the outside hatches open or unlock. The costume itself has sensors woven within the fabric of the gear in order to disallow error.

If ones wish to disembark in unsuitable atmosphere, then this is only possible with the use of the protective dress suitable for the atmosphere in point along with breathing apparatus, heat-shielding, cold-shielding, etc.

As the craft reaches the stratosphere of a given "world", where the atmosphere vanishes, then the outside of the onboard screens, "windows", becomes totally transparent and differs visually hardly from your own clear glass windows.

The screens also automatically shield out all radiations resulting in no danger from this source of hazard unto the crew.

For purposes of observations, we have our control mechanisms, which allow us much better observation than looking out through the onboard windows, because the pictures will likely be unclear, especially during the time the screens may be colored by atmospheric conditions. We have very sophisticated dimensional view scanners constantly projecting on surround-screens--any portion of which can be broken down into microscopic visibility.

ABOARD CRAFT

We are continually amused by the pictures projected by your so-called space vehicles with your crews all floating around like bobbing corks. Much of that show, you must understand, is for your visual benefit to mislead you and those particular pictures are taken, usually, within the vacuum training systems. Our craft are pressurized, etc., to allow for same stability anywhere we are, just as would be present in our home environment. I fear many, many tricks are played on your senses to delude you to truth of even that which is available on your placement.

For our beloved Wally Gentleman, who will produce, etc., our motion picture, we have given great detail regarding the outlay of a typical Mother Ship which houses people for long periods of time as in a city. We have well-prepared fully self-contained living facilities which have gardens, fields, parks, living quarters, food preparation centers, etc. All needs are provided for from survival needs to schools and thus and so. Perhaps I can herein request that if that document written by pen for Wally can be located in copy, we can interject it within these pages for interest of the readers.

CONTACTS AND INFORMATION

The contacts are meticulously trained and groomed and the information monitored constantly and accurately. We respond to personal queries and exchange much personal conversation but we are most careful to not allow misperceptions to go forth in documented format for our thrust is for accuracy and truth--while maintaining security, privacy and respect.

This requires special training and a long working relationship with a receiver so that our intent can be relayed as nearly in meaning as your language translation allows.

All personal and other matters of inquiry, if utilized, are so stated for much knowledge is learned through the questions of your brothers and insight into the training sessions. As the receivers grow in knowledge it is often that their own questions become a better gauge of the level of input of information for which the masses are ready to receive. For instance, Dharma holds all this knowledge, for anything passing through her data system is contained. However, she is not allowed access to that information except as you are basically receiving it. If she is better informed, it is because she has been exposed to thousands of hours of audio and written input--in other words, even if she chooses to not read the documents after the writing; she still has the data stored. We do not allow her access to any information which would represent "fortune-telling" information dangerous to her security and/or anything prior to occurrence in physical projection as regards governmental or military substance--this, obviously, is for security. She bears no information and, therefore, there is no point in trying to get it from her--this is well understood by technicians in your government and military placements. She is simply a scribe of that which we give.

This does not mean that she does not have the overall picture nor fails to see that which will be. Some of you call it prophecy--it is simply "knowledge". Once you understand the mechanism of your passage and experience you all will come to understand that which is projected herein regarding "prophesy". She can in no way be considered either a prophet or a psychic. She receives directly and, therefore, you MAY consider the author of the speeches, i.e. me, a prophet if you choose.

There are safety measures built into our system of communications whereby, should she be utilized as hostage or blackmail against me or our brotherhood--our scanners would automatically be shut down in that I could not give forth security information at any rate. This becomes an obvious necessity. Now, there is other that you all should now be made aware. In these latter days of the cycle of transition, God WILL bring forth truth upon your place--period! It is known by all energies involved in the confrontation and therefore, there are ones, places and things which are a no-no with which to tamper and offenders are not handled with great generosity nor gentleness. It has been a while in reaching such "understanding" but we draw ever closer to perfection in the shielding.

Ours is a Creator-sourced mission and it shall be completed in that total Light. Therefore, we are allowed to protect our counterparts upon your orb and we do not allow ones who work with us in full intent of personal gain, greed or falseness to continue interchange with us. We are extremely disciplined and require total discipline from our ground troops--if personal matters cannot be put aside during our work, then they are relieved of duty until such time as the space is again clear and separate. Our efforts are to never offend if possible but the ego is the first item in forfeit if one chooses to work with us.

If we err in presentation, we shall be first to state such for we function in near human format and we are, of necessity, working with human apparatus and translators--and you, dear ones, have no language of perfect understanding.

We expect recognition of any mistakes which might be projected in error from a scribe or speaker and the errors removed from documentation. It is not a pleasant task for us to constantly trouble ourselves in this respect but truth is our purpose and little errors grow into mountains of confusion.

To our scribes, once we give an "order" or an explanation, then that should be quite sufficient. We are patient during the learning but if individual ego continues to enter into the writings and/or opinions are interjected--the individual is given other tasks or they make their own decision to remove self to other locations and actions outside our teams. As I say, we are most patient--for appropriate time for change and balance; then we are abrupt and decisive for there is not yet time, in perception, for us to continue endlessly with individuals who do not have control of self. There is only one purpose acceptable--God truth. We allow no false and foolish piety to dupe us so the lying lips do not work--we work only from intent of soul-level understanding--not human input. In this group, for instance, we have now reached a point whereby things will not be discussed and rediscussed--facts will be laid forth and homework will be performed and the writings studied diligently by our own groups or they shall simply be finding themselves set to the side. It is a time of pulling off the Earth foolishness of self-orientation.

This repetition and nurse-maiding is extremely time-consuming, illogical and superfluous. We write for 6 1/2 billion separate entities--you readers must glean your portion and stop dawdling about awaiting your private nurse-maid to show up with your digested food. God-truth unto a troubled planet is our purpose--not chewing your food. Social groupings is not in our intent and all children should outgrow the need for emotional crutches for you are in a most critical time of serious change and your social calendar is of not of importance what-so-ever. Will you weep at that which you did not get done for your fellow-man while you socialized at the holiday party? Balance is important--but you might well consider a bit of unbalance in favor of your committed task lest we not get our task finished. What can you do when you have time left from that which you perceive is your active task? Read and study so that you are a professor at the information. Be the source for truth when a brother inquires--and you, dear hearts, in my own ground troops have not even 10% of the information available to your knowledge. How can you expect the world to resolve these heinous problems if you ones do not even attain the information given unto you---how can you expect more from the masses?

By no means do we effort to exercise dictatorial measures or to force our will or our knowledge onto Earth beings. We force no one to do anything. If you do not care for Hatonn--then you are most welcome to go elsewhere. I thrust nothing on anyone--I do require discipline and attention if your commitment is to work with me and I am a hard task-master--would you desire less?

We are here and have undertaken the mission of awakening human unto his plight and give information unto him to allow "remembering" his truth and stature. We come to transmit lessons of truth and give as much service in other ways as will be accepted. Those who wish to accept and acknowledge, utilize and glean worthy and positive opportunity from our farther sight are indeed welcome--humbly welcome. This is done, however, by your own decision and he who refuses our input is most welcome to refuse. We are in service only unto God and Creation--human makes his own choices, be they negative or positive. God promised to send unto the world the WORD of TRUTH and so it shall be given--before the final transition--here it is, coming forth as quickly as we can put it to print. We care not if you deny of it--it is your journey and none of our business save that we are your brothers and ignorance is indeed costly to physical beings--THE SOUL WILL CONTINUE AT ANY RATE--IF YOU DO NOT PRECIPITATE HEINOUS DEATH OF THE PHYSICAL WHICH ALSO IRREVERSIBLY DAMAGES THE VERY SOUL ESSENCE STRUCTURE.

DEFINITE PRINCIPLES REQUIRED

Acknowledging ones must be aware that quite definite principles are necessary to preserve order, thus special objectives and orders must be observed, as well as not omitting certain assistance expected of them.

Man takes it upon himself to edit our material in order to cause less negative responses from, let us say, secular doctrines of churches, etc. We have nothing but God-truth to offer unto your consideration. Earth churches have altered truth and in these closing times God brings and sends again--THE TRUTH--unto you. This is why we accept no alteration or editing of this material.

You ones wish to delete our observations regarding your religions, governments and military intents and controls placed upon you as a species. TRUTH WILL GET YOU GRADUATED INTO HIGHER DIMENSION AND PLACEMENT--NOT LIES NOR OMITTED GAPS IN INFORMATION. If you believe not that which is brought forth, first I suggest you objectively look around at your world and clearly see the problems--then decide for yourself that which you believe. It would be nice of you, however, to allow your brother to come into his own opinion for one day--you who denounce this word and pull your brother from his truth opportunity through your pronouncement of great self-know-it-all--shall surely be pained and in turn denounced. GOD IS INFINITE BUT HE WILL ALLOW UNTO YOUR VERY DESTRUCTION FOR IT IS HIS GIFT UNTO YOU AS A SPECIES--FREE-WILL CHOICE AND "REASON" CAPABILITY.

There are thousands upon thousands of documents, including your Holy Books, which will give you tampered and edited information to soothe, terrify, control and appease--YOU SHALL NOT GET IT HEREIN. GOD IS GOD IS GOD, TRUTH IS TRUTH IS TRUTH--NOT ONE IOTA OF IT SHALL BE CHANGED BY MAN DESIRING IT TO BE OTHERWISE OR CHANGING OF THE WORDS OR PROJECTED TRUTH NOR BY MAJORITY VOTING-IN A "THING". IF YOU WISH TO ONLY SEE AND HEAR THAT WHICH HAS PULLED YOU DOWN--THEN I CERTAINLY SUGGEST YOU READ AND REREAD THE <u>OTHER</u> PUBLICATIONS--FOR YOU WILL FIND ONLY TRUTH WITHIN THESE JOURNALS--WHETHER OR NOT IT IS THAT WHICH YOU DESIRE TO HEAR! SO BE IT.

Some valid contacts have been lost to credibility for this very reason. Earth-persons involved chose to edit, tamper, lie and create models of material and craft and thus truth in wholeness was lost. Unfortunately for the receiver and contact--it rests not with their responsibility as to that which transpires with the material after the presentation. But to a valid and trained contact and/or scribe, to have this perpetrated upon his truth and work is destructive indeed for his life purpose is destroyed and turned into the perpetuation of the lies already abounding. I could name a dozen lost to the work because of the lies and greed of those surrounding them-- it shall not be allowed in this instance--you of mankind upon Earth have no more time for the lies. So be it and selah.

Dharma, allow closure of this segment as the computer has again had tampering. We shall have to consider re-programming or placing more sophisticated monitoring equipment within the apparatus. If you allow constant tending and frequent manual writing of the document we can ease through for a while but you will need be attentive to the signals to call errors to your attention. Thank you. At any rate, this is sufficient in length for this sitting. Good-morning.

There is much work taking place with the location and I suggest that you and Oberli leave for a while this day. You can not long function with the increased noise and discomfort from the signals. Use wisdom, chela, it is better to take breaks away from the location and even into the noise-filled city than to become incapacitated from the constant barrage against you. You are now receiving in a audio range of extremely high frequency and anything of lower pitch or intended ELF pulses are debilitating indeed. We shall simply have to be continually at monitoring and I ask that you observe my requests regarding time away. We, are, at any rate, producing material more quickly than most are assimilating the information. But man shall simply have to become more responsible for we are going to increase the output--GOD IS PATIENT BUT YOUR WOULD-BE WORLD CONTROLLERS ARE NOT! INDEED, MUCH HAS PASSED THE STAGE OF REPAIRING. SO BE IT.

Hatonn to clear, please. Saalome'

CHAPTER 20

REC #1   HATONN

THURSDAY, DECEMBER 13, 1990   8:32 A.M.   YEAR 4 DAY 119

TODAY'S WATCH

Come and let us tarry together on the day of gifted "time". Let us note carefully that which you, Dharma, would put aside. Precious ones, the Earthquake in Sicily is of utmost importance!! Dear ones, this is proving-up the action of Mt. Etna recently. This quake shows current and constant actions building and tremendous activity in the underground fissure system. If this does not quiet, you can expect massive eruptions within the volcanic chain--that, dear ones, will include Vesuvius. Is there a possible connection to the quake in Taiwan this day? Of course--everything is connected to everything and if massive movement happens in one portion of your crust so shall it impact all. 'Tis only the "extent" of activity in point!

You are reaching the point of transition wherein you must look unto these very things for your clues for your leaders are swamped in deception--YOU must return to the basic perceptions in order to allow for "timing".

There ARE NO ACCIDENTS! EVERY COINCIDENCE IS FULL INTENT SO DO NOT MISS OF THE ATTENTION. I WILL SHARE AS CONFIRMATIONS TRICKLE THROUGH TO WRITING SOURCE BUT YOU READERS MUST TAKE HINTS AND AS WE SHARE WITH YOU--PLEASE SHARE WITH US FOR IT IS MOST IMPORTANT THAT WE HAVE A SCATTERING OF INFORMATION FROM ALL POINTS OF THE DIRECTIONS--*IN HUMAN INPUT!*

TO T.D. IN PHOENIX

Thank you, for here in point is exactly that which I indicate above. T.D. has sent much information to this source regarding the most major subjec of late. Rather than give you rundown of contents I shall simply ask printing of the cover letter.

"I feel William Guy Carr's book, "Pawns in the Game" (Emissary Books) is one of the most poignant accounts of the past world wide subversion by Zionism, its thinking and protocols, its revolutionary tactics, its savage barbarism designed to shock the masses and make them docile (emolations in South Africa now), the Satanic betrayals of their own Agenturs, its controlling role in virtually all world revolutions, civil wars (ours) and world wars, its recurring and very effective blueprint to destroy societies, their sabotage and subterfuge of supplies and communications to defeat armies on the battlefield (Napoleon), and their bent on global wars to create eventual stalemates and redistribution of power negotiations all at the expense of the people, their creation of issues, opposing beliefs and subsequent strife and war (we are but pawns), and the world plan to execute most all of us and subjugate the remainder in the most inhuman manner. So also does the author describe the recurring expulsions of these people by national governments. This Illuminist threat to the Colonies (and the World) was the central theme of Pres. George Washington's Farewell Address, also enclosed (from Des Griffin's "Fourth Reich of the Rich", Emissary Books, another excellent book). The Middle East politics and build-up appears to be the use of this same blueprint. Please refer to Hatonn for his use. T.D."

I must say, first of all, that I most certainly leave it to G.G., as publisher of the Journals, and D.G., that which they will carry for your convenience. Please accept the fact, readers, that it is indeed expensive for these ones to obtain a supply of books to which I continually refer; therefore, I leave the books of confirmation to the decision of the reader and the distributor. I do have comment: please utilize the material for that which it is--confirmation from a very basic and fundamental level for the myriad topics we cover in the Journals. You who are avid readers will obtain it anyway--the masses do not read anything--so, if you already are in contentment of the truth of that which we bring to you, I suggest you study the Journals for you need not confirmation. When there is outstanding material available, however, I will continue to give the information. Along the same lines of confirmation and in-depth study of the Khazar Zionist is <u>THE THIRTEENTH TRIBE</u>, by Arthur Koestler, just brought recently to our attention and again, I give thanks to one J. Meeker for sharing the document with my scribe--she does not outgrow the need for confirmation, either--just as any awakening being of human needs the confirmation .

It is most difficult to be the target of abuse and death attempts and the human needs confirmation from its peers. As confirmations of our truth pours forth in these days it becomes easier to give unto you ones more extensive uncovering of facts which are kept from you. If the only point is to bring further and greater attack against my people, I am hampered also, as to that which I can freely open unto you.

Along this same subject line--I thank Dr. L.F. for her contributions of input data--some of which was published years ago but had remained in her library. My appreciation is indeed great and we shall tend of the material carefully so that it can be returned at any time upon request.

It is more than the sharing of information in printed format--it is the closeness of brotherhood that reflects within the scribe and my other workers regarding these Journals and Expresses. It seems a lonely journey indeed, for mostly the abundance of impact is from those who would literally kill these of our brothers to keep you from having information and bring discredit upon the cosmic brotherhood. I humbly thank you ones who seek out confirmation to share. To you readers, we are not simply a publishing company, distributor and/or scribing "place". We are the very foundation from whence truth is given forth--each reader is as/or more important than the scribe herself. It is intended that you "hear your call", if it be so, for you will come into understanding as the sequence unfolds the pathway.

Please allow me the outlaying of another example of follow-up; in a most humorous vein, not directed to me, but reaching me through Dean at any rate. I shall allow the penman to remain anonymous as intended but I especially request that GG make absolutely SURE that our beloved brothers who are in constant touch from Australia and New Zealand receive this writing of today.

You who live in the human form in different parts of this world and feel alone and "missing of your purpose", I plead patience and continuing study of information--for your turn is coming for great service and the way will be made clear in properness. We would never outlay a person's purpose for all the world to see--and allow of the targeting of God's own servants. I like to call it "working patience"--for you have accepted responsibility and you are only in the opening act of the play for the final great show--so please, do be awaiting without turning away as we give unto you in open and public format that which helps to stay the path.

QUOTE: *(AND I AM GRATEFUL TO THE AUTHOR OF THIS LETTER)*

29-Nov-90

Dear Dean,

First of all...I wish to "thank-you" for your unselfish dedication to the Global Sciences Congress(es). They are truly a breath of fresh air in our troubled world. At this point I am going to stay anonymous because I don't know who is reading your mail `first'...? In the process of gathering this information several people have experienced a change in their vibrational patterns...some were voluntary...others were not. (That's "space talk"...I've been reading the JOURNALS.) At the Feb. '90 Orlando Congress George Green made the comment that there was serious construction going on in Australia. Now you'll have to admit that at times it can be a puzzler to separate `fact from fiction'. So I put out some `feelers' about construction `down under'. Wouldn't you know it...I have news that some of the mysteries of life are indeed awesome...and to be feared because of their ultimate function.

The PHOENIX PROJECT is located 426 miles East of Port Hedland and 130 miles South of the Northern Coast. The purchase of this Australian land by "Private Money" encompasses a radius of

250 miles and is being "hotly contested" in the Australian Courts. But you and I know that this will do no good since the "legal thugs" will drag it out until the final chapter is `burned long before it is ever written'. In the meantime construction is moving along at a fever pitch with the aid of 25,000(thousand) Koreans, 12,000(thousand) Indians, 7,000(thousand) Japanese, 2.7(thousand) Americans and 200 Aussies. It's the *best paying job* any of these workers have ever had. There is next to no talking. Everyone keeps their head down and their mind on the job at hand...no questions are asked. They are just there to collect a paycheck. No cameras are allowed...it is an immediate 5-year prison sentence if you are caught with your `brownie' out. This beautiful mountain range is literally in the middle of nowhere. A few Aborigines visit the mouth of the valley for 2-3 months out of the year. Other than that there is only the bush and venomous snakes.

There is a pristine river and an airstrip where **TWA COMMER-CIAL FREIGHT CARRIERS bring in everything**. The planes can taxi into the *hollowed out mountain which is guarded by super-massive blast proof steel doors.* Once out of the planes you walk another 200 yards inside the mountain to reach the start of the living quarters. Home, Home On the Range which entails 10,000 living "units"...some of which are 1,3,5 and 8 bedroom units. The "units" are 3/4 finished...the solid rock is cut out with laser-water cutters in 4' X 4' blocks...which are hauled out with little `crawlers'...to the edge where they're simply pushed over. Big nails are shot into the rock through visqueen...and then gunite is sprayed on and then everything is covered with tile. It looks great! There are already 50 families living in the bottom units...they have their own school for the kids, a swimming pool and tennis courts. There are massive food storage facilities and all of the steel doors are controlled by voice prints and finger prints...SIMULTANEOUSLY!

Everything is powered by solar...which had to be put in sometime in 1989 before the heavy construction started Jan '90. The Photovoltaics are the `tracking type' which sit topside and measure 3/4 by 1/2 a mile and feed a battery room which measures 285 by 160 feet and the battery racks therein stand 12 feet high. The Americans work 60 days straight and then have 60 days off to go home...with full pay. The others work a year straight and then take 5 months off. The airstrip will be taken out around Jan-Feb `92 and then everything will be chopper shuttled in to finish by Nov. '92. (*Hatonn: I cannot allow you to pass this most urgent and important CLUE!!!!*) With tongue in cheek I'd have to call this the 13th Wonder Of The World. No one...and I repeat NO ONE invests this kind of money if they don't intend...no...make that *PLAN TO USE IT*.

Here's an interesting (if you believe in them?) "coincidence" for you...The Photovoltaics have to come from either **AMOCO**

175

(Solarex or Amoco brand) or Kyocera (Japanese I think?). **AMOCO** appears to be the common denominator; so could this `down under' project be collaboration between The GREY MEN and "nasty aliens"? *(HATONN: NO, GREY MEN AND NASTY HUMANS!)* Now that's opposition with a capital "O"...! Is this what we're up against...the ultimate BIG BUCKS and BIG BRAINS all going for the BIG BANG!? Dean-O...I don't feel so good...

As I understand it...our "Brothers of the Light" cannot intervene unless the fireworks go above 150 miles. Hey, it's the first 150 that's the killer. We're coming up on the short end of this dirty stick. Alert the public! How? The **PHOENIX JOURNALS** are great, but 30% of The American population are functional illiterates. These good folks hold down jobs and raise families but have been shorted in the reading and writing department. Don't they count? Do only the `literate' get the word? Of the remaining 70% that can read...only 20% actually do which means that 14% of the American public is hitting the print. And only a fraction of those know about the **PHOENIX JOURNALS**. There's a reason newspapers are going broke. And besides...how in the heck are we going to get enough people to read 20+ **JOURNALS** plus the **NEWSLETTERS**? I haven't figured that one out. But I do know how the American Public thinks...and that means that if it doesn't happen on T.V. then it never happened and it isn't true. There's a reason `why' manufacturers are willing to pay `millions' per minute to advertise during the Super Bowl. Well...sorry, but that's the American Mentality...such as it is. Now if we want to reach these people...turn them around and turn them on...then we need a little `half-time show coast-to-coast' without interruption! I'm a volunteer willing to contribute my puny 2% to the Brotherhood's Brain Trust. For some reason I get the feeling like we're colonies of `ants' with bad manners. I also think it would be wise if we got some `fresh prints and tapes' of various craft. Billy Meier's work has been beat to a frazzle and we need a new approach. Don't worry, my camera saved your `bacon' once before. If needed, maybe I'll have the whole story and some `pics' for you in January...?

Stay safe...

P.S.
I would like the powers that be to consider a `nice and effective' gesture to The Super Bowl Fans...or for that matter to everyone in T.V. Land..."Why not give everyone a souvenir which when looking at themselves, their neighbors and friends will constantly remind them of their ultimate responsibilities in life and with which whenever opening their mouths they will have to speak and spread the truth? Why not change their mercury amalgam fillings to gold?" A little gift of love...a rememberence...

END QUOTING, PLEASE

I acknowledge, I hear and I respond:

Dear "Anonymous", You have just given your brothers quite a bit more than your "puny 2%", brother.

First, I shall respond to an interruption in the Super Bowl. Good idea-- just as soon as it can be done without blowing up your entire world! Many things are afoot and the first thing that man must come into, is some understanding, without fear, that he is USED! This requires a building of knowledge that that which we bring unto you is TRUTH. The cover-ups are massive and continue even as we speak. I shall now refer to further private correspondence from your document, directed to Dean-- but I consider it extremely important.

QUOTE:

"You're going to "love" Dr. Arthur Robinson, Oregon Institute of Science and Medicine P.O. Box 1279 Cave Junction, OR. 97523." (Hatonn: I include this herein because we have already given forth this resource to your readers--he wrote <u>FIGHTING CHANCE TEN FEET TO SURVIVAL</u>. We greatly honored him and Gary North in <u>SURVIVAL IS ONLY TEN FEET FROM HELL</u>. You may also obtain the book from America West if you do not yet have a copy.) "He's really down to earth and his message is BLAST SHELTER SURVIVAL for ALL Americans! The cost...$150 per person and another $100 for a year's supply of food. The Swiss were so well dug in that Hitler didn't dare invade. The Chinese have put more man hours and materials in their 200,000 miles of underground tunnels (30 ft. down), hospitals, cities and stores...than their Great Wall. They have the largest system...the Russians have the most "hardened" or blast proof. I might also mention that the Swiss have the most "elaborate". We Americans have "ZIP"...we are set-up by our politicians to take a serious fall in favor of one world government. Bomb shelters were the "rage" in the '60's...so why have the public libraries been cleaned out of all reference material on the matter? Check it out! Arthur must be stepping on some toes because his 5 kids were taken sick for a week and then his biochemist wife suddenly became ill and died under mysterious circumstances within 24 hours. (1988)" (*Hatonn: And Dharma has been literally given death by cardiac arrest, four times within this past three-year period; not to even mention the laser attacks and the staged event of two weeks ago. I mention these simply because there have been numerous witnesses involved in the incidents--there have been countless attacks never brought to attention, which we have diverted. WE GIVE GREAT HONOR UNTO ARTHUR ROBINSON--HUMAN-ITY WILL OWE THEIR VERY EXISTENCE TO ONES SUCH AS DR. ROBINSON--I WONDER HOW MANY WILL EVER REALIZE AS MUCH?*)

END QUOTE

PUBLIC INFORMATION

I must respond to the subject of "HOW DO YOU GET THE PUBLIC AWARE AND READING?" Probably we don't to great extent--but if a few who can afford to make change by input of funding, we can! Our full intent--on the drawing board--all architecture and leadership in place, is to build a communications center in this location which shall service the globe. But, it costs some $240 million to do the project. Ones are already working on scripting for the pictures and we are giving forth technology, etc., for the finest holographic filming you can imagine. However, the publisher, writer and developer of our projects for this transition, are exhausted both financially and physically. Ones who can, must help by taking up the banner and moving a bit further. Remember, also, dear ones, that there is constant, unyielding attempts by laser pulses, ELF barrage and all manner of business blockage to prevent our bringing this truth unto you ones. We were doing pretty well until we came against the wall of deceivers set forth from your Government in the form of terror tactics laid forth by those who would claim defection from the Government, CIA, etc., i.e., pictures of 9 ft. aliens, etc. That, dear ones, is directed at the Pleiades brotherhood because man just doesn't continue to bite on "Little Gray Aliens"--although, we shall now speak of this data because I am continually barraged by inquiries.

I would like to ask "Anonymous" to keep his camera `brownie' handy because I can promise you that physical outlay of observation will likely NOT be in the area of my scribe--YET. I would no more further jeopardize these one's lives than provide a great rapture for Satan. I ask that pictures and contacts be shared with these ones for they too, are lonely for the touch of seeming reality--but, I shall guard them most carefully in the interim--until man comes into some recognition of truth.

As man comes into truth, he will automatically begin to request shielding from the barrage of programming beams directed against him by your governments. These shielding systems are perfected "WITHIN" and further, if you want them reinforced, we must be ASKED! It is hard for ones who don't believe we exist except to destroy and suck your blood, to ASK! *IT IS THROUGH CONFIRMATION OF OUR TRUTH THAT MAN WILL BEGIN TO HEAR AND SEE FOR HE HAS SLEPT TOO LONG AND BEEN TARGETED MOST EFFECTIVELY. HOWEVER, AGAINST GOD, THERE IS NO ABILITY TO STAND IN DARKNESS- -THEREFORE, YOU OF GOD STILL HOLD THE TRUMP CARDS! IT ULTIMATELY REQUIRES, HOWEVER, A CASTING ASIDE OF THE LIES REGARDING BEHAVIOR AS WELL AS GOVERNMENT, ETC., AND A CONCERTED EFFORT TO RETURN INTO THE LAWS OF GOD AND THE CREATION--IT IS THE PRICE OF THE TICKET, SO TO SPEAK. WE NEED NONE OF YOUR BASE BE-*

HAVIORS AND NONE SHALL BE ALLOWED. WE ARE NOT SENT AS THE HOSTS TO "SAVE" YOUR ASSETS--WE ARE COME TO "SHOW YOU THE WAY" AND "YOU WILL DO IT". SIMPLY "KNOWING TRUTH" IS THE STARTING POINT OF THE REVOLV-ING AGAIN INTO TRUTH IN ACTIONS.

NINE-FOOT ALIENS!/ROBOTICS

You do have "Little Gray Alien" REPLICAS on your planet. You now also have very tall REPLICAS on your planet. There are exact likenesses of myself on your planet--having been replicated from basic RNA/DNA cellular duplication. NOW, HOWEVER, FOR THAT WHICH YOU MAY BE QUITE UNPREPARED: *YOU ALSO ARE GOVERNED BY AND RULED BY A ROBOTOID ARMY! EVERY FUNCTIONING PERSON OF IMPORTANCE TO THE EVOLVEMENT INTO ONE WORLD ORDER IS A REPLICA. I SHALL UNFOLD THIS TECH-NOLOGY LATER FOR I KNOW THAT YOUR PEOPLE ARE NOT READY FOR SUCH. YOU HAVE BEEN SUBJECTED TO THIS TECHNOLOGY FOR WELL OVER TWO DECADES AND NOW YOU ARE REAPING THE FINAL CLOSING OF THE TRAP UPON HU-MANITY.*

I am not, herein, going to outlay who is who and what is what--watch, and you will be able to discern. Is Bill Cooper with his 9 foot alien pic-ture real or false? Would he know if he were not? Likely not!

The "Big Boys" are getting ready to SHOW YOU a whole bunch of very "Earthly" space ships and little and tall aliens. They are going to even bomb some of your cities to bring you into terror of our presence--for they know that with our presence--GOES THEIR DOMINANCE! Through causing the mass of mankind to fear God's hosts, you bring fur-ther confusion and destruction upon selves. YOU HAVE ONLY GOD-NESS COMING FROM THE COSMOS IN THE FORM OF COSMIC BROTHERHOOD--DO YOU ACTUALLY THINK THE ONE WORLD RULERS WILL ALLOW THAT KIND OF NEWS???

To make my point, of all the Journals of Truth in your oppression and lack of truth--HOW MANY OF YOU HAVE A TICKET OR RENTAL AGREEMENT FOR ONE OF THOSE APARTMENTS IN AUS-TRALIA?? I THOUGHT NOT! THOSE ARE VERY EXCLUSIVE LIVING FACILITIES, DEAR ONES, PLANNED FOR THE VERY ELITE AND NOT ALL OF THEM. A GREAT NUMBER OF ELITE WILL BE GREATLY SURPRISED AS THEY MAKE FAST ASCENT--RIGHT AFTER THE BOMB GOES OFF! THERE IS NO HONOR WITH SATAN, DEAR HEARTS, AND YOU HAD BETTER BEGIN TO RECOGNIZE HIS HANDMEN AND MAIDENS!

179

Do not concern yourself with refusal of Billy Meier through his spokes-men--actually, they speak not for Meier--I suggest you all begin to pay attention to the status of one, Billy Meier, and be prepared for painful recognition. He has been placed into helpless incarceration by those claiming to be his own protectors.

Dharma, STOP! Note that which the computer is doing! Now you can know another "subject" which triggers the computer to destroy the docu-ments--and, hopefully, you as well. I will write further--simply stop and begin a new document, please.

CHAPTER 21

REC #2   HATONN

FRIDAY, DECEMBER 14, 1990   3:31 P.M.   YEAR 4 DAY 120

YOU BE THE JUDGE!

I come forth in service unto God, unto the Creation and unto you--my brothers in higher Universal human form.

A book has just been published by UFO Archives and Genesis III Publishing Co. by Stevens--Elders--Welch.   This book is supposedly published documentation, Vol 2, of the Billy Meier notes from Pleiades. My preference is simply not to respond to inquiries for I have absolutely no interest in further cover-up, conjured-up and literally made-up, material. I am saddened for Billy Meier who was a valid contact and who does not in any way sanction use of his material. This volume is published in spite of his request to be left alone and not publish any further information in the United States.

"Well, Hatonn," you will ask, "How can we know what is truth and that which is not?" Easy!! I will give you clues to look at and then you be in your deciding.

First, let me say that the material is in great part factual. However, I will herein tell you at onset of the discussion that Pleiades Command does not inter-work with ones who utilize material for personal gain on the market which would ever deceive the public in any manner what-so-ever.

Many things went "wrong" with the original contacts with Billy Meier and Billy stated that he had stopped the contacts. He later said that he was informed Semjase has been killed--these are not so and there is absolutely nothing wrong with Commander Semjase except that she is completely overworked. There reached a refusal to participate with ones who entered into contact (from Earth) with Billy Meier and who now utilize his material, fabricate more and give incorrect information.

There will be found a portion in this volume in which supposedly Semjase gave information "FOR THE EYES OF WENDELLE, LEE, BRIT AND TOM ONLY". This entire outlay of information is totally fabricated. The information deals with the massacre of the Jim Jones cult group.

I have given you detail by detail description of that which happened in Jonestown. This will be listed as a contact with cosmic brothers prior to the Jonestown happening. I merely state the fact that this is false information, fabricated by these ones to mislead you the public and make gain in material manner from you innocent, trusting public. I suggest that the entire section called Contact 115, "PROPHECIES", are total nonsense and foisted upon you the unsuspecting for reasons of deceit. The ones who have brought this particular set of documents forward do so without permission and with full intent to deceive. This is an affront and deliberate assault on the credibility of one Billy Meier, who had forfeited his connection to higher source prior to this supposed transmission and, more importantly, becomes a deceiving discredit to one of my most respected and revered Commanders.

George, I am pained to bring this to your attention for these ones have been at some point reckoned among your friends and colleagues. Son, they do you great dishonor and disservice. They have practiced in ill-behavior in the past and continue the deceiving unto the public. Their intent is a point of personal gain but the result is far more treacherous--it discredits the very truth of that for which we stand. Morally, these ones would never come into our sphere of contacts and, quite frankly, but for the pure deception perpetrated in these latest volumes--I suggest that all but a fragment of that which has come before is absolute hogwash!

I realize, George, that your own intent (don't be embarrassed) of the material was to test as to the credibility of one, Hatonn. It is fine, son. To fulfill our mission we must have total understanding of truth between us for neither of our tasks are easy but, instead, filled with great pitfalls and direct attack. None-the-less, it pains me greatly for you have paid enough at the hands and whims of these ones who would call themselves your friends and then stab thine backside. As you ones riffle through the pages I warn you of another false projection. You will find reference to ones working with George Hunt Williamson. I believe that our beloved Sister Thedra of ASSK can enlighten you on the projection habits of GHW and Brother Philip. Not that all the information is untruth--but any volume projected to the public as truth--must be truth in all manner of presentation. This volume is one major discredit from beginning to ending.

Are there valid inputs? Yes, but the information had been given in prior "contacts". I speak now regarding metals and vibrational cold fusion of the metallic craft skins, etc.

In view of continuing events we shall set records to straight and honor Billy for that which was given in truth and the public shall have to use the discernment of truth as God gives insight unto them. I find that almost forty dollars for a book of trash is a bit steep, however. George and Desiree', simply hold the original notes in tight security--get them away from your selves and into third party lock-up. We will bring justice unto the truth regarding those contacts when the time is appropriate. I know that you find it difficult to confront that which has occurred, especially Desiree', for her trust is so tested already--please know, son, that we are right on top of it and that which is put forth comes back a hundredfold in kind. Test me all that you will, son, for I believe you will find that I shall stand the testing. I hold you in my trust and in my love for your missions are great and I am honored to serve with you. So be it.

Did the errors come from Billy or from the Group as mentioned--you be the judge for you know both parties involved in the deception! It has been ever thus, dear ones. Ones play at games in magnitude that they give no thought unto the consequences. Is it deliberate deception--yes! Why? Many reasons and none of which matters greatly for truth always stands in the ending. Blessings unto you who stand and dare to counter the lies and demand truth.

WHAT OF THOSE METALS TO WHICH I REFER?

The Pleiadians brought forth samples of metals which have been analyzed from every direction and the method of melding the minerals has been totally elusive to you of Earth. The method of blending is absolutely simplistic in technology. It can be compared to that event called liquefaction in your Earthquake situations. Vibrations of proper frequency impacting substances simply break them into component atomic particles and, when they are merged with other substance, become fused as an amalgamation. The process is cold in nature, simple and can be formed into shapes impervious to penetration. As I mentioned yesterday--our ships simply cannot be opened by you ones if we do not intend that you do so. The shell will simply absorb and neutralize every known laser cutter that you have. That, dear ones, can be confirmed right on your good old hard Earth! Ask someone who has tried--and surprisingly enough, there are several ones around who have been there and tried.

An amusing side story in this procedure of metal production is quite fun to share with you. Lead in your air is most polluting and dangerous to you. To begin to gather our substance for a desired metal, for instance, we utilize the atmosphere. We begin with a substance which begins to gather and condense lead particles from the atmosphere--this eventually gives a product of solidified lead. The second process extracts from the resultant metal all dangerous radiations. Then the lead is fed into heat-converters, which, without the addition of metals, but exposure to various minerals, converts the lead, through several processes, into an alloy. Therefore, you can see that lead is a rather dandy item to have around for it can be converted into almost any metal known.

First you have liquefaction and then the alchemy is achieved. I am not going to give you formulae and "how-to" instructions. We also have a rather "old-fashioned" manner of alteration of metals and substances which converts through heat-converters, and the end result is achieved after some seven processes. The metal becomes liquified in what I suppose you would call furnaces--we would more clearly recognize the term Kiln-- then the liquid is subjected to specific and distinct oscillations until a specific desired frequency of the material itself is attained, next the final product of each segment is pressed by great pressure through a cooling "spiral" and at this point the metal comes forth in small pieces. These can now be put into components for whatever alloy is desired and put into what you ones call bullion or "dore" bars.

The cooling spiral contains water which is quite pure and obtained by a method of condensation, which you call "distilled", so that no impurities are introduced and therefore specific "frequencies" can be utilized to "roll" the metal. The metal bars are simply liquified again by pulses and basically "molded". The finished product--say a craft--appears to have no skin seams. This is a fact for our connecting, or "welding", apparatus is based on oscillation techniques which liquifies the metal in a cold state and allows the substance to simply flow together and thus merge, by which it is completely without seams for a single piece is thusly formed. We use no "grinding" operations for we have no joined seams of demarcation from one part of the pattern of the craft from another.

Once the method is understood and the proper oscillation frequencies isolated, it is quite easy to further understand the total operation of dissipating matter and reassembly of same.

WHAT KIND OF METALS DO WE UTILIZE?

Depending on the use of the substance, many varieties of alloys are in use. I gather what you are most curious about are the craft skins. Some portions of the craft are Mercury-steel and another consists of a nickel-silver-copper-gold alloy. We utilize a lot of gold for we are able to easily convert base metallic substance into gold. It then is easy to manage, malleable, harmless to the touch, beautiful and very conductible as for electricity transmitting.

We gather the components from many things, as for example, from lead-containing atmospheres of stars, from water in different places, from different plants and thus and so. We utilize the decay of different ore-stones of stars in the process of destruction. Through the process of collection, as I have mentioned, we convert the lead substances assembled into the soft metal, lead, which is then changed later by the further mechanical-chemical-electromagnetic processes into a hardened substance. This hard-metal is harder than any substance known to Earth--it is much harder than the substance you call steel, or carbide steel.

To further utilize the substance, as for starships for instance, the alloy must then be polarized. The final product is an alloy of tremendous strength, beauty and smoothness.

The question, of course, is always--"Do we have the necessary stuff on Earth?" Yes, but you continue to gather your minerals in a most primitive manner--you continue ore-mining which is so destructive in many ways.

Ore mining or other mineral mining on a planet or another star is done by us only in extreme emergency, because this process is basically equal to the destruction of the star itself. All mineralization exists in natural placement for specific reasons. For instance, to move uranium from its proper placement causes inability of the mineralization in the original placement to continue break-down in its natural sequence. Further, the stockpile of misplaced ore is then dangerous in its own right. You ones simply do not understand the unbalance you cause by your senseless and foolish alteration and destruction of your own planet.

We never exploit a planet or star in a form as does Earth-man. What you Earth human beings do is equal to the total destruction of the foundation of the planet itself. The first effects of this destruction began to show massively several decades ago as you moved into your technical revolution. The Earth human then began to exploit the Earth by taking petroleum products, minerals and all manner of different ores and removing the under structure of water and oil leaving tunnels which cave-in and can literally cause shifting by actually triggering quakes and fault alterations--either by the blasting entailed or simply the evacuation of the underlying substances.

ATOMIC TESTING

By far the most damaging and dangerous activities which you ones play at, is the underground testing of atomic devices, hydrogen devices and particle beam projections. Thusly, you now have products of nature, life substance itself, which effects an explosion of many thousand times greater than what you refer to as the Atom bomb. Brought to explosion in the suited circumstance, a chain reaction can be induced by which the Earth falls within only some seven to eight minutes into a total firestorm and is atomized. If the chain reaction is started and runs uncontrolled, rescue attempts would be useless--for if a chain-reaction of such nature gets beyond even our ability to control, there simply is not time enough to evacuate all. This is a constantly monitored possibility--moving into probability as your factions face off each other as if you were playing at mumble-peg with your primitive pocket knives.

How can you change your future? Well, we have spoken of many ways and we find that mankind desires not to give up those things he considers his birthrights--sex, automobiles, televisions and beer.

For far too long you have been deluded by beings of human form who rule by force and power and deceit. Man has allowed himself to be fooled by those responsible so he can now achieve nothing more by peaceful means, it appears. On your placement the force is embodied in politics, religions, and the sciences. It is this power that must be broken, otherwise you march directly into the path of the end, not only by war and eradication, but as well by the atomization of the planet if this current direction is pursued. You are going to simply have to return to living according to the natural law, that of God and balanced Creation.

There will be consequences to be paid, at any rate, for the Earth, herself, is sorely damaged and she is boiling and writhing within her very being.

Regardless of man-made damages there will be natural upheaval, great quakes, volcanic eruptions, climactic alterations, storms, tidal waves and accidental events which will make their world appearance in these impending days. Whole countries will sink down into the seas, and numerous human beings will find an evil ending. Most of all, you must realize that war is basically irrevocable--if not this month or year, then later--and later comes with the more heinous forms of killing.

6 6 6

Your prophecies and Biblical stories relate the numerals 6 6 6 and this becomes a common term to cosmic brothers as well as Earth projection. Just as the number represents that which will be on your Earth plane, it also represents that which came from off your Earth--which, of course, by definition indicates "extraterrestrial", but don't get crazy, for anything off terra is extraterrestrial. The symbol 666 will continually and more frequently come into your attention as you move along. The "anti-logos" represents the "lie", the "untruth". This lie is given forth from deceivers, religions, charlatans and greedy, power-hungry ones. In this instance the number 666 does not actually equate with an actual person, and the thinking and doings of this long-separated Earth "human being"--but the *delusion*, which he represented and still represents in your cultures.

You ones already recognize this symbol as being of what you refer to as the Anti-Christ. You always seek a name, a single being or person. You must think beyond that which would be shown as obvious for you are captured by the beast and yet you still see it not. It is indeed difficult to see where to begin your climb from the pit for you have been taught that that which is lie is truth and you recognize not that which you must do.

Mankind must re-arrange his thoughts and actions for himself. He has to find the truth himself, to liberate himself from all mystic nonsense. In this respect, man has a most difficult way to walk, because he is still very much imprisoned in his cultic-religious and mystical matters for which reason in these last months and years he has joined more into base and cultic beliefs and rituals. I ask that you ones not get entangled in the "what if's" and the distraction of sorting out the symbols--if you turn unto the truth of God, recognize that which you are up against in this moment-- then we can isolate a resolution into action. If you continue in the tending and pondering of the tiny fragments of the puzzle--you will be still working at the puzzle after the game is finished.

It is interesting that as your world spins ever closer to destruction you still quarrel over whether or not you evolved from apes. The human form of life accords to a special act of creation, and in consequence is unable to degenerate by any natural or unnatural metamorphical process. You ones ponder upon the large ape/human creatures of which stories are birthed and propagated. These entities do indeed exist in certain places. They are not creatures of "human" kind as you recognize the human Earth species. They are faunic creatures whose origin traces back to the flora-world. They indeed reached the highest developed animalistic forms of this type on Earth, but they are not that which you call hu-man in the definition of "higher" "universal" "man". You most certainly DID NOT evolve from apes and monkeys--the difference? God! God is the difference in all instances--you were given the gift of free-will reasoning capabilities and the ability of creation--a gift given unto man as a reflection of God Himself. The animals and plants were given unto you for your pleasure, balance, nurturing and survival needs--all stemming from Creation and Nature Herself As Creator, what have you created, little chelas? Are you pleased with that which you have created? Do you realize that your only lasting form of creation is that which is gifted in the re-creation of self--the child, and you mass-murder your own wondrous creations by the truckloads. Are you pleased with that which you have done as caretakers unto your wondrous gift of Earth planet? How long will you turn from truth and unto the lie while your world goes into destruction? So be it--for so shall it be--exactly as you decide it shall be.

It is time to close this segment. Hatonn to stand-by, please. Good evening.

CHAPTER 22

REC #1   HATONN

SATURDAY, DECEMBER 15, 1990   7:42 A.M.   YEAR 4 DAY 121

TODAY'S WATCH

I see that you don't allow your soldiers in Saudi Arabia to do "this" or to do "that" and through a "glitch" even the flag patches were removed from uniforms of the U.S. WHAT HAPPENED TO GOD? WHERE HAVE YOU HIDDEN GOD? I note that now your great military leader says the "flag matter" has been cleared up and that the "Saudis don't have any objection, so flags will again be provided!" The plan was to replace the patches, if at all, with UN symbols. However, there is actually so little support from the UN nations that the action was cancelled.

You object to me saying you "..invaded Saudi Arabia to gain control of her wealth!" I regret that you object but I suggest someone look very carefully into the matter. Why does someone not inquire into the testimony of *your former U.S. ambassador to Saudi Arabia James Akins who presented and proved a PRE-EXISTING PLAN TO OCCUPY THE SAUDI ARABIAN OIL FIELDS, REGARDLESS OF THE CONSEQUENCES FOR THE POPULATIONS OF THE AREA -- OR THE CONSIDERATION OF WORLD (AND/OR U.S. CITIZEN) OPINION!!*

This very day there is a stupid and nitty quarrel going on as to who will meet whom, when and where! I suppose 50,000 nice new Christmas Body Bags for America--(to help your sagging economy)--is apropos?

Does it not matter to you-the-public of the U.S. that the U.S. herself prompted by England's great leader, Maggie--lured Iraq into occupying Kuwait?

Does it not matter that you, the U.S. stand actually alone in the Middle East? Does the U.S. have the right, as President Bush asserts, to militarily intervene in any area where there are raw materials it considers vital to its economy? Oh yes, that is EXACTLY WHAT HIS LIPS STATED!

Doesn't this "NEW WORLD ORDER" of President Bush and Mrs. Thatcher dictate of denial of life-saving technologies to all Third World nations, to be exercised through a dictatorship of the United Nations Security Council--of which Mr. Bush intends to be dictator? Well, I have terrible news for Mr. Bush--Mr. Kissinger also plans to have that little slot to his King-ship!

Can the U.S. justify going to war to *restore a ROYAL FAMILY THAT HOLD CHATTEL SLAVES? Is this what America is all about in these "modern" days of modern living styles and modernized religions?*

I suggest, beloved ones, that these are indeed important points to ponder

GENOCIDE POLICY

I am going to outlay something which I think you had better consider most carefully as you are bombarded with the false double speak. Let us consider the overall picture behind the mouths.

Bush talks incessantly about bringing Iraq's Saddam to trial for *war crimes, as the Nazis were brought to trial at Neuremberg--oh sorrowful day for "justice".* But some of Bush's own friends and colleagues could find themselves on the docks of justice if you acted in justice, first. They are chargeable with the crime of genocide.

For decades, top elite figures in the environmentalist movement, just to isolate one grouping, like Alexander King of the Club of Rome, have screamed about "overpopulation"; privately, they say that means *eliminating black, brown, and yellow "USELESS EATERS"* in Africa, Asia, and Latin America. Meanwhile, the U.S. government under Presidents Carter, Reagan, and Bush has carried out a consistent policy of denying technological development to Third World nations.

Bush's shriek that Iraq's Saddam Hussein is developing nuclear weapons (which he already has) becomes a silly support of truth--the component parts for such weapons has come from the U.S., Germany and even cycled through Israel, along with other European countries such as England and France. And what of the Hydrogen bomb capabilities given into the hands of the Israelis--do you think they want this capability to use for power production?

Well, these little helpless countries have now been completely cut off from all possibility of having nuclear reactors and thus massive portions of these countries remain without power supply even for purification of water supplies.

In addition, international financial institutions led by the IMF and the World Bank have consistently crippled development programs in African, Asian, and Latin American nations by forcing them into repeated currency devaluations, cutting off their investment in infrastructure, and lowering the educational levels and living standards of the people who are any economy's indispensable use.

Anyone who doubts this truth is in deliberate intent of genocide need only look at America's so-called "inner cities"; many of them look like bombed-out combat zones, populated with the casualties of induced drugs and AIDS. Or do you simply turn you head away and hope the gangs don't move into your neighborhood tonight? If there is no intent to destroy the dark-skinned people, then why is this what is being driven upon the American populace?

IS RUSSIA PURE?

Why you ones continue to bombard me with my possible support of Russia--I suggest that you have not "read my lips". Not only is Russia not pure but is the largest perpetrator of murder upon a populace. Russia has the greatest abortion rate of any nation in your world! Do you actually believe this is in accordance with the Laws of God? I suggest you all stop "reading the insane lips" and start seeing truth!

NOW PLEASE, FOR YOU HAVE ANSWERS FOR TRUTH

SPREADING

Please do not take exception to that which I am about to present. We get mail every day--in great amounts with great advice regarding our failure in distribution of truth. It comes in forms of letters as I outlaid two days ago in wondrous intent--but alas, without full understanding.

We KNOW that many do not read! We KNOW that unless something is placed under his nose in prime time under the guise of violence and stupidity, that he won't tune it in. We KNOW that if we can't get it onto the screen it won't be watched. We KNOW that you think brotherhood of the cosmos should manifest all of that which you need and you can go right on in your misbehavior in your dream-time. Sorry about all those things that we already KNOW!

Yes, something has to be done to bring about these things. Do any of you have any idea of what it costs to simply publish a book? And, how else do you propose we get the original information unto you? WE DON'T HAVE TO CHANGE OUR BEHAVIOR FOR IT IS ALREADY ACCEPTABLE UNTO GOD AND WE LIVE IN BALANCE WITH THE CREATION.

I defend my workers in this unit because, as with George Green and my people in this very location--they have, without whimper or expectation, given all they have and borrowed more. They do not live in mansions all paid for--they get by as best they can until you of the populace are allowed the touch of truth. We have ones who work short-handed into the wee hours of the nights and then take up collection to give unto you stamps for the very mailings--and they do it without complaint and along with a collective projection that some of you see and hear and act.

We KNOW what we need to do--but this little Earth group cannot do more. Does this indicate that we do not appreciate suggestions--oh no,

190

please--we treasure every tidbit of correspondence of phone connection--even if negative and blasting--for it is the only indication that the word is being received! Please do not think we complain unto you who offer expression and help. We are touched to the very heart by those of you who write encouragement and send gifts unto our people--for the gifts are turned into stamps. We have one who now works through the nights on old equipment--just to get the Expresses out on the same day written--within 24 hours! Then ones gather and volunteer their hands to fold and ready for mailing. I kneel on bended knee unto these precious and faithful ones--who then go into their places asking what more can they do? I want to take this opportunity to thank them for we have little time to even meet in these pressured days in personal contact--and that must continue for we must write more and more and more.

These ones are doing to the limit of that which they can in most instances--it is now up to YOU THE READERS AND RECEIVERS OF THIS TRUTH TO SUGGEST AND THEN HELP US. But each is gifted with choices and free-will actions--we demand nothing.

I am humbly touched by my brothers here in the nucleus of the writing. For I have just told my scribe to cut out all social inter-action for both safety and to write at double receivings. This means, dear ones, that the publisher, distributor, and volunteer editors will hardly sleep at all in effort to get this to press. Our press-people work with IOU's which are never paid current and we must keep them even in secret as to location and label to insure a bit of security. Every Journal brings the impact of open aggression against them and their presses. We put to print out of this state in order to protect the resource.

Please accept that we receive in grateful appreciation, the input and suggestions, and understand that we are doing that which is possible and beyond Earthly production. You ones can only touch on the bare surface that which is brought against our workers in this place--the computers are continually under tampering, the equipment is continually attacked by electronic surges--and now there is dedicated assault against these ones even being able to obtain loans, etc., to continue the publishing.

It should be noted that there has now even been conjured up records from high sources within your government to build a negative dossier on these ones--which, when ones desire to invest (I did not say donate--I said "invest". You see, God desires that you have return and reward for contribution and gifts from your hearts); the lawyers involved tag the information and present it to the considering parties. If you desire proof of that, I believe we can outlay dozens of instances as proof.

As a matter of fact the first groups to obtain this information are the surveillance and police groups. To them I suggest that the truth is also for them--I see very few of them bearing tickets to the secure underground in Australia or anywhere else--and, human police and agents die as easily as do any other citizens--and frankly, even more quickly if you become a bother to your Elitists. I suggest that the computer monitors of this apparatus listen and watch most carefully--for YOU know the truth of it, better than the other citizens of the world who will receive of it. I further announce as I regularly do, that we have these ones in protection and we are given permission to protect them at any rate. WHO WILL PROTECT YOU?? I suggest you surveillance harassers think most carefully as you go home to your families and consider the plight you are ACTUALLY WITHIN! So be it.

You children of the lie, can turn this thing around only through coming into unified intent to do so. Further, if you keep into the truth and move with the instructions as we will outlay them unto you--you need not get the great hot-foot in the final analysis. WE CAN GET YOU OFF AND INTO WONDROUS SAFETY IN A PREPARED PLACEMENT--BUT, YOU WILL ASK, AND YOU WILL COME INTO THE WORKING LAWS OF GOD AND CREATION TO BE IN ACCEPTANCE ABOARD.

P.S.: Any contribution of size is automatically treated as investment-- BACKED BY GOLD IN PLACEMENT--IN COLLATERAL RESERVE AT THE BANK. Can the gold be confiscated? Yes, I suppose, but we stay pretty much on top of what is in the planning for imminent action within your government. Then the funds are funnelled into publishing, businesses for food production, earth material building units, architecture for durable and recession/depression housing, media center and production of information for your T.V. and motion picture theaters--with the central NEW media center for assurance of production and distribution. The first production is in script preparation--so bear with us, we work to the full extent of human ability.

YES, WE NEED HELP! WE RECOGNIZE OUR OWN LIMITATIONS IN THE HUMAN FORMAT--AND WE ARE NOT ALLOWED TO DO IT FOR YOU. SO BE IT. SO BE IT!

Let us return to your PLEIADES CONNECTION.

DECEIVING ELEMENTS

I have already gone through this subject but I suppose it cannot be presented often enough nor stressed enough, to reach unto you all.

These ones who receive this truth are under constant attack from ones who do not understand, do not even read the information and deliberate attack and misinformation perpetrators. These bombardments come from all quarters--not the least of which, are religious circles who pronounce contempt against truth. You see, chelas, as you come into truth regarding God and self--the religious cults loose their power over your being! Therefore, they must insist that you not move out of the limitations as laid forth for your information.

As we are writing, for instance, for the direct contact with the one you called "Jesus", we will receive of mail demanding that we cease the Satanic outlay and "move back into the truth of Christ!" I suppose there might be considered some humor in this except that it constitutes such "sick" humor.

Now the punch-line of course, is to openly discount the work. Then comes the "...oh my goodness, this is proving to be truth!" and the barrage heats up so as not to allow disclosure of the idiot projections of those who did the pronouncing of "LIES" upon the work. In other words, if we prove to project truth--they will be openly accused of deceit and cover-up. This has happened over and over again. It happened in the case of contactee Billy Meier and the cover-up and concoction of lies continues to flow in a steady stream when practically NONE of the information is any way connected with Pleiadians nor Billy Meier. False books, false information, false pictures, etc., have flowed like water through the sands to discredit the truths we brought unto that man in original contacts--just as ones barrage against this work as projected in these Journals.

Well, sad facts confront you the people of Earth place. It no longer is our problem if you allow discrediting of all this information! Our task is a final one--to give it unto you--you do with it that which you will. Then, we will continue to work diligently and constantly with those who desire truth and transition and so be it! God gave us commission to "TAKE FORTH THE FINAL WORD" AND SO SHALL IT BE GIVEN! Salu.

There are perhaps misperceptions and interpretations of our words which can be misunderstood, I suppose. In respect to there being differences in the truths in the way that our explanations and interpretations would correspond with only a "part" of truth in your objections and projections, as would appear, under confrontation with other explanations and interpretations of other "creatures" supposedly coming from outside your world travel to this Earth, and also who are in station thereon--I suggest you look more deeply into facts. Our truth will not vary one iota from the truth of another "creature" of truth. If it varies in otherwise manners, I suggest you study again the Laws of God and The Creation and check it for self as to WHO might be giving false information.

At this time, Pleiadians are the highest developed creatures who from outside your world travel to your Earth. There is a reason for this as we have outlaid over and over again. In conjunction with these brothers come we of the Hosts of etheric stature--the emissaries of God to remind you of truth and allow your awakening so that you might come into understanding and "remembering".

There are still other creatures penetrating into your Earth space and some even have bases thereon for the final purpose intended in the higher PLAN. However, there has been a disallowance of further damaging energies in Satanic form from actually coming from the outer cosmos unto your place. The activities are isolated now, into the spaces in and around Earth and nearby moons and planets--as research centers. You are basically isolated and pinned to your planet--does it touch your hearts in sorrow to realize you as a species are unacceptable unto your cosmic neighbors? The evil and Satanic troops are all now working among you in total take-over of your globe--just as outlaid by the prophecies of ancient beginnings. Your "little gray aliens of destructive intent" are creations of your human Satanic construction. God allows no evil to come forth in these days upon your placement--from the cosmos for it is the time of awakening, transition and reclaiming of HIS wondrous Kingdom.

The brothers and kin of Pleiades represent the highest evolution of human-kind who will be present or approach your planet at this time. Mind you, I said "human". The etheric beings of higher dimension are of different consideration and we come in the service of you and ONLY OF GOD. We are come with your humanoid brothers because YOU MUST HAVE PHYSICAL RECEPTION PLACES TO FILL THE NEEDS OF YOUR PHYSICAL MANIFESTATION. WE OF THE HIGHER DIMENSIONAL ETHERIC STATUS DO NOT AND THUSLY WE ARE IN COMMAND--BUT WORK IN TOTAL UNITY WITH THE HUMAN COUNTERPART OF YOURSELVES. I, PERSONALLY, SHALL SERVE WHERE AND HOW I PLEASE--NO MORE AND NO LESS FOR IN MY HIGHER BEING I HAVE NO PEER NOR HIGHER AUTHORITY. I, Hatonn, CHOOSE TO SERVE AS A PLEIADIAN COMMANDER! Wrathful God? No, a JUST God! A God who allows his fragments to experience in free-will choices! However, a God of discipline and expectation of a return unto His outline of Laws to insure balance and non-destruction of other of His creations--such as a planet and species. Laws are quite suitable for the needs of each placement and each creation--YOU OF MANKIND ARE THE DESTROYERS AND PEOPLE OF WRATH AND VIOLENCE--NOT GOD AND NOT CREATION. IF YOU PERCEIVE PERSECUTION--I SUGGEST YOU TEND THE ATTENTION MORE CLOSELY! I COME IN SERVICE UNTO THAT GOD OF CREATION AND I HAVE BUT ONE ENEMY--THE EVIL OF SATANIC INFLUENCE AND DISREGARD FOR THE LAWS OF CREATOR/CREATION.

We force nothing; we simply bring truth and you will decide that which you will do about it. Cast it aside and move into the darkness in separation from God and Light---OR, move within the Laws and INTO THE LIGHTED AND WONDROUS PLACES OF GOD. IT IS YOUR CHOICE ALONE--EACH INDIVIDUAL, EACH ENTITY!
The next highest civilization behind Pleiades is several thousand years, as you count, behind Pleiadian evolution and you must have help--NOW!

When we transmit explanations and interpretations, from the Pleiadian society, these accord to the highest level of recognition and knowledge and to the highest known truth, which not any explanation and interpretation from lesser developed creatures, under confrontation, could lead towards greater truth--and Pleiadians don't have it ALL by any imagination otherwise!

When matters in consequence that are transmitted to you, it is the highest known truth from them--I hold higher stature and I bring higher truth at this time of cycle for you, as a species, are about to collectively "thought" manifest destruction upon your entities and placement.

Your Pleiadian brothers who have brought truth to your world prior to this, brought the highest known truth which they bore and that has been prior to now, given unto you--how many of you have heard and/or read it? They have given you truth within their level of spirit, which also results that in respect to the formerly mentioned deceptive elements, can only be revealed the effective truth. The brothers of Pleiades must remain with that truth as given. if persons doubt their explanations in this matter, they must sooner or later recognize the truth of the words.

Little ones, this includes ones who pretend and speak in world-wide outlay of adventures and contact with human beings of your neighboring planets such as Venus, etc. You have suffered in the pits of deception while deceivers have made fortunes at your expense. I remind you that God needs no intermediaries and ultimately--IT IS JUST YOU AND GOD, MY FRIENDS--JUST YOU AND GOD! I care not what your star-sign is, nor your special "numbers"--IT WILL JUST BE YOU AND GOD AND THE WORD OF TRUTH. GOD IS THE WORD AND THE WORD IS TRUTH IF IT BE OF GOD AND NOT A THING SHALL CHANGE OF IT! 'Tis alright, Dharma, I know, precious, that the mammoth portent of the task is incomprehensible to you--let us not stop now, for thine brethren must be given this word. So be it, chelas, all of you who recognize not your placement in this final play in revelations. Simply remember--"..the Greatest never recognize their greatness and that, dear ones, is what makes them Great!" I touch ye ones most gently in your own awakening to purpose. My wings are large enough to bring shelter to all mine flock! Be it done!

TIME SHALL REVEAL TRUTH OF THE FALSE

INFORMATION

It will now become evident to you by your own sciences, etc., that on these other planets and upon your own, that there exists no human creatures of the forms described by deceivers, neither spiritual nor material forms. If our explanations are refused by different Earth humans then this is of no importance, because the Earth scientist know well as do all the governments, etc., of your place that these ones do not exist as travelers from the cosmos--only constructed to deceive and mislead you of the Earth-man. The different pseudo-contactees will prove themselves to be deceivers and liars--truth will always stand, beloved ones--always!

For the sincerely interested Earth human, we want to trouble ourselves to give important explanations with respect to the specific planet Venus" Often the Earth's solar system is passed by comets and wandering planets or wandering stars, about which the following is an explanation: Comets appear in different forms; one time as wandering planets and as wandering stars, which by the great attractive powers of other stars and planets, and by suns, are drawn into their sphere of influence. Because of their great speed they usually rush through the gravity belt and distance themselves again, whereby the increased friction of the planetary, solar and star forces their surface is liquified and loses matter. This matter often forms itself as a very long tail behind the fleeing comet. From solar energies, etc., the emitted particles then become visible as a shining "tail".

On the other hand, the so-called "empty space", is not empty, because it is alive with innumerous particles and other things, which by the constant friction with the wandering planets, stars, etc., cause their tails to shine. Yet there exist besides the comets the veil-like cometic bodies.

Comets, in general, have rather eccentric courses, and circle, like the system's planets, around the sun, but upon very much larger courses. These system's comets develop themselves normally at first near the sun with their impressive long tails, which often can be many millions of kilometers long. But truly gigantic comets are quite rare, for which reason the greatest number of all comets is not perceivable by the naked eye.

Dharma, stop NOW. The computer is destroying the information and I do wish to finish this subject in this portion. Please just begin another document.

CHAPTER 23

REC #2   HATONN

SATURDAY, DECEMBER 15, 1990   10:07 A.M.   YEAR 4 DAY 121

COMETS
(Continued from prior document.)

Only the really great and rather close-to-Earth comets are perceived by the mere eyes of the Earth-human. The average comets are nothing more than small and very weak sphere-shaped clouds of light without tails. But of this sort or comet are innumerous ones. The veil-like comets are the most frequent ones, and they possess three main characteristics: They are surrounded by a veil coma, without or with inner central densification; then the core and then the tail. The forms of the coma can be very different: elliptical, round, or drawn out in any direction. The central densification appears that way, that the coma becomes brighter and more compact on the inside.

The core itself forms a brightly shining zone and embodies the essential comet, which can measure a few hundred meters in diameter up to many thousands of kilometers , while the total diameter of the comet's head, measured together with the coma, amounts often to many hundred thousand or even millions of miles.

Each, from the sort of comet and the influences, consists in the tail of dust particles or of forms of gas, mineral substance (from which, for instance, we glean substances), or of all these particles formed together. Tails of merely gas, keep themselves within much closer dimensions than do the dust particulate tails, which only appear in greater brightness and these are tenuously enormous.

The system-connected comets have very long elliptical courses which extend themselves very far out into the cosmos. These courses lead very often half way or even more, into other systems, until they begin their return flight again towards their originating system. But the courses can also run so far that the way may pass through one or several systems and the path becomes longer accordingly. Because of the great distance of these courses, the comets often require multiple decades of years before they return to their home systems, while on the contrary, system-wanderers, comets which fly about through different systems, hold orbiting times of many hundreds of thousands of years. Like all planets, so also are comets subjected to the laws of gravity, thus they also form their courses accordingly.

These different courses and their lengths of cycle are decisive for changes and occurrences in the differing systems of stars and suns, even as such occurrences and changes are only rare.

197

In less detail I have already spoken to the subjects outlaid herein--and have pointed out that your solar system partners in the form of planets have in most instances suffered the same cycles as has Earth--only to end up at the destruction of the very life-forms aboard. When you have topography which can only be created by water--on a planet which appears to have no moisture but, rather, temperatures of incredible degree--it is truth before your eyes. If your own atmosphere ignites and fails to blow apart your planet orb itself--there goes Earth!

BACK TO VENUS

This comet explanation is to allow movement into explanation regarding Venus wherein at this time no human life runs about and plays upon her surface. Millions of years past, a huge dark star destroyed half of a planetary system many light-years distant from your solar system. After the destruction of that distant system, the wanderer rushed out to the widths of the Universe, and took up its course towards Earth, where it was forced by the great planets and the sun into a new orbit which in consequence of that brought it on again and again into your system. I suggest you pay very close attention to this lesson for it has great impact on your very existence--that same comet continues its cycling.

At that time it was recognized by a label handed down through the oral traditions as "the destroyer"; it followed its new course and produced for itself in the course of millions of years, a stable orbit to some extent--but with these travelers, there is never "permanent stability". This course led the destroyer uncontrollably close to stars and other systems, and on to other wandering stars and comets, which were by its own gigantic size then forced out of their own orbits or were attracted by its gravity and were for all practical description--kidnapped.

This happened only a few thousand of your own years ago, when this immense destroyer drew an object into its gravity and course and led it over many millions of miles toward the Earth's solar system. This comet, now of immense size, passed very far outside the reach of Earth gravity but the object trailing in its gravity field passed dangerously close to Earth and evoked great catastrophes.

The whole of your solar system was plunged into disorder and chaos at that time and all its planets were pushed into new orbits. This represents massive destruction, dear one--MASSIVE! THE NEW OBJECT DISTURBING THE HARMONY WAS FORCED BY THE GRAVITY OF THE GREATER PLANETS AND THE SUN INTO A COURSE BETWEEN EARTH AND WHAT YOU HAVE LABELED MERCURY AND WAS UNABLE TO LEAVE THE SYSTEM. That orb, being the brightest and most reflective planet of Earth's solar system, circles since then around the sun and is called by the Earth humans "Venus".

I might add herein, that we choose the very orbs for our orbiting "anchors" of tremendously large craft placed between you and the orb. We can function in full visibility without any of you taking note to any extent at all--the astronomers know we are there but the information is not allowed distribution. So be it.

These events, where Venus was held by the Earth's solar system, happened almost four thousand or so, years ago. By the events of the time Venus was guided into a very quiet course, for which it has one of the least eccentric orbits. This is the essential effect of that ancient close passage to Earth, by which the rotation of Venus was also influenced. By the gravity of Earth, the rotation of Venus was slowed and it started rotating in the opposite direction. And in effect of the very short time of passage through Earth's gravity, the rotation of the slowed planet was not able to increase itself, for which reason it attained an extremely long time for only one rotation, and maintains from that time the slowest rotation time in your whole solar system.

Since then, one day in your counting on Venus has a duration of approximately 117 Earth days, while the time for rotation around the 30 degree inclined axis of the poles amounts to some 243 Earth days.

By the gravity of Earth Venus was robbed in its flight those thousands of years ago of its own rotational energy, and there arose a very great heat of friction. And this frictional heat is also the cause of the physical conditions which presently reign on Venus--not having been destroyed in the same manner as other inhabited planets originally having life-forms.

When we refer to bases on a given planet, we speak of what you would call satellite bases--or platforms. We do not speak of typical life-forms as humans as you recognize your species. There is no physical life form able to sustain in those physical conditions which presently are in reign on Venus. The physical conditions alone show the falsity of all those who would affirm that human life exists on Venus--much less some great voice and/or contact from beings based on that placement. If ones come from Venus--they do not come from the surface thereof. God does not alter natural laws of physics. The physical conditions alone show the falsity of all those who would affirm that human life exists on Venus itself. The matter thereof is completely outside the frame of natural chance, because the environmental conditions on Venus' surface and the atmosphere are absolutely deadly of human creatures or any of the other conjured forms of life as presented unto you. Any forms on such a placement would, of necessity of existence, be etheric in form--oops!

The surface of Venus as measured by temperature guages measures at a depth of some 32 kilometers, is presently registered at 457 degrees Celsius in your language--yes, we can measure quite definitively and travel through the atmosphere quite comfortably for we are entirely self-contained. We utilize much material from such star entities.

This is also the reason why all the water of this planet has turned to vapor and forms the very thick stratum of clouds. That also produces an atmosphere so dense that the pressure at an accepted sea level is some 334 times higher than of the air on your Earth. Interpreted in your scientific terms, the atmosphere of Venus is also a danger to the life of human creatures, because it consists by volume of 87% carbon dioxide, while the percentage differs in some places. There are life-forms in other places which can handle an extreme level of carbon dioxide--but not on Venus, dear ones. You have, however, invited in some of these very beings who came to assist you with your increasing levels of carbon dioxide--and you simply incinerated them for their goodly efforts to respond to you. Oxygen exists at present in the lower stratums in only some 4.23%, and nitrogen and rare gasses are reported to be 55.47%. Water vapor is very rare indeed and the atmosphere is considerably greater than that of your Earth. The actual pressure of the Venus atmosphere is about 107-110 times greater than the pressure of your Earth's atmosphere. This is also a matter which is very hostile to human forms--or any life-form for that matter. By this tremendous pressure, human forms of life would simply be squashed to indiscernability and destroyed as trash in a compactor. Even metallic forms suffer the same fate. In explanation, I wish to reveal herein that we have found on Venus, Earthly apparatus, which by the immense pressure of the atmosphere of Venus was completely squashed and damaged even before reaching the surface of that planet. Therefore, all subsequent bases are set up outside the atmosphere and simply identified as Venus bases. Russia, by far, leads the pack of your nations of Earth in dumping debris all over the landscape of Venus in various degrees of "squashness".

Venus has a magnetic field of very low measurement, and also what you call the "Van Allen Belt" is expressed very low, in consequence of which what you call the "solar wind" factor is not screened to any extent at all. They must be regarded as well the very high temperature, which injures the belt. But also the lack of water has its consequences in nourishing the hostility against all life-forms of the planet. From the event of those thousands of years ago, the planet is at present in the first phases of recovery and restoration. Slowly, over the course of millenniums, natural conditions for life and forms of life of the most primitive kind will begin to develop, as those are usual on each emerging life-developing world. Thus, for even the most unreasonable one, it is evident that we are dealing, in the case of Venus, with a planet that is making its first move within the status of ability to produce and sustain life. Eventually it will be housing life-forms and even human.

With regard to the planet itself, it must be explained that especially in its equatorial regions it is very flat with structured relief regions far away. Concerning the temperature, day and night sides are nearly equal, while there are great differences in the strength of the wind between the lower and the higher regions. At the surface itself the wind is still, and first develops in the higher regions. At still higher regions the winds increase very much and reach velocities of some 117 meters per second. The lower level of clouds exist at about 43.17 kilometers above the surface but this can vary because of atmospheric storms, pressures etc. This is especially likely over those regions where the winds are pressed down wards and reach the surface and blow against the mountain, which themselves reach heights of 2.3 kilometers on average.

The climate and structural weather are on the whole very constant on Venus, but nevertheless show certain differences. Thus it is that human life on that planet is up to now still impossible if not accorded technical means for survival in great protection.

In this sense then, mentioned by deceivers, no life, in fact, exists on Venus as projected by would-be "channels" and authorities on metaphysical and "New Age" stages of disinformation. There are other forms of life which do exist thereon, but there can be no manner of comparison between these and human life-forms. The planet is still extremely wild in nature and it could not be otherwise in the natural evolution of only a few thousand years. For example, look unto your "Moon", as when you look at it you have nearly a copy of the Venus which presents itself below the thick stratum of clouds. You have, effectively, a created imitation Moon, dear ones. When we, or other forms of life go to Venus, which is rich in different minerals and other materials, it is only possible for us by using highly specialized protective gear to function in any manner--that hardly indicates that you humans of Earth technology romp around in your sunsuits tossing out words of wisdom to your Earthbound brethren.

Our protective gear is most sophisticated indeed and, furthermore, we do most of our exploration from aboard ship. Great protective measures must be taken to preserve the life-form from the dangerous influences of the Venusian atmosphere, the great heat, and as well, in regards to the differing forms of poisons and gasses which move as deadly clouds over the planet. Because the planet is subjected to certain differences, we must also take this into consideration, as for example, for different locations where the temperature increases to more than 500 degrees CELSIUS directly on the surface, and where also the values of carbon dioxides, of nitrogens, helium, argon and neon gasses change values; while also the atmospheric pressures differ between 88 up to 107-110 atmospheres (AT).

These are, therefore, the basic explanations which I have to offer in respect to the ability of human or similar to human life-forms existing on the planet Venus. If I had to describe other planets of your sun system, then by regret also there I would have to refute at different planets the deceptive information of certain elements and substitute for it the real truth, because other supposedly inhabited planets of your system contain no such forms of human life at this time--either. Depending upon the reason for this loss of life sustaining format, there is often great histories of great civilizations having at one time lived as well as you of Earth upon their orbs. There are, however, bases on some of your planets in your system put there by some aliens and some of your own peoples. Russia, has by far, the most advanced abilities in that direction, than any other nation on your own orb.

So what of the information coming from so-called dependable "channels"? I have no further comment--DO YOU WANT GAMES AND MYSTI-

CISM OR DO YOU ALLOW THAT TRUTH MIGHT SERVE YOU FAR BETTER? SO BE IT. BUT YOU ONES HAD BETTER TAKE NOTE OF THAT DANDY COMET WHICH DROPPED OF VENUS INTO YOUR SYSTEM--IT'S STILL RIGHT ON COURSE!

Let us close this segment as it has grown far too lengthy.

I hereby move to stand-by,

Hatonn to clear, please. I do further ask that you not mistake my own identity and/or service. My attachment is with one recognized as Aton and it will serve all my brethren to hold that closely in your hearts! Saalome' and Salu.

Please remove yourselves from this placement the remainder of this day. It is not safe as this subject is most unwanted in circulation. Get away and allow us to tend of the electronics in your absence. Thank you.

CHAPTER 24

REC #1   HATONN

SUNDAY, DECEMBER 16, 1990   6:20 A.M.   YEAR 4 DAY 122

TODAY'S WATCH

Good morning, in the Light of Radiance. Hatonn at ready.

Rather than "watch" this day, I shall simply give you ones a thing or two to ponder and then we will effort to finish this beginning dialogue regarding Pleiades.

You desire to argue about my terminology of "invading" and "occupying" Saudi Arabia. Yes, that is exactly what I said. Why do you think your major banks are going to arrange to fail and/or have their subsidiaries fail? I knew you knew; go back to the investment programs set up by the Middle East Oil Producers--to gain control of the money, the banks HAVE TO FAIL! (See <u>SPACEGATE, THE VEIL REMOVED.</u>) If you nice citizens have to lose everything you have worked for, so be it! There has to be military "occupation" because the countries are not going to LIKE the news that the U.S. and World Banks have stolen all their money and the only thing that will save those Royal Rip-Off leaders who sold out their countries and the U.S./World Banks (Cartel) is military presence in such massive manner that no one dares make a peep about it. Do not expect your troops home soon no matter what comes off in Iraq. I told you long ago that this would happen because there would be some hangings in those countries when the masses found out what the leaders have done. These nice high-level coalitions are the bacon-saving measures.

You have allied with the most dastardly leaders on your planet--including Saddam. Come now, you don't really believe it is JUST a disagreement over days of meeting to "negotiate". There are many things at play here-- but money and oil money are the point. Money and world domination through total force.

IRAQ

How can you as a people denounce Iraq for not meeting Mr. Bush's schedule of non-meeting. Mr. Bush, Mr. Baker, Gen. Powell, etc., etc., have announced to the world that there will be "no negotiations"--the meetings are simply to give Iraq no alternatives except to meet Mr. Bush's <u>demands</u>! Now, Mr. Bush wants those demands announced on his schedules--what would YOU DO? I am very serious! WHAT WOULD <u>YOU</u> DO? What ARE you doing? What ARE you parroting? IS

AMERICA REALLY ACTING IN REASON? WHY ARE YOU OVER THERE?

HELP

Why do you think your UN nations are not actually paying the money for support of this adventure? They have not paid even a fourth of that which the US pronounced as "each one's portion". Why does not Japan give more participation, "Because Japan receives over 70% of her oil from the Middle East"? BECAUSE, DEAR HEARTS, IF THE U.S. GOT OUT OF THE MIDDLE EAST THEY WOULD HAVE ABSOLUTELY NO SHORTAGE OF FUEL AND THE PRICE WOULD HAVE RE-MAINED QUITE MODERATE! WHO DO YOU THINK YOU FOOL WITH YOUR "I AM THE GOD OF THE WORLD" ATTITUDE--YOU AMERICANS WHO HAVE TO HAVE SPECIAL RECIPES FOR FAT REDUCTION TO KEEP YOURSELVES FROM OVERWEIGHT? I promise you--overweight is NOT a big problem for most of your world! Neither will it be a big problem for you ones very soon now--a morsel of food will be precious indeed.

GENETIC ROBOTOIDS

I have actually lost some readers because I announce that many of your leaders are replicas. I intend to enlarge on that subject but we have se-quence problems here. We can only write as much as my scribe can han-dle--so please, do be patient.

I will, however, ask Dharma to reprint a paragraph from one of your own news publications. *U.S.NEWS AND WORLD REPORT:* Nov. 19, 1990, from an article regarding the DEATH OF A NATION (RUSSIA) entitled *The Last Hurrah*: I suggest that you pay attention to terminology in sev-eral respects within this statement from *a Jewish journal, VESTNIK*, by Viktor Yakushev, a member of the group, Pamyat. He denounced "...`Zionists/Masons'--*as bio-robots, programmed for self-destruction. This is a scientifically proven fact, and we have arrived at such evidence through experimental means. In addition, 6 to 8 times more Zionists are .....*"

I simply remind you--THE SOVIETS HAVE LONG HAD THE CAPA-BILITY AND THEREFORE, THEY SHOULD KNOW! You of the citi-zens of this world have no idea of that which you are up against and most will make death transition never having known. So be it. Please allow us to continue on our original subject, chela. Science Fiction? Oh, you should be so fortunate! It is NOT fiction, dear ones.

204

I suggest you spend <u>some</u> of your time asking God to request to the nice Pleiadians not to abandon you to your foolishness--for they have the right to do so if you continue in your hostilities unto them. They have the prerogative of simply picking up their brethren on your planet and moving out and watching the rest of the show unfold. So be it for I would hope a word to the wise might be received as given. God, the one you recognize as the Messiah (Christ) and the higher energies will NOT abandon any of the entities of their own--I suggest you re-read your books! NO EVIL SHALL BE BROUGHT FORTH INTO THE KINGDOM OF GOD, FROM EARTH! We are in the process of telling you explicitly and emphatically that which will be acceptable behavior and that which will not be acceptable. You continue to confuse idiotic mysticism, false teachings and BS for truth. We care not which you choose--but to get off of that planet in physical form and transfer is going to require a return in intent at each soul vortex--unto the LAWS! SO BE IT! We will continue to outlay how it really is, and then you will be in the deciding where you want to put your little tootsies and assets.

You ones keep efforting to place finite limits on everything and then turn about and make your own foolish rules of acceptable behavior against the very thing that allows you infinite and unlimited potential. Strange indeed, are you Earthians. There is NO limit or "end" to the Universe--you only have "barriers" of various energy separations, of Universes which comprise various aspects and conglomerates.

George, for instance, personally ponders what I outlaid a few days ago regarding the entity, ASKET, whom I announced was from the DAL Universe. This is simply recognized as another universe of another polarity opposed to yours, which counterbalances yours in manifestation. Ones from that vortex arrived prior to the Pleiadians in this time of encounter to prepare some of the earlier contacts for the Pleiadian contacts which would be coming shortly--and now, here they are! The Pleiadians and the DALs have been in contact in association on projects of various kinds with each other for a very, very long time.

Contactees are ones from past experiencing with beings from the various aspects--they come and function on your planet specifically for contact purposes although this is not readily recognized until just prior to need of service. You of this group desire to go back and use Billy Meier's contact with our brotherhood as a guideline. It is difficult for so many things came to change the situation as is the case if the opposition can pull down or discount the contact. Billy was not a Pleiadian in last passage--he was a DAL(ian) and having lost ability to inter-relate to the DAL(ians) got into great trouble with credibility. You see, the first contacts, even though they worked totally in conjunction with Pleiades Command, were not considered threatening to the Elite--it was anticipated B.M. could simply be discounted as a "nut". When Pleiadians entered the picture--the entire scenario changed for that was to be the big event of truth-bringing and the discounting and discrediting had to be pushed into high gear.

It is not separation in the Universes as such, for Pleiadian ancestors, and YOURS, come from a common heritage, descended from the refugees, if you will, from the great sun-system--some of whom fled at one time to the Pleiades, some to the Hyades--oops!--and a number of other places where they found hospitable planets in their escape from destruction--oh yes, human entities have a hard time getting the point! But in the ending--the point shall be thoroughly gotten and the lessons of behavior--well-learned!

You of Earth must stop efforting at discounting receivers from this dimension by errors we might pronounce as regards things such as names, labels and attitudes of various planets, systems, etc. For instance, allow me to give example: "IHWH-HATA"---what does this mean to you?? I thought not! It is what we call that energy polarity system which is translated into "The Eye of God". As we scan your astronomical books, we find that you refer to this "Eye of God" as being with a constellation called by you, "Lyra", and you call it "The Ring Nebula of Lyra" or, in more mathematical identification--"M-57". Now, the next thing is always for you ones to say, "OK, but give me explicit distances and miles and light years and absolutes!" Why? You would not know whether or not I speak truth. If you have nothing upon which to compare or relate--you have been given nothing! You ones will learn to stop asking me for explicit information for I shall be lessening input of specifics as we move along--explicit information will be given through mind reception and transmission--that which will be technical information. This is the intent of this mission--security whereby several will hold portions of most critical survival and transition information and ones shall be pulled together to share these portions at the proper sequence of events. You will not need magic formulas from space. So be it.

While we are close to the subject of travelers let me clarify a point of contention used as a discrediting point against the Billy Meier material. It has been claimed that the one Semjase was actually a woman seen about the city--and was assumed a model. No, Semjase made frequent jaunts into the city for various reasons--Munich being a frequent point of contact with other contactees who still remain silent witnesses and busy workers.

SEA LEVEL?

Oberli, in monitoring yesterday's writing, had a most logical question--how could Venus have a atmospheric pressure of some 107-110 AT's at one statement and then at "sea level" have a pressure of some higher than 300 % more than Earth. It is a difference only in the way you measure vs. how we measure altitudes, for instance.

You can't know altitudes exactly, for you start from the reason-based premises of that which appears to you to be a starting point from which to measure. For instance, your scientists count the height of a country or of a given mountain, in "meters or miles or feet above the level of the sea". What a foolish starting point. The starting point for all measurements must be from the center of the planet, which never changes. This is because planet forms are not exactly round, but tend more towards an ellipse shape. For another example, let us say that you say Mount Everest is the highest mountain of Earth, then this is correct only so far, with respect to your sea level. But in truth it is around 2,150 meters less high than the highest mountain of your world. When you measure Earth mountains, then the center of the planet is decisive, and measured from that point of reference, you will see, the highest mountain of Earth planet is NOT Mount Everest. Pressures also vary greatly from one perceived altitude to another just as you have great pressures at the bottoms of your oceans so, if you have no oceans, you have great pressures increasing as you move toward the center of the planet.

OTHER VISITORS?

We are further developed forms of life, and no longer are able to move in such levels of mind perception as do Earth beings. This is not a pretentious point on our part, but simply a law of Creation. It is the same with all forms of life; also with Earth humans. They, as well, are no longer able to move within still lower, to them, levels, thus they are not able to integrate in any manner with lower beings. The concept would be insane. To adjust to all tasks in the existing laws of Creation each world creates, according to its level of evolution, one or more creatures of advanced development through whom necessary facts may be transmitted. These higher developed creatures have been called "Prophets" on Earth who, unfortunately, in their times, were almost without exception persecuted and pursued, which condition still has not changed. And because this is the way it is, there is no necessity or intention to make ourselves further known to all ones.

Besides us, there are still other extraterrestrial intelligences who move in the Earth realm, but who are in uniquely different positions in evolution than are you, and who are sometimes advanced over Earth humans by only a few centuries. These creatures may thus come into contact with Earth humans and reach total integration. Because some of these intelligences are not much developed beyond Earth mankind, they may behave like "Commanders" and such, and more advanced creatures may actually participate with humans of Earth to prevent evil consequences.

Some Earth humans do have real contacts with such extraterrestrials, and others take such reports and elaborate them with fantasy, thus creating new stories. There also appear lesser developed intelligences who thirst for command and want to keep the scepter over Earth humans and, conscious of the affinity for religions on Earth, they learn to apply them for their own purposes. These advanced, let us refer to them as negative(for lack of better description) beings who would manipulate the human populace are indeed clever and, being advanced in technical knowledge and abilities, are able to influence and direct your own species. These ones have become great menaces to Earth man's development for they are basically destroyers. Earth man can begin to better sort out the tools of these ones by observation at times when wars and catastrophes befall them. The powerful leaders of Earth at this time are unconsciously, or consciously, or in absentia, led totally astray by such intelligences.

To understand the relationship of Earth beings and your cosmic brothers, you must use logic and the gift of true reasoning deduction processes. I'm sorry, chelas, but the stories you have been given are simply not even logical and furthermore, they form a mystical aura about God and Creation which is absurd. Why do you have to couch God in mysticism when there is none? The wonders of the Universe are so magnificent—why require it to be mystic and magic?

Specifically, extraterrestrials or star-people, whatever you desire to call your cosmic counterparts, are very much like you. Knowledge and "WISDOM" are superior to yours, as well as technology—no more and no less—each moving through experience. Space and time are not overcome by space and time—BUT BY SPACELESSNESS AND TIMELESSNESS, which means that space and time collapse into one another and become equally directional to zero-time. By that, a few fractions of a second are enough to rush through billions of light-years, practically without loss of time, because the zero-time neutralizes space and time simultaneously. We do not even need to discuss "etheric" beings at this point, nor thought transference—good old space and time will do nicely.

Many deceivers pretend they are in contact with other planetary human beings of your solar system, and even having flown with or in their ships. That is nothing more than false, as most of the stars (planets) indicated are so desolate that human life is no longer possible on their surface or, as with Venus—the star itself is not old enough or evolved enough to sustain life-forms of human. It is most unfortunate that the contacts which might well be valid are discredited by lack of understanding of the truth by the receivers themselves. Of course this is the total intent of the base energies efforting to control your planet.

Our mission is to alert you to the presence of the deceivers and warn you of your declining ability to reverse your negative path—these are not "little gray aliens" from somewhere "out there"—they have become real and incarnate beings with intent for control and destruction of your planet as you know it. THAT is NOT mystical.

The time of conflict with these energy forms is coming in imminent experience and you are, by great numbers, at disadvantage if you are IN truth and just behavior. You have become dominated by evil intent and actions, your human spirit is greatly underdeveloped and the lessons of false teachers continues the decline of the overall.

Above all, there remains but ONE that possesses the power of life and death over each creature. This is the CREATION alone, which has laid its laws over ALL. Laws which are irrefutable and of eternal validity. The human being can recognize them in nature when he troubles himself to do so. They expose for him the way of life and the way to spiritual greatness, embodying the goal of life. While the human indulges in his religions, and by this a heresy, he pines more and more away--in spirit--which finally leads to a bottomless pit--abyss.

The human being may recognize that a God can never take over the part of the Creation or destine the fate of a human being. God is NOT the CREATION, but as well, only a creature of it, like all Creation-dependent creatures. But the human being hunts for his religious wrong beliefs and affirms God being the Creation ITSELF. He goes even further and pretends a normal Earthman by the name of "Immanuel", who is also called the "Jesus Christ", is God's "son" and the Creation itself. Still different sects of the new time go on to maintain these same things, which already approach total delusion and the stories get more and more wild in presentation.

It is pathetic for, as already mentioned, deceivers also walk in the same direction and put out incorrect perceptions and total lies unto the world of man--that your cosmic brothers and sisters from other planets of the cosmos would come at the "order" of God (with whom they actually mean that one, "Christ") and integrate into one element of definition, those "beings" with that of THE CREATION. This is total bunk! Ones misproject and attempt to allow you unthinking and seeking humans to believe such trash. There are ones who come with the cosmic brothers who do attend these matters of higher dimension and are a higher integration with The Creation. These ones come in attendance at this time with the higher teachers in preparation of return of God upon your place in order for the reclamation.

The CREATION itself gives the commands, dear ones, in ultimate measure, because IT embodies the greatest power in the Universe, and never is in need of commands or silly religions. Religion is only the primitive work of human beings, in purpose, quite frankly and honestly, to lead them into suppression--for exploitation--to which only spiritually deficient life can fall.

Our further mission at this time is to bring this truth to the light of the world and make it known. If this does not happen, then mankind will slowly destroy itself and fall into complete spiritual darkness in separation from God and Truth.

God is one thing, Creation another--it is the total lack of balance with the laws of Creation which has brought you down. The Laws of Creation as given unto the human species are presented by God of Creation as guidelines by which you can remain in balance and harmony with that which IS The Creation and you have broken and rewritten them all to suit your lustful, greedy and very base human desires. So be it.

Dharma, this is a good place to break off this Journal for we have reached the number of pages beyond which the readers will not even "begin" the Journal. I cannot finish this in properness in this sitting so please allow abrupt interruption and we will simply move on to a second volume regarding your PLEIADES CONNECTIONS--RETURN OF THE PHOENIX!

THE TIME IS AT HAND WHEN YOU MUST NO LONGER LOOK THROUGH THE EYES OF THE CHILDISH FANTASY. IT IS TIME TO COME INTO MATURE UNDERSTANDING (AS THE CHILD WITH CURIOSITY AND OPENNESS) INTO TRUTH--FOR THE CLOSING OF THE CYCLE IS AT HAND. SAALOME'

I realize this information is a bit difficult to swallow and perhaps two doses of the medicine will go down the easier? Please be in relief as you come into understanding--it is far easier to believe, change and meet the need of that which is "REAL" than to continue in the lies and deceptions of those who would simply deceive and mislead you by their false projections. God and The Creation are totally balanced and very logical, it is time you see Light instead of hazy, mystical aberrations.

May we walk together in brotherhood, though this wondrous journey called "life". I extend my hand--who will accept of it? Salu.

Hatonn to clear, please.

SIPAPU ODYSSEY
Dorushka Maerd

The Sipapu is the opening (gateway) through the Kiva to the "nether" lands of the ancient Anasazi Indians and their decendants in the southwest. This sensitive love-story of the "end-times" brings together a returning tribe of the Ancients from the past, a Pleiadian Space expedition from the "future", and some "awakening volunteers" from Earth's present. The plot climaxes with a "Gathering" at which many "Masters" from the higher realms speak about the Prophecies and Revelations in these end-times. This manuscript was written in early 1987 as a movie and is being published at this time to protect the copyright.

AND THEY CALLED HIS NAME IMMANUEL - I AM SANANDA
by Sananda and Judas Iscarioth

The story of the life of the one commonly known as Jesus of Nazareth as told by Jesus and the disciple Judas Iscarioth. Absolute clarification of the numerous falsifications, misrepresentations, lies and misconceptions concerning that time period and Jesus' teachings are presented. Mary seeded by Gabriel, Guardian Angel of the Sons of Heaven. The actual teachings of the Master are given as spoken at that time. Clarification regarding God and The Creation. The Laws of The Creation and The Commandments are given in clear definitive language. The name of Judas Iscarioth is cleared as not being the one who betrayed Jesus. Statements by Jesus are provided, as spoken at that time, concerning falsification of his teachings over two thousand years. Strong warnings regarding false teachings. Words of great strength, power, light and healing at a soul-level.

SPACE-GATE: THE VEIL REMOVED--by Gyeorgos Ceres Hatonn

Facts are provided concerning the governmental cover-up of extraterrestrials visiting our planet, and crashing on our planet, as early as the late 1940s/early 1950s. Historical perspective of the period from the late 40s to present is put forth with many surprising, startling and troubling details of secret actions by governmental agencies and representatives. Disclosure of various "secret" agencies and societies, such as the "above top-secret" MJ-12 (Majestic 12), The Jason Society, The Bilderbergers, the secret government, the "grey-men" and details regarding their stretegies and operating methods. Past cover-ups are exposed. Clarification of the ongoing peaceful intent and involvement of the beings from space. Signs of the times, prophecies and the involvement of Satan and Christ in these "end times" are clearly stated. The correlation between Christ and extraterrestrials is clarified.

SPIRAL TO ECONOMIC DISASTER
LIFEBOAT MEASURES - IF YOU ACT NOW
by Gyeorgos Ceres Hatonn

Waking-up to some economic realities. Exposing the "grey-men" and the secret government, their manipulations from a historical perspective, the degree of their diabolical capabilities, and the perfection of their plan on the unsuspecting "masses". Depression imminent. Get ready, it is coming down fast. New currency and some solutions for not getting caught in the new money and debit card system. Get your hands on cash (under 50s) and stash it (not in a bank). Financial strategies across the board. The solution of Incorporation (for everyone). The Nevada secret. Prophecies of these times previously given. Sananda and Aton state 'how it will be'.

FROM HERE TO ARMAGEDDON--by ASHTAR

A multi-dimensional perspective, offered in precisely clear language. Some noteworthy cautions to "receivers". Clarification of the Ashtar energy, of etherian beings and of the difference between space people and spirit people. Earth as a school of learning, of the lower grades. Great insights into the purpose and state of "man", of the planetary condition and the governmental attitude toward "higher" beings. Demystification of the planetary cleansing and evacuation process. Turning the cards on evil through understanding their methods. The true origin of the species of man. The "dark brotherhood" is real. Pitfalls are plentiful, the path steep. There's no turning back. Christ's teaching gave us example. The nuclear threat is real. The powerful forces of Spirit at work within man during this 'end-time' where final choices must be made. Closing statement by Jesus Christ.

SURVIVAL IS ONLY TEN FEET FROM HELL--by Ashtar

Ice-water thrown in the face of nuclear misconceptions. Clearing the air for some true understanding. We (U.S.A) have no defense. The China nuclear threat and example. The Russian nuclear threat and example. The Switzerland model. Shelters, shelters, shelters...where are our shelters? Nuclear war not likely, probable. While there's still time. Tunnels, plan ahead and store. What of the rebuilding? More hard realities on Russia. God's involvement in this entire process. Earth changes and shelters. If you don't do it, it won't get done. The nuclear deterrent once available to the U.S. has been abrogated by the failure of the U.S. government to protect its citizenry with bomb/radiation shelters. The Russians and Chinese have access to organized and maintained shelters, leaving only the Americans unprotected. The United States is wide-open for nuclear blackmail. It may not be too late, but action must be taken.

2

THE RAINBOW MASTERS, "THE MAGNIFICENT SEVEN"
by The Masters

A manual for living the life blessed of God. Insightful to the heart, offering hope, direction, promise, guidance, love, discipline, clarifying long clouded issues and illuminating concepts of higher reason. Stilling troubled waters with penetrating clarity. Cutting to the core of the nature of man, yet offering such gentle direction filled with compassion beyond measure. Words which resonate as musical chords within the very soul essence. Each energy uniquely powerful, yet in accordance, together they form a team of One. Offering insight into the planet, our purpose, God's involvement and will, our journey here, our process as a collective, the Greater vision. Unbending in strength, these words renew hope, instill love, and give 'trust in God' a deeper meaning.

AIDS - THE LAST GREAT PLAGUE
by Sananda, Hatonn, Ashtar, Nikola Tesla & Walter Russell

Assessing the situation. The World Health Organization (WHO)'s involvement. Virus review. T-Cells and HTLV-1 through HTLV-5. The African Green Monkey. Animal retroviruses in humans/bovine leukemia cattle virus/visna virus (brain-rot) of sheep. Viruses jump through condoms. Asian Tiger Mosquito. Forget the vaccine option. Recombinant retroviruses replicated at 9,000 to the 4th power, minimum. It's all around you and spreading fast. Safe sex? And you thought the common cold was easy to get. Will AIDS naturally die out? Viruses are crystalline structures and are therefore affected by sound vibrations and light. Dr. Royal R. Rife. Electromagnetics. SEM waves. Antoine Priore's machine. Sir Walter Russell speaks on the 'secret of light'. Electricity. Octaves. Atomic structures. John Crane. Mr. Cathie. Nikola Tesla speaks on 'light and applications'. There will be assistance from Divine Source to bring forth a cure, but man must do the work with the tools and "clues" provided. Start work now.

SATAN'S DRUMMERS--THE SECRET BEAT OF EVIL--
SATAN IS ALIVE AND WELL
by Sananda

In this deeply troubling book Satan is revealed bluntly, not as an abstraction. Satan's presence is documented with specific cases, examples of evil, control, power, death and murder, and the sacrifice of babies, children and animals by the Satanic cults.

Satan's "commandments" are exactly opposite those of God and the Creation, he is the Master Liar of the Universe. It is time to wake up to the LIE and know your enemy. These are the "end times" when each soul makes a choice of "dark" or "light"; guidance is offered in this book.

PRIVACY IN A FISHBOWL--by Gyeorgos Ceres Hatonn

It's a lot worse than you thought, they really are watching, everything. The government's thirst for information on its citizenry is unquenchable. Is privacy possible? This document contains very pragmatic 'how-to' and tactical suggestions to help you legally "fade into the background". The financial collapse is imminent. Preparing for financial melt-down. Commentary on a variety of related topics including: S&L's, the real estate market, oil, bonds, precious metals, interest rates, money laundering, home security systems, the Internal Revenue Service, and the new (traceable) currency. As the screws tighten. You the consumer. Credit card nightmare. The War on Privacy. Putting your affairs in order. And what of drug screening, lie detectors, on the job surveillance, medical history, credit history, the public mail system, your telephone records? Incorporate citizens, incorporate. The Right to own firearms, for how long? What are the ways to conceal money? This document is more important than you may realize. Reading it is your decision, of course so are the consequences of not.

CRY OF THE PHOENIX
DEATH RATTLE OF FREEDOM
THE PLAN "2000"--by Gyeorgos Ceres Hatonn

The four horsemen of Revelations have been loosed and are ravaging the populations of the world TODAY. If, as told in Revelations, two thirds of the population will be killed by wars, pestilence and plague, some four billion people will "die prematurely" in the next few years.

Most of us already wear the Mark of the BEAST; the BEAST will be recognized in 1990. The government of the United Staes of America is now firmly in the hands of the elitist Cartel, including the world bankers, who are dedicated to the collapsing of all nations into a One World Government by the year 2000.

The Constitution and the Bill of Rights are to be "abolished" in favor of the Soviet-Constitution-based United Nations Universal Declaration of Human Rights. The hour is late but perhaps not too late to preserve those precious freedoms guaranteed by our Constitution and Bill of Rights. As in the Communist nations there will only be two classes, the ruling elite and the "workers". If you are not guaranteed a place among the elite this book describes your future and how you might help change it.

4

CRUCIFIXION OF THE PHOENIX
by Gyeorgos Ceres Hatonn

God promised Mother Earth that she will be cleansed, this time by fire. Out of those ashes will rise the Phoenix, a renewed earth born into a "Time of Radiance".

But first the "ashes", the trials and tribulations, the destruction and carnage of the Plan 2000. Will humankind somehow "be forgiven" and avoid the atonement? No, the raft is in the river and Satan has the helm; the Apocalypse is now. But the fate of each soul is the choice of that soul and no other---free will---remember?

And the **WORD** will go forth.............. And the WORD is going forth, herein.

SKELETONS IN THE CLOSET
by Gyeorgos Ceres Hatonn

"I scatter things from extra low frequency beams to counterfeit money via German Nazis in the Antarctic funnelled through Japan and flooding your markets because I desire to shock you into attention--and then we can take the events in sequence that you can recognize the truth of the Journals."

"The twilight of the United States is guaranteed that it is humanly impossible for the U.S. either to turn aside or to win a war with the Soviets, for instance-- and that is only for starters. Only a miracle could do that--do you deserve a miracle?"

"You simply cannot believe the incredible weapons available for your annihilation---." "--YOU ARE NOT FREE, YOU HAVE A POLICE STATE AND ARE *COMPLETELY CONTROLLED!*"

"The Kremlin has committed itself to a step-by-step clearing of the decks for war and so have your government participants who work with them under the covers. They have left you without even the ability to have a shelter system in which to survive--YOU OF THE U.S. HAVE BECOME THE EXPENDABLES. "THEY" CANNOT GET RID OF THE AMERICANS AS THEY ARE GETTING RID OF MANY AFRICAN AND THIRD WORLD COUNTRIES, THROUGH FAMINE AND DISEASE, AND WEATHER AND DISASTER CONTROL. OH OH! HATONN HAS DONE IT NOW-- WEATHER AND DISASTER CONTROL?"

*RAPE, RAVAGE, PILLAGE AND PLUNDER OF THE PHOENIX
by Gyeorgos Ceres Hatonn

In truth there is Hope. "The truth will set you free." Do not turn away--join together and find truth and come into community and demand a return to Godness and your Constitution as given forth by your forefathers for protection of your wondrous freedoms.

-----As America falls so falls the world for the Plan was well laid and the Plan includes the whole of the globe.

The takeover is so insidious and deadly that man does not even realize he is being enslaved in mass. If this Satanic cartel is allowed to continue and fulfill their mission, it will be the start of the darkest ages your planet will have ever witnessed--there will be mass annihilation of mankind by the billions and YOU have no recourse.

God, my petition is that you of the masses be given into the hearing and see-ing, for you can stop this thing if you want to do so. If you act not, then I bless you and pray for mercy for, as free people, you will be finished!

RAPE OF THE CONSTITUTION;
DEATH OF FREEDOM RRPP-VOL. II
by Gyeorgos Ceres Hatonn

As you journey through this passage, this may well be the most important single Journal you will ever read. It is of physical importance and impacts your soul growth tremendously, that which you do in this cycle of experience. This book is not pleasant--it was not written for entertainment; you are on the edge of the abyss in your nation and the "anti-Christ", of which you have waited, is upon you. Rarely are things as you expect or at first perceive for it is the way of the enemy of Godness.

You ask and again ask, "What can I do?" Herein we tell you that which you can do. The time for letting "someone else" do of your work is finished--you will stand forth and participate in the journey of God or you will be passed by. Your Constitutional rights as written by the Founding Fathers are being re-placed by the New Constitution which is already in operation without your realization of same.

You have a right and obligation to know that which is in store for you at the hands of the conspirators for The New World Order, and further obligation as a citizen, to act. You have been people of the lie far too long, my friends, and it has all but cost you every vestige of freedom. What you do now can change your world. Do nothing, and you had better increase your prayer time, for it is serious indeed. The projected prophecies are at your door and it is time you recognize your enemy!

THE NAKED PHOENIX HOW, WHO, WHY, WHERE, WHAT AND WHEN THE BIRD WAS PLUCKED A GUIDE TO DO-IT-YOURSELF FEATHER GROWING
by Gyeorgos Ceres Hatonn

The subject of this Journal is the Federal Reserve System and the Federal Reserve banks. This is the one most important deception and subterfuge ever foisted upon the world. It actually is only the conduit through which the Conspirators have perfected their "PLAN". The Journal would be ten times this length if we unfolded details but while we would be unfolding you would be consumed. Let us please take the information, confirm it if you will, and allow us to move into action.

Let us quote Congressman Louis T. McFadden in a speach before Congress June 10, 1932:

> Mr. Chairman, we have in this country one of the most corrupt institutions the world has ever known. I refer to the Federal Reserve Board and the Federal Reserve banks. The Federal Reserve Board, a government board, has cheated the Government of the United States and the people of the United States out of enough money to pay the national debt. The depredations and the iniquities of the Federal Reserve Board and the Federal Reserve banks acting together have cost this country enough money to pay the national debt several times over. This evil institution has impoverished and ruined the people of the United States; has bankrupted itself, and has practically bankrupted our government. It has done this through the defects of the law under which it operates, through the maladministration of that law by the Federal Reserve Board, and through the corrupt practices of the moneyed vultures who control it.
>
> Some people think the Federal Reserve banks are United States Government institutions. They are not government institutions. They are private credit monopolies which prey upon the people of the United States for the benefit of themselves and their foreign swindlers; and rich and predatory money lenders. In that dark crew of financial pirates there are those who would cut a man's throat to get a dollar out of his pocket; there are those who send money into states to buy votes to control our legislation; and there are those who maintain an international propaganda for the purpose of deceiving us and of wheedling us into the granting of new concessions which will permit them to cover up their past misdeeds and set again in motion their gigantic train of crime.

Yes, there are things you can do to take action and we have laid them forth. Will it be easy? NO! You will need to start at "home" in the community and unify and get rid of the thieves and conspirators which you continually send back to be wardens of your prison and robbers of your property. They, too, are vulnerable to the nuclear bombs and confiscation--they just have forgotten as much. Your Senator is as physically mortal as are you and will die as quickly and suffer as greatly from the collapse which is coming. Preparation?

You have all but waited too long, but you still have time, while the elite vie for position to see who will outdo who and gain the ultimate control--the messages, unfortunately, of the prophecies tell you who that will be and those ones will bring devastation of physical nature--not just glean all property and wealth.

In for a hard time? Yes! But also a wondrous time of unity, brotherhood and freedom from boredom and degradation as fed to you by the silver spoons of the puppet masters.

Which will it be, citizens of World Earth? Freedom or enslavement? The choice is yours, for God so loves this world that he again sends his Hosts and his being to show you the way! Who will see and hear?

BLOOD AND ASHES
YE SLEEPING CHILDREN OF THE LIE,
WHO NOW HEARS THE PHOENIX CRY?
by Gyeorgos Ceres Hatonn

You are sitting upon the bomb ready to be burst and you hide within the lies This book is truth and we are now writing in sequence so that you might see the correlation between the lies of one decade heaped upon the next--but the play is the same. Satan intends to win or pull as many with him as is possible--there will be many, dear friends.

To understand the lies given unto you this day in your "Middle East" you mus know of the lies told you by your government during the decade past. The traitorous Zionist plan to win world domination through an American nuclea first strike on Russia has not been abandoned, even though Russia ha thwarted several attempts.

The "Biblical Prophecies", written not by God but by Satan, are being playe out by a mankind brainwashed and blinded to believe them to be "inevitable" They are not. Mankind, hearing God's WORD, can re-write the script to fi God's plan, a much more wholesome scenario.

We come forth as the Hosts of Heaven, sent to bring you truth and show yo the way for God would never leave his children in darkness. We come wit instructions for your journey--who will receive? Who will walk with us into th light?

Know this, in thine truth--BEFORE THE PHOENIX CAN RISE--FIRS MUST COME THE ASHES. GOD ONLY PROMISED THAT TH WORD OF TRUTH WOULD GO FORTH IN THE ENDING TIMES--H DID NOT SAY YE HAD TO PARTAKE OF IT. HOWEVER, IT WOUL SEEM OF GREAT WISDOM TO DO SO.

8

FIRESTORM IN BABYLON
THE TIME IS COME
by Gyeorgos Ceres Hatonn

History is repeating itself--in ever shortening cycles. It is he who can learn from history who will prevail.

This book is a review of the several attempts to start Nuclear War I during the past ten years and how that relates to the current (September, 1990) Middle East "Crisis in the Gulf"

The world teeters on the Abyss of total all-out nuclear war, the military bases of the U.S., foreign and domestic, have been stripped of men and equipment, and the news media (controlled by political and financial cartels) work diligently to obscure the truth.

FOR YOU WHO STAND IN TRUTH--THERE SHALL BE PEACE IN THE VALLEY FOR YOU! GOD EXTENDS HIS HAND; HE HAS AGAIN SENT HIS "SON" AND THE "HOSTS" AFORE HIM. WHO WILL TAKE OF HIS HAND? WHO WILL THEN TAKE OF THINE BROTHER'S HAND?

THE MOSSAD CONNECTION
HOTFOOT FOR THE PHOENIX
By Gyeorgos Ceres Hatonn

Americans, to understand how their Constitution, and Nation, are being stolen from them (and who is doing the stealing) must understand the MOSSAD CONNECTION.

The "Thirteenth Tribe" of Israel, now self-designated as "ZIONISTS", is in control of both Israel and, through its political influence over some sixty percent of the U.S. Congress and its working relationship with the White House, the United States of America.

This book identifies those connections and clearly outlays the only potentially successful course of action open to the people of America to regain control of their Nation.

CREATION, THE SACRED UNIVERSE
By Gyeorgos Ceres Hatonn

In this latest "JOURNAL" we are given day by day information of important events going on in the world and especially about Russia, Iraq, Israel, the Middle East and the U.S. and how these tie into the major prophecies of the end-times.

We are given information about the history of this planet and origins of the humans here.

We are also given a response to the "Middle East Prayer Alert", put out by many well known "Christian" leaders, by Jesus Sananda.

Many other topics are covered including: Our origins -- The moment of "no time" -- Cities of Light -- Pres. Bush and the "New World Order" and its consequences -- The geological processes involved in Vulcanism -- Learn how water (Babylon's Achilles' heel) will play a major role in the starting of Armageddon -- The "Global Agenda" and how oil control is of key importance -- More about Noriega -- Why doesn't Saddam give up? -- Russia's real role with Iraq and the Middle East - Russia's superior weapons determines what we can do in space -- The POW's we abandoned -- The origin and purpose of the Bird Tribes -- Some history of Earth and the settlers that came here 70,000 years ago and the consequences.

THERE IS ALSO MUCH MORE.

BOOK LIST

THIS BOOK IS PART OF A SERIES PRESENTED THROUGH "dharma" BY ENTITIES FROM HIGHER REALMS TO ASSIST HUMANKIND IN UNDERSTANDING HOW TO MOVE THROUGH THE "TIMES OF TRIBULATION"

THE BOOKS IN THE SERIES ARE:

SIPAPU ODYSSEY

AND THEY CALLED HIS NAME IMMANUEL, I AM SANANDA

SPACE-GATE, THE VEIL REMOVED

SPIRAL TO ECONOMIC DISASTER

FROM HERE TO ARMAGEDDON

SURVIVAL IS ONLY TEN FEET FROM HELL

THE RAINBOW MASTERS

AIDS, THE LAST GREAT PLAGUE

SATAN'S DRUMMERS

PRIVACY IN A FISHBOWL

CRY OF THE PHOENIX

CRUCIFIXION OF THE PHOENIX

SKELETONS IN THE CLOSET

RRPP*
*RAPE, RAVAGE, PLUNDER AND PILLAGE OF THE PHOENIX

RAPE OF THE CONSTITUTION

YOU CAN SLAY THE DRAGON

THE NAKED PHOENIX

BLOOD AND ASHES

FIRESTORM IN BABYLON

THE MOSSAD CONNECTION

PHOENIX JOURNAL EXPRESS VOLUMES I & II (BOOK)

PHOENIX JOURNAL EXPRESS VOLUMES III & IV (BOOK)

CREATION, THE SACRED UNIVERSE

PLEIADES CONNECTION--RETURN OF THE PHOENIX VOL. I